After
Extra Time
and
Penalties

After Extra Time and Penalties

Mike Ingham

The Book Guild Ltd

First published in Great Britain in 2019 by
The Book Guild Ltd
9 Priory Business Park
Wistow Road, Kibworth
Leicestershire, LE8 0RX
Freephone: 0800 999 2982
www.bookguild.co.uk
Email: info@bookguild.co.uk
Twitter: @bookguild

Typeset in 12pt Minion Pro

Printed and bound by CPI Group (UK) Ltd, Croydon, CR0 4YY

ISBN 978 1913208 080

British Library Cataloguing in Publication Data.
A catalogue record for this book is available from the British Library.

In memory of
Brian Dunkley and Steven Cooper
and for
Lorna, Marshall and George;
now you know where I was.

Contents

Foreword

IT'S A CLICHÉ TO SAY THAT THE PICTURES ARE BETTER ON the radio, but they're only better when there's a great voice at the microphone.

Mike Ingham has that great voice, and he used it to cut through the noise and the hype to bring radio listeners (like us) into the ground where the game was being played.

A true fan of football and music, which is a combination that his friend John Peel also possessed. Good company, indeed.

"Anyday of the week – when Saturday comes."

Michael Bradley and The Undertones – May 21st, 2019

Introduction - D.N.A.

"There's been no pattern to England managers in the past. We've gone from the foreign mercenary to the big-hearted Englishman."

Former FA Chief Executive Officer,

Martin Glenn – Sport Business Summit 2017.

SO THERE I WAS, LUXURIATING IN THE VACUUM OF MY retirement, deliberating over which flavours of cat food to mix and match from the 'buy one get one free' offer, when over the supermarket Muzak could be heard the plaintiff sounds of a Howlin' Wolf, Robert Plant embarking on the climax to Led Zeppelin's 'How Many More Times'. My son Marshall, who understands such technology, had made this the ringtone on my phone. Normally I would let it run right through to '...*cause I've got you in the sights of my... gun,*' before answering, however, I was more than aware of a lady in the same aisle, who obviously preferred 'The Hunter' by Paul Rodgers and Free. She fixed me with a Queen Victoria glare, and so I put her out of her misery and took the call.

It was a familiar voice at the other end belonging to the former head of media at the Football Association, Adrian Bevington. He wanted to know, two years into my retirement, if it would be all right to pass on my contact details to someone who might as well have been attempting to work out why his numbers hadn't come up yet to win the Euro Millions jackpot. Instead, as a consultant on team culture in sport, having worked closely with the New Zealand All Blacks, Owen Eastwood was trying to get to the bottom of why the country that gave the game of association football to the world, England, had become classroom dunces. *Best of luck with that one*, was my first reaction, but then on reflection, I was chuffed and flattered that, after covering the national team at thirteen tournaments and working with ten full-time England managers, anybody would want to canvas my opinion. This had never happened before. At the same time, I was instinctively consumed by cynicism. My experience had taught me that any FA initiative of so-called root and branch, forensic analysis had usually amounted to a pile of leaves and twigs and now the new theme apparently was going to be DNA, which for the FA normally stood for 'Do Not Alter'.

I have no idea whether or not any of the thoughts I subsequently expressed when I received my phone call from Auckland were ever documented and so I will try and summarise them here.

I was asked first of all if the modern England players were conscious of the history and heritage of the shirt they were wearing. I replied that not only were they aware, but some had appeared to be overwhelmed by it. When was the last time an England team went into a World Cup without being reminded of Moore, Hurst, and Peters? Whenever the England players line up in the Wembley tunnel, they do so in front of a bust of Sir Alf Ramsey, something that should motivate and stimulate but never intimidate. I was facetiously tempted to quote England's Rugby Union head coach, Eddie Jones, when he said so accurately, "Nobody owns an England shirt. You borrow it. You're lucky to get it back again, and if you don't work hard enough with the right attitude, you won't get it again."

In terms of being aware of history and tradition, the FA, in the new corporate world, are as much in need of a lesson on this subject as the players and proved this more recently with a willingness to sell off the home of English football, Wembley Stadium. I obviously didn't have that information at the time of my telephone interview but instead concentrated on the fact that the FA had routinely failed to tap into the experience of so many legendary former internationals, who were often present working for the media at tournaments. Bobby Moore and Sir Bobby Charlton, for example, were both in Sweden covering England's abysmal Euro '92. I will always remember one of Brian Clough's party pieces to try and lift his Nottingham Forest players before a game. Whenever word reached him that Denis Law was at the ground working for us on BBC Radio, he would summon him to the dressing room, much to Denis's embarrassment. Clough would then introduce him to his forwards and say, "Gentlemen, I want you to meet a real goalscorer," in the hope that some of his stardust might rub off onto their boots.

I was invited to comment on whether the team had a sense of identity. I tried to explain that the identity of any side is ultimately moulded by and is a reflection of the manager. Logically, if the manager is not English, it will be more difficult to project an English identity. Furthermore, if the manager has an insecurity complex, then this will be transmitted by the team. If man-management is weak, then there is unlikely to be much togetherness, and if he is not tactically astute, then the result is usually disorganised chaos. If a manager, though, is not handicapped in any of those areas, then there's just a chance you might get a team to be proud of.

There was also a discussion about perceived English traits and the characteristics I was presented with were 'fearless, creative and composed'. I did my best to explain that England were always fearless in the build-up to any tournament. They were world champions of preparation, facilities and soundbites and then when the game started, couldn't keep the ball. Tommy Smith, Steve Bruce and Billy Bonds were all fearless and between them rewarded with one cap. Charlie George and Howard Kendall were creative, Steve Perryman and John Hollins always composed, and their combined caps totalled just two. Seven marvellous English players with a grand total of three caps. There are many other examples I could have used.

Passion, which hadn't been mentioned, had always been regarded as a more traditional English hallmark, but then I reminded the All Blacks consultant that whereas his team prepares for action with a Maori war dance, England's footballers nowadays habitually mime their way apologetically through 'God Save the Queen'.

In the end, though, it is all a bucketful of bollocks. All that is required is a manager who understands the mentality of the English footballer, can cultivate a spirit of unity, and help the players to do themselves justice and perform in the way they do for their clubs. I suppose if you are going to fail to retain the services of Terry Venables, who managed to achieve all of those things, then the next best thing is to find someone who was profoundly influenced by him, and that's where Gareth Southgate came in.

I remember interviewing Gareth on the day he was appointed manager of the England under-21 team. He had been a convivial member of our media entourage when working for ITV, even joining in with the beach cricket on a trip to San Marino. What impressed me about him though on this day was the way that he gently but firmly managed to reimpose his authority in our interview. Not an easy thing to pull off, but he did it through force of personality and in quite a subtle way repositioned himself in our working relationship. It was done naturally and commanded respect, so I was not surprised when earlier than he might have expected he was asked to upgrade to the senior team. His shoulders were broad enough and self-belief strong enough to rise to this daunting new challenge. Southgate was able to draw on the experience of playing under four very contrasting England managers at four different tournaments. It was a bit like that old advert on TV: 'It's the fish that John West rejects that makes John West the best', as Southgate embraced methods that had impressed him and distanced himself from those that had not met with his approval.

There were a couple of ominous moments early on. Harry Kane is such an admirable role model for his country and a real throwback to the days of the old-fashioned centre-forward. When his England team had not only contrived to surrender the lead but then faced defeat away to Scotland after conceding two almost-identical late goals from free kicks, Kane managed to rescue a draw in added time and observed, "A crazy end to the game, but that's international football for you." Well, actually it's not; that's chaotic British football for you. I got palpitations when I heard another of Southgate's impressively professional core players, Jordan Henderson, after the game in Malta doing his best Andy Capp impersonation, describing his manager as 'the gaffer'. Press officers need to step in at this point. Today's top footballers don't have 'gaffers'. Indeed, some of Henderson's contemporaries wear watches that can cost over £20,000. The gaffer went out with Sydney Tafler and Arthur Haynes on black-and-white TV, but they are minor gripes when there is a World Cup to be won.

I didn't agree with Gareth Southgate when he said that base camps don't win tournaments. I know what he was getting at, but dysfunctional base camps can lose tournaments, and there is no better example of that than South Africa in 2010. What he was able to do in Russia was set about recreating the spirit of the best camps he had been in as a player. He took a leaf out of Terry Venables' book by ensuring that, with his assistant Steve Holland, he had perceptive and trusted eyes and ears around him. It was clearly an advantage to him that he had overseen the development of a number of his squad at under-21 level and so there was a continuity there that rarely exists.

There was no extravagant final preparation for Russia. The build-up could hardly have been more understated. Expectations were low and so when momentum started to build there was unscheduled euphoria as the equally unexpected summer sun beat down at home. Football doesn't go in for shades of grey, unless you are Gareth Southgate, and that is what was most impressive about him as a potential pathway to the final opened up. At no time did he lose a sense of perspective and pander to the overreaction. The only time he flirted with losing the plot was the momentary paranoia over a published photo that had appeared – wrongly, as it turned out – to indicate a possible change to his team to face Panama. It actually did him a favour in spreading some disinformation, but he didn't see it like that at the time. "The media has to decide whether they want to help the team or not," was his complaint. Well, with respect, they don't. That has never been the role of the media, which is to report unrestricted and objectively on performances and unearth as many illuminating stories as possible which will provide some background and insight from the England camp. Whether or not a story helps or obstructs the team is irrelevant, provided it has been properly sourced, professionally handled and is a matter of public interest. Over the years, if the England football team had done their jobs as efficiently and diligently as the English media then there would not have been such gross underachievement.

It felt so strange not being involved after thirty years or so covering the national team. Such a sense of detachment, yet still able to identify in the summer of 2018 with what was going on in Russia. I missed it more than words can say, although the considerable compensation was to be able, for the first time in my life, to watch it all unfold in the company of my two sons, Marshall and George, and my wife, Lorna, who tunes into football every two years for a major tournament. Don't underestimate the part that network television played in helping to whip up a frenzy that I had never been able to experience before back home. It should never be assumed that every household has BT and Sky, and World Cups and European Championships must be available for all to see, if they are going to grip the public at large. When the 2019 Women's World Cup was staged in France and received blanket coverage on television, the interest generated at home was unprecedented. A few weeks later, Sky's generosity in allowing Cricket's World Cup final between England and New Zealand to be also shown free to air on Channel Four, allowed this momentous occasion to go into even more homes.

I suppose the withdrawal symptoms took hold of me most of all when the anthems were played just before the kick off and memories came flooding back of the job I was so lucky to have without always appreciating it. I was reliving again the adrenalin surge you felt in stadiums alongside colleagues and friends. It may not always have been Club England with the players, but it most certainly was among those who wrote and talked about them. I could sense from afar the nervous anticipation that my successor John Murray would have been feeling as he squeezed his long frame into his seat for England's opening game. It doesn't matter how many matches you have commentated on, there is always an extra edge and a tingle when it is the World Cup. I am recalling the generous acts of kindness and support shown to me at my final World Cup in Brazil from cherished members of our close-knit team. Ian Dennis, the BBC's chief football reporter, who like Eric Morecambe could make the sun shine on the dullest day and our producer, Alastair Yeomans, who had such an unenviable task of taking over from the ever-popular Charlotte Nicol, yet managed to get on famously with everyone, even though he was a Chelsea fan living in Yorkshire.

There were many more lows than highs covering England, but right now I am only remembering those upbeat times when we celebrated Platt's volley in Bologna, the four first-half goals against the Netherlands at Wembley and the Owen hat-trick in Munich. All those traumatic penalty shootouts and now finally in Russia, defying World Cup tradition, England manage to prevail in this ritual of fine margins against Colombia. A psychological breakthrough that gave the team impetus, to take them into what turned out to be the one truly admirable performance against Sweden. Once again, though, almost inevitably they fell just short against the only top-quality opposition they faced, Croatia, and then in the meaningless play-off against Belgium. However, the squad had regained an identity and restored some pride back in the shirt, and isn't that what the DNA test was supposed to be all about?

A year later, there would be another reality check in the inaugural Nations League semi-final in Portugal losing to the Netherlands, who didn't even qualify for that Russian World Cup. This defeat reinforced the theory that in Russia, England had ultimately failed to capitalise on a freakish opportunity that might not present itself again for a very long time, with so many of the leading countries having fallen by the wayside. However, another success in a sudden-death shootout, this time against the Swiss, in the pointless game for third place was further confirmation that the team had been clearly just waiting for me to retire before perfecting the art of taking penalties!

The fever pitch reaction at home served as a timely reminder that there is no other sport quite like football. It's all very well a BBC Ofcom regulator decreeing that there should be live radio coverage of at least twenty different sports, but this should not be funded at the expense of the national game. It is also utterly scandalous that English football's governing body, for all of its shortcomings, should be called to account by Parliament and questioned about its fitness for purpose. Talk about living in glass houses and throwing stones. Football can unite the country; politics only divides it.

A funny thing happened to me the morning after the semi-final between England and Croatia. I was undergoing my morning ritual in Cornwall of walking up a very steep hill to buy the newspapers. A token exercise to be able to justify the two slices of toast on my return. Normally I would only encounter boisterous seagulls, bread delivery vans and dogs being pushed in prams, but on this particular morning, in a yard about the size of a penalty area, were two schoolboys kicking a football to each other, increasingly rare in this present day and age. They had been bitten by the World Cup bug, and it gave me a flashback. That could have been me. Once upon a time, it was…

Take the time to make some sense of what you want to say
And cast your words away upon the waves
Sail them home with acquiesce on a ship of hope today
And as they land upon the shore
Tell them not to fear no more
Say it loud and say it proud today.

I Will Light a Fire for You

As far as chat-up lines go, it was a best original screenplay nominee. Certainly knocks spots off that old village hall barn dance belter: "Wow, you don't sweat much for a fat girl." It wasn't rehearsed either. Like all the best one-liners, it was unscripted and spontaneous – just like Mr Wolstenholme's in 1966, though first, he had to observe that some people had prematurely come onto the pitch before delivering that sentence of immortality, one certainly not prepared in his hotel room the night before. It was the sort of early 1940's seduction scene that could have featured in one of those classic black-and-white wartime movies, though this was to be no *Brief Encounter*.

I've only really been aware of three Madge's in my life: Madonna, Dame Edna's bridesmaid and my late mum, Madge Fearick, a policeman's daughter and on this day in question a secretary in the town clerk's office in Macclesfield, Cheshire. She was still a teenager and fourteen months older than the trainee solicitor Marshall William Ingham, who entered the room and her life on a wintry day without central heating.

As Marshall waited in a characteristically low-profile manner for his municipal appointment, the typist with the Celia Johnson hairstyle and the world's lowest blood pressure sighed what should have been a conversation stopper: "Isn't it cold in here?" Her future husband, needing no second invitation, looked up from his *Law Society Gazette*, whipped out his box of Swan Vestas and sealed a relationship that would last for over seven decades with seven killer words: "I will light a fire for you." It was not so much a fire, more an Olympic torch that would burn well into the next century. By the time he had vacated the by-now blast furnace of a typing pool, he had done the decent thing and arranged for the pair to have a *majestical* night out – at the Majestic Cinema in Mill Street, epicentre of the Macclesfield social scene. Mind you, he managed to undo some of that Cary Grant charm by suggesting that they meet 'Outside the Butcher's'.

When darkness descended on the back row of the stalls, there they sat passively, inhaling an auditorium of cigarette smoke, nibbling on choc ices, with yours truly eight years before my time already no doubt an embryonic twinkle in my dad's eye. Maybe my future mum's aversion to any celluloid that didn't correspond to her world and her language was nurtured that night. Their film entertainment was Michael Powell's *One of Our Aircraft is Missing*, with its 'B for Bertie', 'permission to speak, sir!' and 'teaching Jerry a good lesson'.

Soon after that for my mum, it was not so much a case of one of our pilots is missing, but one of our sailors as my dad went off to do his bit for King and country. First, on board the old aircraft carrier HMS Furious before transferring to minesweepers and small gunboats. Most of his service was spent in Egypt, India and finally Singapore, where he attended some of the War Crimes Trials at the Goodwood Park Hotel. War was declared the day after my mum's sixteenth birthday. It was difficult for her generation to imagine what lay ahead, but she remembered a deep sense of foreboding from her elders who had already endured sorrow and hardship two decades earlier. Whenever she looked back at those times, she recalled that people were much kinder to each other than now and had more time for one another in adversity. Her own father, Jack, had volunteered underage for army service during the First World War and only survived that appalling conflict when he felt a shell ricochet off a notebook that he had with a metal casing in his breast pocket.

In the Second World War, one of my grandfather's domestic duties was to escort UK-based Germans and Austrians to the Isle of Man for internment. Many of these poor souls were Jewish refugees who had fled their homeland for their own safety, only to become prisoners of war themselves. I have only one photograph of myself sitting on my grandfather Fearick's knee before he died suddenly in his mid-fifties. He had been a gregarious pillar of the community in the Cheshire Constabulary – a Dixon of Dock Green with biceps. In 1921, after two years on the force, he was awarded an RSPCA silver medal for bravery – stopping two runaway horses in the centre of Macclesfield. An honourable mention for him as well in a 1929 edition of the *Macclesfield Express*:

Joseph Carter, a labourer, pleaded not guilty to having stolen a walking stick and soap dish belonging to Jack Johnson. Mr Johnson had left his property to run an errand, leaving the door locked and the windows closed but not locked. PC Fearick passed by the house that night to find one of the windows wide open. Carter was standing in the living room holding the soap dish and walking stick, and when confronted told the police officer that Mr Johnson had left for good and told him to take whatever he wanted. He was arrested and later found guilty and fined twenty shillings.

For years, I thought that my mum's brother Frank Fearick had been a Chinese admiral – that was what he told me he did when I asked him what he had been in the war. He would tour the town in his greengrocer's van, which to me carried far more kudos than being the mayor or chief constable. Our time together was too short but very sweet.

Nowhere captured the essence and spirit of Macclesfield in those days better than 43 Coare Street, home of my mother's two aunts and spinsters of the parish, Nellie and Nancy Gilman. Two up, two down and if you wanted to do number twos you had to leave the house and freeze to death in the communal lav up the alleyway. Gas lamps for street illumination, neighbourly net curtains that fluttered with nosiness should any stranger ride into town. In a movie, Nellie would be played by Dame Judi Dench, elegant and attractive, a surrogate mother to my mum, who was the daughter she never had. Nancy, more in the Peggy Mount mould, pressed the panic button every time her younger sister got to within touching distance of the opposite sex. Their own father had flown the family nest when they were young, and this meant any male suitor attempting to make his intentions known towards Nellie would, in Nancy's eyes, be tarred with the same brush. It was tragic to behold – like watching a female version of *Steptoe and Son*. Even if Clark Gable had attempted to cross the threshold, he would have been met with Nancy's withering assessment that 'he'll only let you down', or rather it would have been 'me-mawed' in the Cissie and Ada style of Roy Barraclough and Les Dawson.

Both sisters worked in the Silk Mill and so loud was the clatter of machinery that communication would have to be mimed, especially if the subject matter was a trifle delicate. In any conversation or rather gossiping it would always be, "Have you heard about her at number thirty-seven?" She would never be named and neither would the fancy man almost always involved. The banter that followed would always be mouthed and not spoken out loud and I could have watched it all day. Magical, just like my smoky image of industrial Macclesfield captured in a 1947 John Mills film, *So Well Remembered*, premiered where else but the Majestic Cinema.

My dad went into the legal profession, following in the footsteps of his own father, Charles Ingham, an old-school solicitor in Stockport. Sadly, no pictures could be taken of the two of us together – he died aged sixty in 1947, two months before my parents' wedding. Charles was by all accounts shy and retiring, and his quietness by nature was perhaps not surprising when you consider some of the advice he was given as a youngster in the church choir. Handed down to me was his *Little Help for Choirboys* book, published in 1902, which offers the following guidelines for behaviour at a church service. It included the following gems:

> You cannot attend properly if you have been chatting and laughing about some outside subject immediately before. Do not come too early or you will get tired of waiting.

Like his son Marshall, Charles also served in the Navy in the First World War and his younger brother Harry, my great-uncle, was a gunner in the 317th brigade of the Royal Field Artillery. Harry was killed on October 17th, 1917 manning a battery near St Julien, shortly before the capture of Passchendaele. He was just twenty-three. After his death, a letter was sent to his brother Charles, my grandfather, from his own mother. It was mailed to him at the Royal Naval Depot at Crystal Palace, dated December 12th, 1917 and sent in a white envelope with a black cross on the back. What is so striking about this letter written by a mother who has just lost her youngest son is how matter of fact and formal it is:

> Dear Charlie,
>
> I received your welcome letter. I was glad to hear you were all right. I don't think I should be so content in bed when the air raids are on. I suppose you think you are as safe in one place as another.
>
> I think you are one of the lucky ones. Everybody seems to think you will come out all right. Poor Harry did not know how to dodge or else I think he would not have got killed. I feel sure he was lagging behind and got caught.
>
> I will close hoping you are all right, with love from all who remain from your family.
>
> MOTHER – E. INGHAM.

Before my dad died in 2014, he received a letter from a Mr John Clark in Macclesfield who had led a group from Sutton St James church to visit Uncle Harry's grave near Ypres. They had laid a wreath on his gravestone and said prayers. I retired from the BBC on the day he received that letter and he died four weeks later. By coincidence, the first project I was offered as a freelance after retiring from the staff was to present a documentary about the footballers of the First World War and the so-called Christmas Day truce. The centrepiece of the programme was recorded in Northern France, accompanying two relatives of the former Grimsby Town captain Sid Wheelhouse, who was killed during the First World War. It was their first visit to his grave and was a profoundly moving pilgrimage. I would have loved my dad to have heard it and would have liked to have done more programmes as meaningful as this one for the BBC, but it wasn't to be.

Had my grandparents employed computerised dating, then it would have led to wife swapping! But in their case clearly, opposites attracted. Jack Fearick, the jovial policeman and life and soul of the party, married to Edith, for whom the glass always appeared to be half empty. Charles Ingham, taciturn lawyer, married the profligate Elizabeth, with the Mollie Sugden purple rinse, who lived every day as if it was her last. Belle Vue Circus, Chester Zoo, pantos at the Palace Theatre in Manchester – her chronic asthma never got in the way of her sharing any of those treats with us.

I wonder if it was something in the water of Macclesfield's River Bollin, but my roots were a melting pot of chalk and cheese personalities; put them all together, though, under one roof and add Mackeson and Babycham, and it was as convivial as VE Day. Disparate characters united by love and affection; the embodiment of family values. For some, no doubt the town is just another dot on the map, but not for me. It was very probably where I was conceived – I like to think Christmas Eve, 1949 – bearing in mind I was born nine months to the day on September 24th, 1950. Well, that's my story and I'm sticking with it. I thought Macclesfield was the coolest place on earth – and then I had it confirmed; the godfather of British blues, John Mayall, was born there in 1933.

Going to the seaside once a year, castles in the sand
Going to the fairground with my pennies counted in my hand
Going to the circus crying if I saw a clown
Walking on my six-foot stilts and never falling down
These are the things I still remember from so long ago.

"Memories"

Words and Music by John Mayall

Saint George Music Ltd. (PRS)

All rights administered by Warner Chappell Music International Ltd.

Sosban Fach

I DON'T HAVE ANY RECOLLECTION OF BEING POORLY, BUT I must have been. I can't remember the illness, but I know it caused concern. All that has vividly remained was that feeling of temporary solitude.

Being taken away from your parents is difficult to comprehend when you are only four. I can't imagine what it must be like for an infant parted from one, and sadly sometimes both, for an even longer period of time. For my young brain, just three weeks' separation seemed like an eternity, intensified by the fact that I would only be allowed a glimpse of Mum and Dad for half an hour on a Sunday afternoon looking through and tapping on the window behind my bed. I suppose what made it more traumatic at the time was to see them both being visibly upset.

I was in isolation at the Hill House Hospital in Sketty, a leafy suburb of Swansea close to the home we had moved to with my dad's job in 1951 just a few months after I was born. We travelled from the silk mills of Cheshire to the sandy beaches of South Wales, a journey that in those days took as long by car as a flight would now to California. A different world, a different country, and the benefits for a toddler were palpable. What's not to like about dipping your toes now and again into the saltwater that lapped against what I consider to be the most striking beaches in Europe?

My 'butter wouldn't melt in his cute mouth' speciality on those summer days at Caswell, Three Cliffs or Tor Bay, would be to break ranks and supplement our family picnic by pilfering more attractive options from our neighbours. I would make my escape from my minders while they were preparing our feast of what was usually white Nimble bread, pickled onions, potted meat and Sandwich Spread which looked like vomit – even the wasps gave that the body swerve.

I would return with a, "Look what I've got, Mummy," producing a chocolate teacake still just about wrapped in silver paper or a Penguin biscuit. My dad would then have to make peace with the victims, explain that he wasn't related to Fagin and assure them that his son hadn't actually eaten any of the almost-melted and squidgy teacakes being returned to its rightful owner. It was an idyllic existence – until, that is, I paddled and inadvertently drank from a contaminated swimming pool that had been piddled in opposite my nursery school and was diagnosed with *dysentery*. Highly contagious and requiring immediate quarantine. The only other flashbacks I get from that enforced internment, in what I assume was a children's ward, was the sound of music: 'Early one morning just as the sun was rising', 'Ten green bottles hanging on the wall', 'They're changing guards at Buckingham Palace', and that Uncle Mac *pièce de résistance* 'Gilly, Gilly, Ossenfeffer, Katzenellen Bogen by the sea'.

Strange isn't it, how your senses appear to be at their most acute in those fledgling years when you are less able to interpret the information received? You are probably more aware than at any other time of your life of the beauty of the world around you but too tender an age to rationalise it all. Does that make sense? Unless you are a freak of nature, you are more than likely to be existing as lilliputian – even the overfriendly sheepdog towers over you like a terrifying triceratops. Being so diminutive, though, does yield a harvest of blessings. You are able to smell and wonder at the bluebells and red campions, and want to blow on every dandelion, all at eye level. On the downside, you also walk into nettles but soon discover the healing power of a dock leaf. The soil beneath your feet cries out for excavation, and you unearth spiders, worms, snails and ants going about their daily chores. As far as I know, they are all still doing their stuff today, but I barely give them a pause for thought or work ethic appreciation. In those rudimentary years, your young senses and imagination work overtime, especially if there are bushes for dens. All you need is your Davy Crockett hat, the tool shed becomes your Alamo and the cabbage patch your wild frontier. Santa Anna probably didn't realise he'd been to Swansea.

I did cheekily revisit the old house we rented on Derwen Fawr Road, and I'm so glad that I did. We were tenants on the top floor, and I was blissfully unaware that you could get a distant sea view from the living room window, but then you had to be to over four foot six to access this vantage point!

This was the room where I did my Disney jigsaws, played with the plastic toy soldiers from cereal packets and sang along to 'The Little Shoemaker', 'Oh Mein Papa' and 'Black Hills of Dakota'. Musically, I was not exactly backward in coming forwards, precociously interrupting the builders next door with a rendition of 'Wonderful Copenhagen' or 'I Can't Tell a Waltz from a Tango'. Still can't.

Back at my little Blackpill Nursery School – which no longer exists – on the Mumbles Road, my dose of dysentery was put firmly into perspective one Monday morning. Instead of starting our day by singing, "*Summer suns are glowing over land and sea, happy light is flowing, bountiful and free.*" We were gently told by our teacher that one of our classmates had fallen from a cliff over the weekend and had gone to heaven. Apparently, when my mum picked me up from school later that day, I was so confused emotionally that she couldn't understand a lot of what I was saying; I had used some of the Welsh words we had been taught. A bit like the law I would study later in life, this knowledge has fallen, alas, by the wayside. Had we stayed in Wales a little longer, then who knows? I still get very nostalgic whenever I hear 'Land of My Fathers'. My sister, Christine, probably even more so as she was born in Morriston Hospital in Swansea.

For me, sitting in all of those national stadiums around the world, it was always the most stirring of anthems, and reminded me of Cliff Morgan and Peter Jones.

My parents' rarity value acquired during my enforced absence soon dissolved and things came dramatically to a head one holiday morning. Quite frankly, I had had enough and decided that it was time to up sticks. So I stuffed my little satchel with *Playhour* comics and made it known that I was off to find my own way in the world and meet up with Noddy and Big Ears. A passport would be unnecessary; my journey of all of 100 yards took me to an overgrown copse out of sight, I thought, of my bound-to-be-heartbroken mum – who unknown to me, with her built-in CCTV camera, had followed my every move. She did have the decency to allow me half an hour of independence before amplifying her gentle voice and called out to the postman, "Well, I don't know where Michael has gone – I was going to cook him some beans on toast." Sorry, too much temptation, my truancy days were over.

If I had emulated Dick Whittington, then apart from missing out on being raised by very special parents, I would not have experienced my early radio indoctrination. That little, magical box of knobs and dials was always on – relied on by every household during the war. A soundtrack to my childhood – ever-present in my ears.

"What are you listening to, Dad?" I would ask on a bitter January morning while he was breakfasting on Laverbread and Camp Coffee. You could barely make out a word anyone was saying as the sound faded in and out. I knew that we'd already had Bonfire Night, but this was apparently something to do with the Ashes. Before setting off for his Guildhall shift, my dad was just making sure that Edrich and Hutton were still getting the upper hand against Lindwall and Miller, as they did in that winter of '54–55.

Cricket just won the sprint to be placed first in my sporting subconscious. On the way to those sandy, thieving days out in the Gower, we would always drive past the General Store in Park Mill, and my dad would point out in a brainwashing way: "That's

Don Shepherd's place." The same Shepherd who captured 2,218 wickets in a monumental career and would no doubt have been an England regular, had he been with one of the establishment counties. The great man was involved on the day I attended my first sporting event. Monday August 6th, 1951, a month short of a first birthday candle. Trapped in my pram and taken to St Helen's for Glamorgan against the South African tourists. I'm told that I became distressed by the ear-splitting roars every time a Springbok wicket fell, and fall they did – only needing 147 to win, they lost by sixty-four, their only defeat all summer against a county side. All completely lost on an eleven-month-old bairn. I was too sensitive, and it was the same reaction at the panto – *Jack and the Beanstalk*. 'Fee-fi-fo-fum' scared the living daylights out of me – not helped by my dad's 'I smell the blood of Michael Ingyum'. Slept with the light on that night, oblivious to the fact that this show was the last production ever staged at the Swansea Empire before it became a supermarket!

My ears were far more receptive to the radio music my dad always cranked up after tea on a Saturday. I still get goosebumps when I hear it. No idea what the song was about, but my dad tuned in to get news of the Swans – but not the birds in Singleton Park or the feathered friends introduced to me by Danny Kaye.

I was concerned when I found out that he was being taken to the Vetch Field football ground as Mum let it slip that this was next to the prison. Dad was taken by a colleague as a treat while he was recovering from a broken leg. He had been knocked down on a pedestrian crossing during a visit to London. The driver didn't stop but was clocked by an American tourist and later charged. Dad, still on crutches, must have been a spectator in a special enclosure because on his return, he couldn't stop talking about sitting near to John Charles – the first footballer's name I ever heard. Swansea-born John was injured and missing from the Leeds team, so had come down to watch brother Mel, not to mention Ivor Allchurch and Cliff Jones. I couldn't understand then why my dad was expressing such schoolboy delight; years later it became only too apparent. The Gentle Giant, now why couldn't he have been in *Jack and the Beanstalk* instead?

Dad's radio programme started with a rousing chorus. It sounds like a terrifying call to arms and is one of the most passionate pieces of music I have ever heard – but it only works in Welsh.

Here's what I heard in *Cymraeg*:

Sosban fach yn berwi ar y tan
Sosban fawr yn berwi ar y llanr
Ar gath wedi sgrapo Joni bach.

Words: 'Myndogg', Richard Davies / Music:
Talog Williams, 1873

In English:

A little saucepan is boiling on the fire
A big saucepan is boiling on the floor
And the cat has scratched little Johnny.

May the Welsh language live forever.

'Semper Fidelis'

PEAS FROM THE SAME POD, CHIP OFF THE OLD BLOCK, LIKE father like son; you know you don't have to have that kind of synchronicity to guarantee a happy family. I had a wonderful dad, but we were as different as Wallace from Gromit. He had been one of the lads, served in the Navy, went to the pub, enjoyed playing cards, had a great sense of humour; but do you know, in my presence never once did I hear him swear, don't recall ever seeing him worse the wear for drink and never ever wearing a pair of jeans. If only my sons could say the same about me. My father had the patience of a carpenter, the calmness of a surgeon, had the greenest of fingers in any garden and made a career out of law. Not only that, he made his own wine; I just consumed it. He took an interest in football but didn't live and breathe it. He liked to support his local club, but it didn't make or break his weekend. Paternal instinct, though, alerted him to the possibility that this was going to be more than just a passing phase for his only son and so he took me to every home game until that day finally arrived when it was no longer cool to be seen out with your old man.

My dad had moved another rung up the local government ladder and now, back over the border in England, was in Plymouth where he had spent some of his national service during the war. He would bring home an Amazonian forest mound of paperwork, and there were so many other things he might have chosen to do to unwind on a Saturday afternoon, but he took me to Plymouth Argyle's Home Park come rain or shine. If it rained, which it regularly did, then standing behind the goal at the uncovered Barn Park End, you would return home looking as if you had just sailed around Cape Horn. I've always saved football programmes from my games, and one of my most treasured is from the Plymouth Argyle v Bristol Rovers match on December 5th, 1959, played in a monsoon. My saturated programme was almost reduced to *papier-mâché* but, frayed and crumpled and still just about intact, is nostalgically irreplaceable. But I've leapt forward a year.

In early 1958, my growing awareness of our national sport was transported to another level following the horror and tragedy of the Munich air disaster. If John Charles was the first footballer's name that I heard, then Duncan Edwards was the second. Like Charles, a colossus of a player who battled for survival for a fortnight after seven of his Manchester United teammates had been killed. I remember my mum telling me that she was going to pray for him at church and that the rest of the country would be doing the same. At school, we were given the news that a great young life had been extinguished. I obviously didn't know him, had never seen him play but fully absorbed the national grief.

Family friends back in Macclesfield of the red persuasion had managed to get tickets for the FA Cup final only three months later between United and Bolton and my mum thought it would be a good idea to watch on television just in case we could see them in the crowd. This was the first match that I ever saw and introduced me to another name to add to my growing list of football personalities, Nat Lofthouse.

My school, Hyde Park Juniors, simultaneously stimulated my newly discovered passion. My best friend Peter Davis introduced me to bubblegum cards of players and teams – with such evocative names like Wilbur Cush, Ambrose Fogerty, Len Duquemin and Bedford Jezzard. Even more significantly, as an Argyle season ticket holder with his dad, Peter would regale me with a blow-by-blow eyewitness account of their weekend exploits. I felt that I could already visualise some of the names he was bringing to life: Gauld, Carter, Anderson and Williams. Peter, probably more than anyone else, was responsible for nurturing my love for the game and I would like to thank him for that. The picture that you see on the front cover is of the two of us posing before recreating one of Argyle's heroic victories in the back garden. Peter, looking characteristically cool, was an infinitely better player than me and a natural sportsman. To overcompensate for my athletic shortcomings, I am the one impeccably kitted out, fully convinced that it could be only a matter of time before Roy Race and Melchester Rovers came knocking on my door.

His parents, Gwen and Ted, were friends at that time with the Rowleys – Vi and Jack. On one Sunday afternoon, we all met up for a picnic and a game of French cricket in Yelverton, a cattle grid away from Dartmoor. Jack was quite competitive and good fun. I liked him a lot and we got on well, but I didn't know very much about him, apart from the fact that he was the Argyle manager, not something that I was then able to identify with. What I didn't know, and he certainly wasn't going to offer the information, was that he had scored 182 league goals for Manchester United, and before he left Old Trafford played in the same team as the immortal Duncan Edwards. Jack Rowley did lead Argyle into the old Second Division, and that was something I would be able to relate to, but the next inevitable stage in my coming of age had to be put on the backburner again for medical reasons.

This time it wasn't a contagious illness. I had been born with two brains – well, that's what my dad told me. A cyst about the size of a billiard ball on the back of my head had to be removed before I turned into the Elephant Man. So I was admitted to Freedom Fields Hospital, an austere-looking building with a tower that began life as the Plymouth Workhouse and formed part of what used to be Greenbank Prison – nowadays it's an Aldi supermarket. This time I was allowed visitors and, having been Davy Crockett as a four-year-old, was now a nearly eight-year-old Cochise with a head bandage to protect my wound, but still too young to appreciate that contrary to Hollywood propaganda, the Apache were not necessarily the bad guys. The good guys at Freedom Fields were the sisters and nurses, the most undervalued members of our society, who kept my spirits up and sang their songs, though the beat was changing from 'Runaway Train' to 'Wake Up Little Susie'.

Plymouth in 1958 was still rebuilding after the wartime blitz that had flattened so much of the naval city. Several nurses and children had in fact been killed during an air raid in 1941 in the hospital that was now taking care of me. Although I was missing my freedom at Freedom Fields, this was not an upsetting experience and all I have to do, even today, is run my finger across my little indent of a scar to remember that time when I was reduced to having only one brain.

I more than made the most of my regained freedom once the bandages had come off and I was back in our home, the first one Mum and Dad had been able to buy themselves, so it was a big deal for them. A pity that the survey, if such things existed at the time, didn't warn them of the perils of having a flat roof, especially in a coastal city that can attract winter storms. Every time it rained rather than producing pennies from heaven, buckets had to be strategically placed to catch the unwanted drips.

The home had an unobstructed view across to the village of Eggbuckland – looking over a valley with a babbling brook, hedgerows and fields now filled in by the four lanes of the A38. On days off school, we would play from sun up to sun down. Incredible to think that 'as long as you're back by dark' was our only instruction. It would be unthinkable for most children now, yet presumably, there were potentially menacing predators on the street in those days too. The only danger we were aware of was the dog next door that, given half the chance, would sink its fangs into our plastic ball. I certainly wasn't in danger from any cars. Very few people in the district had one, and that made it even more surprising that very often on a Sunday morning, Mum and Dad would ask me to go and sit on the garden wall outside and write down in my little notebook the registration numbers of all the cars that I happened to see. They suggested that I spent half an hour doing this and I'm sure there was no ulterior motive behind this request. After all, Dad assured me that he would be passing on all of the numbers to the chief constable.

After the anguish and hardship of the war, there was a coming together of neighbourhoods; many families in our area were still living in prefabricated homes and at our school, there was a cavernous air-raid shelter under the playground which was a stark reminder of the suffering that this naval city had had to endure. Although my dad dropped me off in the morning, even at seven years old I was allowed to make my own way home. The child's bus fare was a penny from Mannamead to the Bluebird pub but a penny halfpenny for the next stop by the Dairy – the walk home could be done inside half an hour. So on a nice, dry day, I could elect to use that coin to buy four grotesque farthing chews from the tuck shop – no wonder the dentists had to work overtime. On a particularly stormy day, I was tempted by the bus stop slightly nearer our home but hadn't paid the extra halfpenny fare. What followed still haunts me to this day sixty years later. As I furtively attempted to sandwich myself in between all the others exiting at this extra stop, a voice far more threatening than the giant in *Jack and the Beanstalk* ominously bellowed towards me – two piercing eyes of interrogation were fixed on me and I was about to get the mother and father of all public dressing-downs. It was, of course, the conductor and he wanted me to explain myself in front of all the other passengers. Those getting off did an about turn to listen in despite the rain – those getting on sadistically relished this unexpected in-house entertainment. Lips quivering, eyes moistening, I was under interrogation by a man in a uniform for whom it was 'more than his job's worth' to be taken for a ride, or rather giving an extra ride to an urchin still in short trousers.

"You know very well that it's a penny halfpenny to this stop, don't you?"

"Yes, sir."

"So don't ever do it again – all right?!"

I was so traumatised by this that from that moment onwards, I cut off my nose to spite my face and would wait to make sure that he wasn't standing on the step before climbing on board for any return journeys home. If he was there, then I would let the vehicle go, imagine a self-satisfied smirk on his face as I waited for the next one and missed the start of *Whirlybirds*.

What does that say, if anything about life in the late '50s? Possibly what was more revealing was that my parents, who loved me dearly, were prepared to let a seven-year-old make his own way home from school. Was that naivety on their part or an illustration of a more civilised and honest way of life?

In Higher Compton Plymouth, I made my Wolf Cub vows and assured Akela that I would do my best. I dib-dib-dibbed with all the other Mowglis every Thursday night in the Church Hall.

"The cub gives in to the old wolf, the cub does not give in to himself." That was the motto, and I broke it. All I could think about while running with the pack was the sound that would accompany our Saturday afternoon fixtures against other local troops. Our pitch appeared to be on a one in two gradient – our goalposts were Baloo's jumpers, and we were in Central Park as close to the Argyle game that was going on as you could get without actually being in the ground itself. That memory of the roar from the crowd still brings a lump to my throat. It was hypnotic – 20,000 voices calling out to me – unquestionably my Road to Damascus moment – that unique, collective *yes* when a goal is scored. Martin Tyler said that he fell in love with football when he smelt the wet grass on a Saturday morning. For me, it was the mystique created by that sound.

The first game that I ever witnessed in the flesh was on Saturday November 15th, 1958: Plymouth Argyle v Gillingham in the first round of the FA Cup; a day that you never wanted to end. My dad and I were in a crowd of 21,759 and it was 100 per cent home support. No motorways and no away fans. We stood behind the goal with the old grandstand and players tunnel to our left. On the pitch entertainment from the band and drums of the Royal Leicestershire Regiment. The match programme cost us threepence, and when I looked at its front cover, I thought how considerate it was of the club to know I would be attending as there was an advert for 'Madge and son – for all your electric requirements'. Also in that programme was news of prices for forthcoming games – one and six admission to the ground – half price for *boys*. Germaine Greer would have a field day with that – an assumption then that football was not attractive to the fairer sex.

The first time you saw the players was when they ran out. There were no warm ups on the pitch beforehand, increasing the anticipation. Argyle, in the grand military tradition, came out to Sousa's march 'Semper Fidelis' (always faithful). Finally, I was able to put faces to names – faces that in those days, possibly because of the war years, looked ten years older than they do today. There was Johnny Williams, still in the British Army with his cannonball shooting; Bryce Fulton, the full-back who had played with the Busby Babes and goalie Geoff Barnsley, who kept asking the crowd how long there was to go. There was only one slight problem: I was too slight – couldn't see over the heads. So what does a dad do for his son? Why, build a little wooden stool to be carried to the game for him to stand on; it'd probably be confiscated by security now, but mine wasn't and has been with me in every home since.

I got my first introduction to the unpredictability of the FA Cup. Argyle were top of Division Three, yet were held 2-2 by Fourth Division Gillingham. In the replay, though, a more straightforward 4-1 win for my new heroes. But a reminder that not everything at that time should be viewed through rose-tinted glasses. Before the replay, manager Jack Rowley had to decide which of his injured strikers to leave out. Jimmy Gauld had a broken toe and Wilf Carter had five stitches in his eye. According to the *Daily Mirror*, "A broken toe could be padded, but it's not as easy to patch up a damaged eye." So Gauld played and cricketer Barrie Meyer came in for Carter and scored a hat-trick. Having to play through the pain barrier with no substitutes available in those days was the norm, and many would pay the price for this later in life. Even in our kickabout games at junior school and in the Cubs, we would be confronted with an enormous leather ball with a lace in it which, sodden by morning dew, was a ton weight to head. Imagine having to do this for a living every day in training; there have been some tragic repercussions and some of these have been sadly documented in more recent times.

But to end the chapter on a more upbeat note – my next visit to Home Park was for my first league fixture five weeks later and five days before Christmas 1958 against Hull City. These would be the two teams promoted at the end of the season. We returned home in time to watch Jim Dale present the *Six-Five Special* followed by *Boots and Saddles* and *Dixon of Dock Green*. Thankfully I was spared the embarrassment of *The Black and White Minstrel Show* and went off to bed oblivious to the fact that around the time Jack Warner had been saying 'Evening all', over two hundred miles away the birth was being confirmed of Lorna Jill Dickinson. It would take another seventeen years for our paths to cross, but it was well worth the wait.

And all I ever needed was the one
Like freedom fields, where wild horses run
When stars collide like you and I
No shadows block the sun
You're all I ever needed
Baby, you're the one.

To Be a Pilgrim

The future Mrs Ingham, an early Christmas present for Barbara and Michael Dickinson in the Wirral, was being measured, weighed and no doubt nourished as I slept in readiness for the tortuous car journey to the county of her birth for our traditional Macclesfield season of goodwill.

Argyle's draw with Hull meant that they were still leading Division Three at exactly the halfway point of the season. Our game didn't feature in BBC television's *Soccer Special*. This was a precursor to *Match of the Day* and was introduced by Kenneth Wolstenholme:

> *Sports-view cameras bring you today's sport; among the film it is hoped to include from Division Two, Brighton v Middlesbrough, and from Division One, Chelsea v Manchester United.*

The programme incidentally was produced by AP (Slim) Wilkinson, who would become my boss a quarter of a century later. I hope that the film it was 'hoped to include' did turn up, otherwise the show would have missed out on fifteen goals. The results were Brighton 4 Middlesbrough 6 and Chelsea 2 Manchester United 3, and there is a reason for my drawing attention to those scores.

In the first game, twenty-three-year-old Brian Clough got three goals for Middlesbrough to add to the other five he had helped himself to against Brighton on the opening day of the season. In the second, twenty-one-year-old Bobby Charlton opened the scoring for Manchester United at Stamford Bridge. I didn't know too much then about that first BC, but the other was fast becoming a household name. What I wasn't aware of was that as an unexpected reward for enduring our expedition to share turkey and tinsel with our nannas, was that I was going to be taken to Manchester United's Boxing Day fixture at home to Aston Villa. Now just try and imagine what impact that had on an eight-year-old; there was nothing more guaranteed to fan the flame of addiction. There would be no going back after this. I was hooked.

This was going to be United's last home game of a year that had seen the club crushed by the Munich disaster and they would be taking on the team that had beaten the Busby Babes in the 1957 FA Cup final. Bobby Charlton, alas, was missing, but that was never going to overshadow one of my most cherished days watching sport. Four other Munich survivors were in action that day: Bill Foulkes, Albert Scanlon, Dennis Violet and the courageous goalkeeper Harry Gregg. It's remarkable now to look back and think that we all piled into my uncle Frank's fruit and veg van, easily parked and paid to get in for what was a bank holiday game. We were a cloth-capped, waistcoat-and-breeches entourage containing lots of honorary uncles for the day, who all seemed to be called Arthur.

There were 63,000 in attendance and it sounded like 163,000. United won 2-1 and the occasion will live with me for as long as I draw breath. Again it was that mix of sound, smell and spectacle all experienced through child's eyes. From the paddock, in front of the main stand, I had to glance up to see the touchline, and when Villa were defending the scoreboard end, I was within touching distance of one of those 'uncles' favourite players, Peter McParland. The whole landscape, as befitting a stadium with a Stretford End, was like a giant Lowry painting. Old Trafford appeared to be shrouded by an almost-supernatural smog, not just the product of cigarette and pipe smoke, but from steam trains passing by and especially from the factory chimneys towering over the roof of the stand directly opposite to us, the sort of industrial revolution pillars that Fred Dibnah would eventually be required to remove. There was a magic in the air that day, so much so that from then on, I would scan the horizon of every town and city that I passed through, either by road or rail, for a glimpse of the floodlights that would enable me to identify another Disneyland Castle of a football ground. That was my idea of trainspotting. I was very fortunate to revisit Old Trafford on many occasions for the BBC and coincidentally did my first ever commentary there in 1984, but nothing ever came close emotionally to matching that fruit and veg van baptism.

It was hard to believe that a fortnight after being so utterly transfixed watching the club that had appeared in the previous two FA Cup finals that Manchester United could be beaten in the third round of the competition away to a team from Argyle's league, Norwich City, who would march on gloriously to the semi-final. This added another dimension to their visit to Home Park just three days after they had beaten Spurs in a fifth-round replay. Standing on my little box, leaning on the crush barrier which was supposed to reinforce our safety behind the goal, made you even more aware of the keepers and I remember having a bird's-eye view of twenty-one-year-old Gordon Banks in his final days with Chesterfield. The following season, after promotion to the Second Division, I was captivated by Sheffield United's Alan Hodgkinson, not the tallest but so agile. The goalscorers, though, were always the focal point of attention. I was able to see the veteran Billy Liddell in his penultimate season at Liverpool, who had just appointed Bill Shankly as manager. It was Shankly's second visit of the season to Home Park. On the previous occasion, he had been in charge of Huddersfield Town who had a wiry eighteen-year-old with the predatory instinct of a mongoose, and it goes without saying that Denis Law scored.

As far as box office appeal was concerned, though, there was nobody to touch Middlesbrough's Brian Clough. You simply could not take your eyes off him. His imperious demeanour invited invective from opposition fans all around me. Yet apart from the odd 'bloody', I can't recall one four-letter word ever infiltrating my impressionable ears and believe me I would have done. Fancy that, a legion of working-class men, many probably from the dockyards, minding their Ps and Qs by watching their Fs and Cs out of respect for the minors in their midst. There was, though, plenty of verbal advice directed Clough's way and he responded by puffing out his chest even more. He may have had a striking partner called Alan Peacock alongside him, but he was the peacock, captain of the team, strutting his stuff, winding up the crowd and, of course, finishing off all of the chances that came his way. Unfortunately for him, while he was helping himself to more goals, unprotected at the other end, the keeper, his mate Peter Taylor, would very often see four or five flying into his net. No wonder when they became the best management pair in the history of the game, they elected to build their teams from the back.

On the Saturday morning of one of their games in Plymouth, Clough and Taylor both made an advertised personal appearance in the sports department of the city's Co-op and so along I went to obtain my first two non-Argyle autographs. Many, many years later, I told them both about that first meeting. "Aye, we remember him don't we, Peter?" said Clough. "You were the one that didn't say thank you."

All joking aside, good manners were encouraged in my childhood. I remember being in a pack of boys and approaching the Argyle goalie Dave MacLaren after one game for his autograph. "Sign this, Dave," demanded one of our number. "Mr MacLaren to you," said big Dave, his senior by nearly twenty years. When he did sign, he had the courtesy to carefully write his name on the scrap of paper so that it could be clearly read. It is indicative of the changing times that so many young fans today get short-changed by their heroes when they obtain signatures which appear to be written in shorthand – a squiggle and a loop to get it all done as quickly as possible. The only clue to the identity of the player is when they attach their shirt number alongside it. It is inconceivable to imagine that former England captains like Jimmy Armfield and Bobby Moore, with their pristinely legible autographs, would have added a number 2 or 6 after their names. Neither would have been presumptuous enough to assume that they owned that shirt. The same applied to Wilf Carter, Argyle's number 8. It wasn't too difficult to get his autograph. He lived modestly across the road from our school and probably walked to the ground from there. No ring of steel or security surveillance to negotiate; a simple, polite tap on the front door and he would emerge and indulge our hero worship. Carter scored 148 goals for Argyle over seven seasons, including all three in my final game at Home Park as a fan against a Leeds team that included eighteen-year-old Billy Bremner. He also grabbed five goals one Christmas at home to Charlton in a 6-4 win. The two teams had met twenty-four hours earlier in London, and it had been 6-4 to Charlton. They don't make them like that anymore.

Back on the other side of the road from Wilf Carter's house at school, now reduced to having that single brain, there was more exposure to radio every week in the classroom joining in with the programme *Singing Together* with William Appleby. Having polio jabs together, though, was not a bundle of fun, but kept us alive during an epidemic, whilst a visit to the dentist after school was like an appointment with Sweeney Todd. Children's TV provided welcome escapism after that ordeal: *Circus Boy*, *Gary Halliday* and *The Range Rider* were among the favourites, though *Whack-O!* with Professor Jimmy Edwards was a curious affair. The star of the show was a headmaster, or rather the cane he used to administer corporal punishment. I was allowed to watch this nonsense yet banished to bed before the start of *Quatermass and the Pit*. Ear pressed closely to the floorboard in the room above the TV set and denied the pictures, I would conjure up images far more terrifying than the ones actually being transmitted, which were about as scary as Sooty and Sweep.

Nothing transports you back in time more effectively than music. I've only got to hear the opening bars of *Hancock's Half Hour*, *Champion the Wonder Horse* or the Harry Lime theme from *The Third Man* with Michael Rennie to place me back in those days as a young Pilgrim when Argyle were at the centre of my universe. When they were not at home, I would go to the reserves on my own, bicycle left unpadlocked by a tree. This was the quickest way to keep in touch with the first team game which was always letter A on a scoreboard. Your heart would be in your mouth whenever you heard the telephone ring, and moments later the recipient of that call would come out of his bunker to update the score, and you prayed that it would mean confirmation of an away goal. On occasions he would tease you, half come out and then go back in again, the phone call presumably having been to ask him what he wanted for his tea. One miserable day, he had to come out nine times, but the Argyle score never changed from zero. That fixture at Stoke was the only away game that my dad ever attended.

Radio had yet to offer their teleprinter service, but there was a weekly second-half commentary on a Saturday afternoon, before the BBC's biggest star, Eamonn Andrews, displayed his versatility by seamlessly presiding over the show that would tidy up all the loose ends of the day – a show that might get a mention or two later.

On TV's grandstand, it's staggering now to think that reporters would have to leave before the end of games, climb into a fast car and get back to the studio in time to deliver their eyewitness accounts; heaven only knows how they would have coped with Manchester City against QPR in 2012. You had to live off scraps as far as live football on television was concerned; that's why FA Cup final day was always the most eagerly awaited in the calendar. I could dash home from school on a Wednesday afternoon if the second-half of an England home game was being screened in those Wembley days before floodlights – provided, of course, my nemesis of a bus conductor wasn't going to be on duty. There were certainly no cameras at Home Park and that just ramped up the mystique. Everything had to be remembered and then exaggerated from your one and only view of an incident – routine tap-ins for Argyle would grow into scorchers from twenty-five yards.

Only now, looking back at those exciting formative Argyle years, am I able to reflect on how potentially perilous they might have been. There was no danger from football hooligans yet, but you did take your life in your hands, especially carrying a wooden stool at the end of a first-team game. What became something of an iconic sign – 'Ten steps start here' – was a bland warning that on the way out with sometimes seven or eight thousand others you would have to descend ten very narrow, steep steps back down into Central Park. You couldn't see your own feet, never mind the steps. Mercifully, Home Park was spared tragedy, but sadly this accident waiting to happen finally did occur in Glasgow at Ibrox in 1971.

I was so very lucky to be able to spend the first ten years of my life by the coast. However, all that was about to come to an end. We were moving to just about the furthest place in the country from the sea. Sensing my sadness, my mum tried to soften the blow with the sacrilegious inducement of 'Nottingham Forest is just down the road'. I had no intention of being recruited by Robin Hood's Merry Men, I had already firmly decided on my vocation in life.

There's no discouragement
Shall make him once relent
His first avowed intent
To be a pilgrim.

'To be a Pilgrim', John Bunyan, 1684

My dad had a new job in Derby, and the *ram*ifications of that would seriously test the resolve of that young 'avowed intent'.

Charles Buchan

FAMILY, FRIENDS, TEACHERS, WORK COLLEAGUES AND THE medical profession can all change your life. Footballers, like actors, musicians, writers and broadcasters can profoundly influence and adorn your life without necessarily altering its direction.

There was, however, one footballer who was responsible for furnishing me with a route map and a pathway to pursue. I never met him and never saw him play, but his publication was delivered to me once a month, and his annual was the only gift requested on my Christmas list.

Charles Buchan had been a league championship-winning centre-forward with Sunderland in 1913. When war intervened, he was awarded a military medal. By the end of his playing career, this England international had scored 209 goals for Sunderland and ended up back at Arsenal in Herbert Chapman's side, but that was only the first half of his story. Buchan entered journalism, worked for the *News Chronicle*, reported for the BBC and was a co-founder of the Football Writers' Association. His vision didn't end there. In 1951, he put his name to and edited Britain's first football magazine. His aim was 'to produce a publication that will be worthy of our nation'. He cared passionately about the sport but was never an apologist for it, never attempted to sugarcoat or gloss over its shortcomings. The publication was to football what *Melody Maker* was to music. Charles Buchan's *Football Monthly* cornered the market; it was embroidered by stunning photography and included features dealing with serious as well as superficial issues written by some of Fleet Street's finest. It was non-elitist; the semi-professionals and amateurs were never ignored. There were articles by referees and even, in the first edition, one by JB Priestley. Buchan was a romantic, for him winning the FA Cup was seen as 'reaching for the dream'. He died on summer holiday in 1960, and while he would not live to see Sunderland win the Cup again, Arsenal do the double or England become champions of the world, he did change my life.

When I knew that thirty days had passed since receipt of my last *Football Monthly*, I would sit Lady of Shalott-style at the top of the house, gaze out of the window and seek out the paperboy. My eyes would follow him in and out of every front gate until just before he approached our letterbox. When that happened, I would run downstairs, trying not to trip over the pet tortoise and with feverish anticipation hope that the thud on the carpet mat would be louder than usual. Oh, the anticlimax if it was just the daily paper.

For me, nothing tabulated or documented the game that I was being weaned on quite like Buchan's *Football Monthly*. Much of the content was a cross between eulogy and doomsday warnings. The impact of the magazine was to make me think, *Well, if I'm never going to play for Argyle and England, maybe I might have a better chance of doing the next best thing and report about the game, even if I am left-handed and smudge all of my writing.*

The material is now lodged in a time warp and I can only just scratch the surface in offering you a smattering of how the game was being perceived in those years when my digestive juices were being so excited.

In July 1954, Peter Morris predicted that the £34,000 paid by Sheffield Wednesday to Notts County for Jackie Sewell, not even a million in today's money, 'may remain forever a British record'.

More accurately, Buchan himself picked his team of the 1956–57 season and selected Brian Clough, who he wrote 'has the makings of a great leader'.

Sadly, the March 1958 monthly went to press too early, because on its front cover with no mention of his death was a picture of a smiling Duncan Edwards tying up his left boot; inside there was an opinion column from Buchan on the fact that there would be no increase in the maximum wage for players of £17 a week, plus £3 for first-team appearances. There had been a call for a return to £20 a week for all, not taking into account the number of appearances. There was a picture of Manchester United's David Pegg, who had also perished in the Munich disaster with a caption underneath asking the now irrelevant question: "Would David Pegg relish a £3 drop in wages through no fault of his own?"

Clifford Webb, a regular BBC contributor in August 1959, under the headline 'You can't make a fortune out of football', wrote:

Why don't the big shots of commerce move in on football? It is obviously extremely difficult under existing regulations for personal fortunes to be made out of professional football in this country.

In October 1960, Peter Morris made this prophetic observation:

The Football League now seems prepared to sell its soul to a medium which really could not care less about the game itself – television. Instead of being no more than a by-product of the game, it looks as though it could take control one day.

This was all being debated nearly sixty years ago, what would they make of it all now?

In May 1963, concern was expressed by Pat Collins – who was the father of one of my favourite sports writers Patrick Collins – over the potential threat to the game from crowd disorder:

"There seems to be a dangerous element creeping into the game, perhaps this is because the spectator is following the trend of aping everything continental, but it is to be hoped that we are still a long way from the ultimate, a continental or South American barbed-wire fence."

So there you have it, our boys were just copying the continentals when they set about looting mainland Europe.

Looking back, it must have been very easy to develop a complex if you were just a normal Homo sapien at that time. "Stop being ashamed of yourself," ordered bodybuilder Charles Atlas in an advert. "I'll prove in only seven days that I can make you a new man. Once I was a weakling weighing only seven stone. I can make you a new man from head to toe in just fifteen minutes a day."

I wonder if anyone was brave enough to ask for their money back. Certainly, nobody would be quibbling over the one shilling and sixpence you had to fork out for *Football Monthly* or especially the ten bob Santa's elves cobbled together for that Xmas Gift Book.

Charles Buchan died shortly after helping to produce the *Football Monthly* for August 1960, which had a colour photo of Chelsea's Jimmy Greaves on the front cover. Among the tributes paid to him was this one by John Macadam in the *News Chronicle*:

"If football has to have a father figure, then this is Charles Buchan."

Hey Up Youth

It was such a culture shock, like stepping out of the TARDIS into an alien land. I know that I must have sounded different; I'd worked that out when my Macclesfield relations used to mimic the way I said the word 'miles' in the way Janice Nicholls used to pronounce 'five' on *Thank Your Lucky Stars*. Any trace of my Devonian twang would be severed from my vocal chords by Derbyshire peer pressure.

My initial impression of Belper, where we had relocated to in the spring of 1961, was one of utter disorientation, a complete disconnect from my coastal comfort zone of the previous decade. This cotton mill town's major claim to fame at the time was to have the deputy leader of the Labour Party, George Brown, as its MP. He was representing a constituency nestled in the River Derwent valley, bordered by the Chevin Hills and was a gateway to the Peak District An essential time-keeping aid on my way downhill to the junior school was at 8:45am, when every morning, without fail, the Midland Pullman Express hurtled beneath our bridge, with no 'leaves on the line' or 'essential maintenance' work to hold it up. It was a community of cobbled streets, corner shops, mill cottages, pigeon lofts and a foreign language. The older generation addressed you as 'Duck', and to your contemporaries you were known as 'Youth', although most of the boys in my class at the Long Row Junior School were also given nicknames by our unorthodox teacher. Tot, Pud, Nellie and Man Mountain – sounded like a Mötley Crüe tribute band.

On my first day after a greeting of 'Hey up youth', I was informed that I was 'frit, nesh' and 'didn't know 'owt about it'. That last bit was certainly accurate. It was like you were stepping back into a DH Lawrence story, though it was more Charles Dickens when lessons began and our snow-white haired teacher instructed us with his version of basic multiplication. "Now what you do is you take the top," reaching forward to crack a front-row victim around the head and then, changing his position but not his emphasis, "You multiply it by the bottom," aiming one of his brogues at the nearest available backside. "So have you got that?"

"Oh yes, sir," we chorused to spare ourselves another bout of masochism. Whether those arithmetical pennies dropped is debatable. There was a mixed bag of success when the eleven-plus results were revealed at the end of term in a manner that was brutal and inhumane. No private correspondence sent home – classroom friendships were about to be ruthlessly terminated as a roll call of achievement was divisively made public:

CROSBY – PASS
HOPE – FAIL
ABBOTT – PASS
COSTELLO – FAIL

and so it went on...

The ones that obviously hadn't been able to get their heads around that multiplication, maybe because their backsides were still sore, were being branded as eleven-year-old failures. By the end of that school day, gangs had been formed looking for revenge over the swots, who had the temerity to reach the required standard. Mind you, for those about to progress to the grammar school in Belper, the emphasis on elitism had only just begun.

There was one graduate from that class who didn't continue his education in the town. We went our separate ways and the next time I saw him was at least twenty years later on TV. Peter Wight went on to become an accomplished character actor and has one of those faces that you will know without necessarily being able to put a name to it. I could, because I recognised this former colleague who had somehow managed to find his own space in the maelstrom of that class, kept his head down and was quietly self-contained. I don't recall him having had any interest in sport, and we barely spoke. Peter more than raised his profile, though, later in life as a performer obviously valued and respected by filmmakers, especially that creative genius Mike Leigh. Peter was never the star of the show but made every cameo moment count. I am sorry that I have never been able to personally congratulate him on an outstanding career, but I am doing that now.

For self-preservation, staying under the radar and keeping your head down like Peter was probably the right tactic to adopt in the company of some tough young hombres from the mining, mill and farming communities who populated that year. If only I had possessed the nous to do the same – but it wasn't in my DNA. I couldn't resist showing off and made several rods for my own back. Guess who was the only cricketer in cap and whites for a game played in front of the whole school? I strode out to bat at number three purposefully like Ted Dexter and spent more time walking to the wicket than I did occupying the crease. Unfortunately, my first delivery was a straight one and uprooted my middle stump. Not even the teachers, especially the one with the snow-white hair, could suppress their laughter.

At this school, unresolved differences of opinion and personality clashes were never up for arbitration but could be straightened out at the Ritz Cinema Saturday Afternoon Club for kids. As soon as the lights were dimmed, it became a free for all and scores were settled against a backdrop of *Zorro* and *Swiss Family Robinson*. I would love to have seen Mark Kermode attempt to review a film in this environment. Nowadays, patrons are respectfully requested not to spoil the enjoyment of a film for others; at the Ritz – which should have been renamed *Fort Apache, The Bronx* – the message would have been:

Please don't set fire to the seats and only one assault permitted per person.

School dinners were an unappealing ordeal. We would be marched up a hill similar to the one in the Hovis advert, to a church hall where our grub arrived in milk churn containers and was slopped out like my uncle Frank's pig swill. Predictably, our dinner ladies were as sympathetic as traffic wardens and would berate the less enthusiastic diners with the same sort of lyrics from 'Another Brick in the Wall': "If you don't eat your meat you won't have any pudding," so we deliberately didn't eat that indeterminate meat to save us from the *spotted dick*.

A session in the Belper baths was about as unedifying as taking a shower at the Norman Bates Motel, from the moment you cranked your way in through a turnstile and observed the big sign that warned 'NO SPITTING'. Verrucas were the order of the day, and if you hadn't yet mastered the art of keeping yourself afloat, you were coached by a formidable woman who had less patience than a US marine drill sergeant.

It was the new age of coffee bars, and Belper had its fair share of these dens of iniquity. The coffee itself was an illusion, a couple of mouthfuls of froth and you were staring at an empty cup. One of these establishments was patrolled by a hostess with a very similar approach to battle-axe Ivy from *Last of The Summer Wine*. "Have you finished your drink, dear?" was her question and if your answer was in the affirmative, you were shown the door and advised to use it. That was a bit of a blow if you were still waiting for your tune to pop up on the jukebox, which was in my case usually something by The Shadows.

Our first family record player arrived in Belper, though my dad came up short with his first choice of discs. Instead of Billy Fury, Del Shannon or Duane Eddy, it was Joe Loss, Nina & Frederik, and 'Mr Custer' by Charlie Drake. Dad must have based his selection on the outcome of *Juke Box Jury* – essential Saturday night viewing – but looking back, how did they get away with it? David Jacobs, a supremely smooth host, pressed a button and a record tumbled from the rack, though never the one you would actually hear. Then the TV cameras focused on the tapping of feet in the audience or close-ups of the four panellists who usually had no connection with the music business. This latest release was then faded, usually before the best bit, after about forty-five seconds. If they had played 'Lust for Life' they would never have got to Iggy Pop's vocal. 'I like the beat' was usually the sign that this was going to be voted a 'hit', whereas a puzzled look and a frown would be the signal for thumbs down and a 'miss'. Such a rejection was guaranteed to make me want to go and buy that record first thing Monday morning.

When I was able to earn money for the first time in my life, it could not be spent on freshening up our pick of the pops; this cash belonged to Lord Baden Powell. All Boy Scouts, of which I was one, had to do seven days of slave labour that was dressed up as 'bob-a-job week'. Imagine eleven-year-olds nowadays wearing shorts and a woggle being encouraged to knock on a stranger's door and ask if there was anything you could do to earn a bob. The best you could hope for was an, "Oh, I can't really think of anything today, so here's a bob in return for one of your stickers." Alternatively, you could just as easily get an, "Oh, I've been waiting for you to call. Go and clear all the weeds in the back garden."

One thing Derbyshire had that Devon couldn't provide was a first-class county cricket team, with its two very contrasting main home venues. At Queen's Park, Chesterfield, with its wildlife and water features, it was like watching cricket in the grounds of a stately home, while at the windswept racecourse ground in Derby on a summer's day, even for the polar bears hypothermia would have set in. In those days, you actually got to see England cricketers representing their county.

Derbyshire had an opening bowler who was deceptively deadly and was short-changed by the national selectors. Les Jackson played one test in 1949, and his second and final appearance came twelve years later at the age of forty in a victory over Australia at Headingley. This was Fred Trueman's match, but Jackson chipped in with some crucial frontline wickets. England moved on to Manchester for the fourth test and Jackson was never seen again; had he played for Middlesex or Surrey he would probably have won 100 caps. The Old Trafford test match was also the cue for my uncle's fruit and veg van to be loaded with family and friends again to take us to the fourth day's play. This time, instead of watching Bill Foulkes against Peter McParland, it was going to be Peter May against Bill Lawry. Health and safety would have had a field day; the gates were closed with over 30,000 people inside. We were allowed to sit on the grass behind the boundary ropes in a sea of discarded boiled eggs, bread rolls and cucumbers with our legs crossed so you didn't need to go for a wee. Fielders dashing to retrieve the ball would often have to hurdle over young heads and land in a bed of squashed tomatoes. We saw Australia, in their second innings, bat all day, Lawry making a hundred. England, though, still had a big first innings lead, and the visitors appeared to be out of the game. However, back in Belper the next day, exchanging my view from the boundary ropes for black-and-white TV, I watched England contrive to snatch defeat from the jaws of victory on what was Richie Benaud's finest day.

That live introduction to test cricket was as memorable as my first visit to the other Old Trafford had been on Boxing Day, 1958. Putting partisanship to one side, though, was going to be a big ask after I attended my first football match at Derby's Baseball Ground on April 8th, 1961. A final score of Derby County 4 Plymouth Argyle 1 definitely tugged at the heartstrings. As much as I still loved Argyle, attempting to get from the East Midlands to a home game in Devon was impractical, to say the least.

The Pilgrims had left Plymouth before and found a new place to worship and now so must I.

When you see a gentleman bee
Round a lady bee buzzin'
Just count to ten then count again
There's sure to be an even dozen
Multiplication
That's the name of the game
And each generation
They play the same.

Tea Leaf Tex

"HAVE YOU BEEN SEDUCED?"

"Err, yes, I think so," I said, still three weeks away from turning eleven. Quite an indoctrination on my first day at the Herbert Strutt Grammar School in Belper, a gabled, Jacobean-style building founded by one of the godfathers of the town's cotton industry. I was the diminutive one at the bottom of a dinner table that was overflowing with rampant testosterone and the bad news was that my inquisitor was to be one of those dishing out the food, with a one for you, ten for me policy. How on earth could this new seat of learning think that this was the best way to integrate undefiled babes into their community? In this purpose-built refectory, the food that did grudgingly come your way was certainly an improvement on the offal available at the Junior School. There would have to be the occasional warning after we had mimed Latin grace that 'this fish may contain bones' whereas, in fact, it was more a case of these bones may contain fish'.

On this introductory day, I felt as if I had shrunk overnight. Having taken the eleven-plus early in Plymouth, I was now officially the youngest member of this establishment. One ceremonial ritual passed down for all male inductees in this mixed school was to be asked if you had been to fairyland. That was a non-negotiable invitation, as you were dragged off to the changing rooms and, fully clothed, hosed down under a cold shower. Character building? Not really, just blatant bullying which always seemed to go unpunished. You could be in trouble with the authorities if your tie was not straight, but apparently had *carte blanche* to perpetrate assault. I would learn that the school had some bizarre double standards when it came to code of conduct. On the one hand, a blind eye was turned to a serial-offending teacher, who routinely flirted with the attractive girls reputedly in his care. However, if you handed in your homework late and in that same week had a button undone on your shirt or had forgotten to put your cap on, then you were caned.

Although I still wasn't sure if I had been seduced or not, I was more than aware of my physical underdevelopment. Authentic shower time after PE was guaranteed to make you feel inadequate when having to expose nether regions as bare as the Sahara, whilst surrounded by torsos spouting more foliage than Kew Gardens. A coming of age process? No, just traumatising.

When we had lived in Devon, one of my dad's favourite haunts was that village of fables, Widecombe-in-the-Moor. One of the customs would be to toss a coin (the one with the robin on it) into the wishing well and then say a little selfish prayer. I would more than often secretly appeal for a Cup final programme or Bobby Charlton's autograph. In Belper, now I would have been prepared to empty my entire piggy bank to be granted a friend that might be able to offer me some school playground protection. Lo and behold, such a guardian angel suddenly did materialise with a jaunty 'Hey up youth' that had more sincerity about it.

Brian John Dunkley wasn't just any old youth either. For a start, he was twelve going on eighteen and nearly a foot taller than me. Brian had been forced to grow up quickly. Like me, he was born on September 24th but in 1949. Like my mum and dad, his parents were born respectively in 1923 and 1924, and they were also married in 1947. Like our family, they had a second child, Andrew, born in 1952. Like my dad, Brian's father, John, served his country during the war and then became such a well-respected employee in the bank that Viscount Scarsdale from Kedleston Hall would always ask to see him personally. John used to enjoy cycling home to Allestree to have lunch with his wife, Edna, but on his return to Derby Market Place one midsummer afternoon in 1956 was in a collision with a lorry and killed.

Brian was six and Andrew just three. Andrew has no recollection of his dad, apart from the occasional flashback to the funeral day of closed curtains and dark clothes. I know how alone I felt just being deprived of my dad for three weeks in hospital; God knows what it must have been like for the Dunkley boys. Brian instinctively tried to fill the void in Andrew's life as a male protector. It was a role that I would benefit from when our paths crossed five years later. Brian despised bullies and at the first sign would be at your side. He influenced my adolescence profoundly and introduced me to music I might never have discovered on my own. Having acquainted you with Alexis Korner and Cyril Davies, he would then suggest you lend an ear to Memphis Slim and Sonny Boy Williamson. In our makeshift band, he christened himself Tea Leaf Tex and one day proudly announced that he had written his first song but wasn't sure about the title. "Why, what's it called?" we asked. Tony Blackburn would have loved it: "AND NOW HERE'S A NEW ONE FROM TEA LEAF TEX AND THIS ONE'S CALLED *I LOVE YOU SO F***ING MUCH I CAN'T SH*T!*" Always a sense of mischief about Brian. I remember following him into a convenience store in Belper one day, handing over his money for a bottle of Lucozade and then promptly asking, "Where is she, then?"

The puzzled proprietor replied, "Who?"

"Rosy," said Brian. "In your window, it says buy Lucozade and feel Rosy all over."

Brian died in Australia aged fifty-one. I was on holiday at the time and wasn't told until I got home. I read his Christmas card, that was waiting for me, knowing that he had passed away shortly after writing it, enthusing that his mother had finally made it out to Perth to spend the season of goodwill with her two young grandchildren from Brian's second marriage. Brian died in front of them all from a heart attack while preparing breakfast. In front of his mum, who had been a widow for forty-five years and had raised him and his brother on her own. In front of his two small boys, for whom now the Dunkley family history was going to be tragically revisited.

Acquiring this enforced maturity and independence, without a father to guide you at home, made it difficult for Brian to come to terms with regimented authority. Disillusioned, he left school as soon as he could, found manual work and qualified for university entry at night school. He saw through the system at Strutts with its focus on streamlining the cream of the crop for Oxford or Cambridge. This became known as the Express Group, a top twenty who would skip twelve months and leapfrog straight from year three to five, a game of musical chairs that would be highly disruptive for everyone else. Many others followed Brian out of the door, some through parental pressure to find work; others, made to feel neglected, just threw in the towel. I don't believe that this elitist concept would have been part of George Herbert Strutt's original thinking when Belper's great benefactor founded the school for the benefit of the community.

The school struggled, and I'm sure across the country, it was not alone in attempting to embrace and understand the revolutionary changes that affected young people in the sixties. Teachers were a cross-section between the traditional advocates of corporal punishment who committed the cardinal sin of making their subjects sound turgid and the more enlightened, fresh-from-college enthusiasts who urged their pupils to do more than just copy notes off the blackboard. Unfortunately, this more liberal approach could backfire. Having been encouraged in history to do as much personal research as possible, one colleague boasted on a Monday morning that he had been able to devour an entire book over the weekend on the Tudor period by GR Elton.

"What, you read the whole work?" said the sceptical teacher.

"Yes, sir," was the equally unconvincing reply.

"Which text?" asked the teacher.

"All of it sir," he insisted.

"Then, pray, what did you discover?"

The next moment will remain in my memory bank until the end of time. "Well…" said the student. "There was Elizabeth…" And that was it – no further elaboration.

Another associate, having done zero preparation for his French oral, sat in painful conversational silence, failing to pick up and run with any of the batons being tossed his way. Finally, he mumbled an apologetic '*je*' and '*oui*'. Suddenly, the teacher, anticipating a possible breakthrough and urging a little expansion, implored '*C'est tout?*' (meaning, 'Is that all?' but pronounced 'say two'). My mate puffed out his chest and knew how to answer this one. "*Deux*," he proudly trumpeted. He would never have got away with that with the fearsome head of modern languages, Miss Saull, who had been at the school for nearly thirty years. Her nickname was 'Tusker' and such was her reputation that even the macho men were cowering at their desks in dread of being taught by her. As it turned out, we didn't know how lucky we were. She was by a very long way the best tutor I have ever had. As with all the great football managers, you wanted to perform well for her. She raised the crossbar, and it was the only time I made any real progress in French. Yes, she applied the metaphorical stick, but there were plenty of carrots dangled your way. I was really sorry when she retired and would have valued another three or four years of her inspiration.

If you weren't in the aforementioned Express Group, it didn't endear you to the rest of your colleagues to get ideas above your station and appear to be visibly making an effort. "What's he trying to prove?" would be a very audible mutter of protest around the class. No better example than the annual mandatory House Competition – Beauty of Spoken English. This involved learning verse and then, as beautifully as possible, reciting it. Although the school had a rich, artistic heritage, not everyone was keen to uphold this legacy. "I'm not bothered," was the order of the day and this would lead to entertainment like this:

'The Tyger' by William Blake.

TYGER TYGER... err...
  Teacher prompt: *burning bright.*
OH AYE – BURNING BRIGHT... err...
  Teacher prompt: *in the forest of the night.*
RIGHT, IN THE FOREST OF THE NIGHT
  Entire class on the floor wetting themselves laughing hysterically.

Performer looks up and catches my eye and mouths at me: "I'll smash your face in, Ingham, after."

Anyone else who had failed to mask their mirth – and there were many – would also be duly served notice that retribution would be sought by this tiger without a tale to tell as soon as the bell rang.

One way of getting this latent violence out of the system was to volunteer to act out the murder of Banquo from *Macbeth*. There was never any shortage finding members of the cast for this scene. Out would come the compass needles and sharpened pencils and in a more than lifelike dramatization, flesh was penetrated, genuine screams could be heard and the floor became a river of blood. This was a school that had nurtured the talent of the great Academy Award nominee Sir Alan Bates who left in the lower sixth. "They would not let me take Maths O level, not good enough," he said. Not exactly a mortal blow; RADA welcomed him with open arms.

Timothy Dalton, before becoming 007, had a licence to dish out order marks as a Strutts school prefect. I got one for not wearing a cap. I saw him playing Sergius in a school production of *Arms and the Man* by George Bernard Shaw and his contribution was reviewed in the school magazine: "This is a part that cannot be over-acted and if anything, he did not pose enough." Well, he made up for it when I met up with him again many years later. My future wife, Lorna, interviewed him for a TV special that she produced to celebrate *30 Years of James Bond*. He was the current Bond at the time, and I went along to ingratiate myself and light-heartedly scold him for that Belper punishment. Unfortunately, he was neither shaken nor stirred, and fixed his attention on someone else in the room of more interest to him. I would like to think and hope that if I had ever had the same opportunity to rewind the clock with my former primary school classmate Peter Wight, that he would have been more accommodating.

Boys and girls were kept at arm's length with separate playgrounds either side of the carpentry room. This was the domain of – and I promise you I am not making this up – our woodwork teacher, Mr Pine. As far as I can remember, there wasn't a Mrs Cook in charge of domestic science, but then in keeping with the segregation, this was for girls only. We had to spend our time doing more useful men's work with a hammer and chisel. But honestly, I could have benefitted so much more later on in life from being taught sewing, ironing and culinary skills. Making a wooden letter rack was about as practical as learning Latin.

I used to love playing school cricket in grounds that are now a supermarket, though if the Saturday morning breeze was coming from the direction of the Chevin Hills, the aroma in the air was essence of sewage works. In my final year at Strutts, I was awarded my cricket colours but never officially presented with them. As the sixties had progressed, so had the length of my curly hair and one day the headmaster informed me in a distinctly politically incorrect way that 'I looked like something from the Sudan' and that he couldn't be seen to be approving of me in public, so the colours would have to be presented by the Royal Mail.

Cricket was seen as the epitome of model sporting behaviour. Whatever the circumstances, you always accepted the verdict of the umpire, who nowadays in televised games has been rendered superfluous by technology. At school, the umpire's word was always final, even when standing at one end was dear old Reg Dean – or Dixie as he was affectionately known – who went on to become Britain's oldest man at 110. One of the secrets behind that longevity was possibly the fact that his 'hills were always alive' with the sound of music, carrying a happy tune with him wherever he went. He was more a *Songs of Praise* than *Test Match Special* man, but he enjoyed wearing his white umpire's coat and admiring the harmonies from overhead feathered friends. I can't ever remember a batsman who had been hit on the pad, not being given out LBW. Back then, if I had questioned a decision and wanted it 'referring upstairs', the answer would have been simply, "Fine, headmaster's office Monday morning…"

School days are reputed to be the happiest days of your life. While not everyone at my school would have subscribed to that, there was never any shortage of laughter in the air. From hundreds of jokes that did the rounds, this one from over half a century ago, is most representative of our juvenile humour:

A bloke goes to the circus and is humiliated by the clown.

"Are you the front end of an ass?" the clown asks him.

"No," is the reply.

"Are you the back end of an ass?" he queries.

"No," again is the reply.

"Then you must be no end of an ass," he roars to hysterical applause.

The bloke is distraught and vows to get his revenge. He enrols in classes offering lessons in wit and repartee, elocution, and oratory skills and ends up passing a PhD in spoken English.

Years later, with all that accumulated knowledge behind him, he returns to the circus fully prepared. The same clown is still there and spots him on the front row and goes through the same routine again.

"I say, my man over there, are you the front end of an ass?"

"No."

"Are you the back end of an ass?"

"No."

"Then you must be no end of an ass," he proclaims and falls over, laughing uncontrollably.

This time the bloke is prepared. This is the moment he has trained for over so many years.

He stands up, puffs out his chest and confidently pronounces:

"F*** off, you red-nosed c**t."

End of the Innocence

AT THE TIME, IT WAS THE GREATEST EXHIBITION OF CLUB football ever seen. I remember watching in awe as Real Madrid beat Eintracht Frankfurt 7-3 at Hampden Park to win the 1960 European Cup. Afterwards, the BBC offered copies of the match film to all ninety-two Football League clubs; only eleven wanted this blueprint of how the game should be played. More to the point, there were eighty-one who stuck their heads in the sand as insularity prevailed. That never-to-be-forgotten night in Glasgow reconfirmed the extent to which much of mainland Europe had not only caught up with the motherland of the game but was starting to forge ahead. Certainly, the entertainment was a marked step up from those days of belting a pig's bladder around a community.

I had moved to the region that gave birth to that concept of the original local derby. Yet Derby County's football team played in a Yankee Stadium-style Baseball Ground and had several squad members who had dual careers as county cricketers. In the fifteen years since that FA Cup triumph for this railway town, the trains had hit the buffers and run out of steam.

In my simplistic eleven-year-old world, nothing embodied the contrast between my former *Life on the Ocean Wave* in Plymouth and my new East Midlands environment of dark satanic mills better than the difference between the two football grounds. Home Park

Plymouth, in its lush, symbolically green surroundings at the heart of Central Park, with its open terraces and spatial awareness, was if anything too inviting for all visiting teams. A smell of pasties and warm hospitality pervaded the air. The Baseball Ground in Derby, on the other hand, was more Wagon Wheels and hot dogs, bordered by terraced houses and a factory. It was an arena fully enclosed with steep double-decker stands behind both goals, trapping and enhancing the wall of sound generated by fans that were almost on top of the pitch. If only the team could have matched this ambience. There was, though, an almost-undefinable stirring of emotion watching this moderate Derby County side that I was never able to feel when experimenting with Nottingham Forest. Forest were a far superior team, playing at a higher level, but maybe it was the detachment of not living there or a sense that I got that the ground lacked a distinctive identity, being in such close proximity to Trent Bridge and Meadow Lane. Who knows, maybe it was the cliché of running out to the Robin Hood music. OK, he's the area's most celebrated former resident, but that sort of thinking didn't compel Torquay United to adopt the theme from *Fawlty Towers*. It felt like the difference between riding on a merry-go-round and a roller coaster. One was infinitely more comfortable but bland, the other not for the faint-hearted but more of an adrenalin rush. The music that heralded the arrival of Derby County in those days was the 'Dam Busters March', used in the film that saluted the bravery and courage of those who carried out and also lost their lives in a series of daring wartime air raids. The Central Band of the RAF's recording of this was prefaded to climax after two minutes – with the entry of the home side. It was all neatly choreographed and stage-managed, but the only problem was that when the game started, the Dam Busters would usually turn out to be the other team.

Two senior citizens were drinking ale together on Saturday afternoon. One looks up at the clock on the wall at five to five and says:

"I see Derby lost again."

"How do you know that?" says his pal.

"Well, it's Saturday," is the reply.

Like this old chestnut, you had to retain a sense of humour following Derby County. My dad and I would watch from the middle tier standing behind one of the goals at the Osmaston End, and on one of those infrequent days of sunshine, you would need to shield your eyes. Directly opposite us behind the other goal, the Normanton End in the shade became for me a much darker place.

When Second Division leaders Liverpool came to the town in October 1961, it was so congested trying to get to our usual vantage point that my dad made a late decision to try our luck at the other end. There were 27,000 there that day; many more than normal were shoe-horned into very tight and compact areas. What should have been one my most fondly remembered days, solidifying my new allegiance, would leave only scar tissue and bewilderment. Derby County had one of those rare days of efficiency and won a rousing game 2-0. Space was at a premium, our view was obstructed and the phrase being pushed 'from pillar to post' might have been dreamt up that afternoon. Derby were a revelation, and a little bit of discomfort was worth enduring as the thrills far exceeded the spills, at least until I found myself momentarily parted from my dad. In an instant, I found myself being clutched uncomfortably where I had never been held before between my legs. It lasted only a split second, and mentally I suppose I tried to dismiss it as an accident in the coming together of the crowd, until it happened again. The invasive hand belonged to a man I can only describe now through child's eyes as having the leering expression of a goblin. I can remember fixing him with a bemused stare and then never saw him again. I had just turned eleven and had no understanding, really, of what had just happened but knew instinctively that it had been wickedly wrong. Looking back, it was the sheer, unexpected, from-out-of-nowhere assault that most upset me. Innocently happy one moment, terrified the next. I never mentioned the incidents to my dad; it was never discussed, and I should have done but felt too embarrassed. All I knew was that I didn't want to ever return to that stand again and I never did. God only knows how many other youngsters might have been targeted by this pervert. I felt a shudder down my spine when I became aware of his presence the following summer while hanging around the kids waiting for autographs at the county cricket ground in Derby. I gave him a wide berth but have never forgotten that demonic face. He got away with it because he knew his victim was not old enough to comprehend what was happening until the damage had been done. Up until that day, football had been a magical, escapist fantasyland of colour, theatre and heroes but no evil monsters. This brought me rudely and dramatically back down to the harsh reality of earth.

The roles of non-disclosure would be reversed when my dad decided to hold back something to save me from feeling hurt, though this was more superficial. The first time that my name was ever printed in a newspaper was when a letter that I sent to the *Derby Telegraph* was published, in which I praised the contribution being made to the team by recent signing Alan Durban. It was signed, 'M. INGHAM, DUFFIELD'. I was so chuffed; my mum bought an extra copy to send to my uncle. Later in the evening, my dad took a telephone call in the hall which left him looking a little bit shaken. He said that it had been the wrong number and was going to have a smoke outside. It was many years later when I discovered from one of his drinking friends from the pub that the telephone caller that night had given my dad a volley of abuse about my letter in the evening paper; obviously not an Alan Durban fan... But there you are – still the early 1960's: a paedophile and a troll – they've always been out there, just never highlighted and exposed in the way that thankfully they are now.

If Alan Durban was my favourite in that era, it was another Welshman from his former club that made a more lasting impression on me. Visiting teams would habitually travel to Derby by train on the morning of the game and then walk from the Midland Station to the ground. When Cardiff City came in November 1963, my dad and I walked part of the way with the team from the station. My dad was excited to see one of his former Swansea favourites, Ivor Allchurch, in the flesh again, but I had eyes only for big John Charles. Imagine that, two of Britain's greatest footballers walking through the busy streets on their way to playing an important game. Imagine too, this tongue-in-cheek scenario nowadays if a major club issued travel arrangements to players the way it was done in 1963.

Club: Right, Derby, away Saturday. Train leaves at eleven – we change at Stafford and when we get to Derby, we'll be walking to the ground.

Players: Walk?

Club: Yes. The chief scout went to watch Derby's last home game and said that all the Cardiff players walked from the station to the ground.

Players: Yes, but with respect, that's Cardiff.

Club: Yes and they have John Charles, who's the most popular British footballer to ever play abroad and would get into most people's all-time greatest team.

Players: Didn't he have any security?

Club: Excuse me? Have you seen the size of John Charles? By the way, our next home game with Stoke, rather than coming to the ground in the coach and having your car pre-parked for a fast-track getaway to avoid the fans, leave the car at the hotel where we are having lunch and then we'll all walk to the ground from there.

Players: But nobody else does that!

Club: Our chief scout went to watch Stoke's last home game, and Sir Stanley Matthews walked to the ground from his home, and he's probably the most famous English footballer in the world.

Players: But wasn't he hassled for selfies?

Club: I don't know what you mean.

Players: You know, when people want to have photos taken on their phone.

Club: Why would anybody be taking a phone when they are going to watch a football match?

Some things are best left to the imagination. When my dad somehow managed to conjure up two tickets from a friend of a friend of a friend for the 1964 FA Cup final between Preston and West Ham, the anticipation, pageantry, goosebumps were intensified by not seeing the teams coming out of the famous tunnel that we were standing next to until they appeared in front of us. We were alerted to their imminent arrival by the volume being cranked up by the fans at the opposite end, who got a glimpse just before we did. Sometimes, as in commentary, less can be best. There is a growing trend nowadays to make membership of an exclusive tunnel club available for the well-heeled corporate fan. However, if you want to gawp at players through a one-way glass like some tacky peep show, then why not just stay at home and watch it all on TV? You get all that access and can drink to your heart's content. 'Getting You Closer to the Players Like Never Before' is the slogan that makes it sound like a zoo. Certainly, you'll get closer than the real fan is going to get when trying to get an autograph before or after the game. 'Unrivalled Backstage Access is on Offer', but too much access can shatter the mystique and illusion and in my case would have detracted from one of the happiest days of my life.

Our tickets were at the Preston End and the experience was life-changing. I was standing next to a fan from Lancashire who was commentating gently for his blind colleague, who was smiling, wearing his North End colours, looking up at the sky, unable to see but living the game through his friend. This was the first time I became truly aware of the power of communication through commentary.

Over thirty years later at BBC Radio Sport, the idea was floated for some of us to make a programme about our favourite games. I immediately decided to focus on that Cup final and fixed up to interview the West Ham manager on that day, Ron Greenwood. These programmes never saw the light of day and that interview was never broadcast, but I kept the cassette. Although it had been my first visit to Wembley, Ron informed me that he'd been several times in his former life:

When I was a working lad, I was also an apprentice signwriter. Our firm did all the signwriting around Wembley Stadium, and when all the cup finals were on, I was always first in the queue. They used to have boards pushed around with the names and the changes, and they had to be written very quickly. So the place wasn't new to me in 1964.

Ron had to make changes of his own on that day – at half-time West Ham were trailing 1-2, and this is what he decided to do:

Walking off the pitch, I made up my mind what to do and say. I set off the game playing Bobby Moore as a sweeper – a continental type of role – but we were losing midfield. Bobby was peripheral, so I switched him into a flat back four – pushed Ronnie Boyce into midfield and it won us the cup.

It was 3-2 to West Ham. Sir Geoff Hurst scored a goal and Bobby Moore went up to the Royal Box to receive the trophy. On the journey back to Derbyshire that night, it didn't cross my mind how significant a dress rehearsal that might turn out to be.

Hector's House

IT'S DIFFICULT TO THINK OF ANYONE ELSE FROM THE SPORTING world with a more appropriate surname than George Best. There was Grand National hero, Bob Champion; Usain Bolt with the lightning speed and who can ever forget world record-breaking hurdler Marina Stepanova. I'll stick with George because he was the best British footballer that I ever saw and would have shone in any era. He was Cristiano Ronaldo and Roy Keane all in one – could score every kind of goal and never shirked a challenge. When he came to Derby with Manchester United in the third round of the FA Cup in January 1966, he was still only nineteen. For a town starved of excitement, this was the most eagerly awaited fixture for twenty years.

Any sceptic still to be convinced about George Best's pedigree now had an opportunity to trot out the old cliché about, "Can he do it on a misty, boggy, winter's day in Derby?" In other words, had he got the bottle? Without question, he had. On a sticky toffee pudding of a pitch, with Derby County's limited defenders getting stuck in like lumberjacks, what I remember most of all from that day was Best's balletic balance as he scored two first-half goals in a 5-2 win. It was another one of those rare 'pinch me to prove that I am not dreaming' days, watching three European Footballers of the Year, Best, Law and Charlton, sharing the same swamp as our more functional hosts. Among that home opposition was winger Gordon Hughes, nicknamed Charlie Drake, and centre-forward Ian Buxton, known to our section of the ground as 'Bloody Buxton'. On that mud, Flanders and Swan might have been more suitable alternatives.

George proved that this was no flash in the pan; a few weeks later, on what was a watershed night in his career, Best scored two even quicker first-half goals away to the mighty Benfica in the European Cup. Just another of many reasons why he and not Eric Cantona should have been voted as United's greatest ever player, closely followed in no particular order by Charlton, Giggs and Law. Cantona may have been the catalyst for change domestically, but not in Europe.

If Best hadn't been playing that day at Derby, my focus would have been on Denis Law, who got his customary goal and was a magnet for attention. Denis was even more motivated for this game, as getting to an FA Cup final at Wembley was always the main objective of his season. However, later in the year when it came to a World Cup final beneath the Twin Towers with two of his United buddies wearing the red shirt of England, Denis remembered that he had an unmissable appointment in his diary that afternoon to play thirty-six holes of golf.

The 1966 World Cup in England provided me with a welcome escape from the humdrum of watching Derby. I watched every black-and-white TV second of that tournament. All the episodes in that drama have been so well documented that there is no need to indulge in any superfluous repetition, except to say that I feel an immense sense of privilege to have witnessed it all. Looking again at Sir Alf's chosen eleven makes it hard for me to get on the same page as Jamie Carragher. In his autobiography when he wrote about playing for England, Jamie's observations probably shed a little more light on why his generation in the national team so breathtakingly underachieved. Carragher's conclusion was that a different culture existed between the northern players in the squad and the 'London Lads':

If you're born near Wembley it's a more natural aspiration to play there – it's bred into you.

Well, looking again at that 1966 team sheet, Bobby and Jack Charlton were born nearly 300 miles away from Wembley. Gordon Banks, Ray Wilson, Nobby Stiles, Alan Ball, Roger Hunt and Geoff Hurst also hailed from north of Brent Cross, two-thirds of that immortal team appearing to contradict Carragher's theory.

Aside from the joy, there is also poignancy when I look again at the official Football Association World Cup Annual that I bought just before the tournament began. The introduction is written by the chairman of the 1966 organising committee Joe Mears:

I assure you, the footballers of England are absolutely determined to give a good account of themselves and make no mistake, we are well capable of winning. What a finish to the football festival if England emerge as world champions.

Twelve days before the opening game, Mears died suddenly while in Norway with the England team for a friendly. He was only sixty and never lived to see his prophecy come true.

My post-World Cup euphoria didn't last long as Derby County made another grisly start to the new season. Former England keeper Reg Matthews was in need of even more crafty fag breaks in the dressing room to calm him down before going out to face another onslaught. Derby County were dining at the Crossroads Motel at an ebb even lower than normal. They reacted by making the most significant signing in the club's history.

In Greek mythology, Hector was the Trojan army's chief warrior, and although Derby's Achilles heel was their profligate defending, they went on the front foot and signed a prolific striker, twenty-one-year-old Kevin Hector from Bradford. I have never seen a player make such an impact in a home debut as he did against Huddersfield on September 24th, 1966 – my sixteenth birthday. Obviously I am biased, so let me try and put it into context. Along with the 15,000 others that day, we had been fed on a diet of lashings of mediocrity. For me, this was the footballing equivalent of watching a James Brown concert at the Apollo. It was Hector's stunning ability to run with pace at defenders and have the ball always perfectly under control that took your breath away. It was as if he had roller skates under his boots. The goal he scored was never filmed and my memory of it has probably been extravagantly embellished. I recall that it didn't even appear to be a half-chance so that when the ball nestled in the back of the Huddersfield net, you thought that it must be an optical illusion. There was never any danger of having that illusion shattered by the reality of television pictures.

In the *Football League Review* supplement that used to be inserted into the match programme, the message in 1966 was quite unequivocal:

> *The view of the Football League towards live television remains exactly the same; it cannot be contemplated.*

On this day there was the first hint that 'somewhere over the rainbow' bluebirds might indeed fly, but not yet. At the end of Derby's season, some people were on the pitch when it was all over, and I was one of them at the Baseball Ground demonstrating our restlessness by protesting, "We want Ward, sack the board." The directors had decided to part company with Tim Ward, the manager who had given us Kevin Hector. Ward, for his part, had grown weary with all the politics that would become a trademark for the club.

I was becoming aware of how the atmosphere at football was changing. The game had received a shot in the arm after the World Cup but was now starting to attract a new breed of fan that a decade earlier would have had national service as a vehicle for releasing any pent-up aggression. Throughout that season at Derby, and especially away from home, I could see the seeds being sown for disorder by a minority of fans. So much so that on that final day of the season, rather than addressing the management issue in the programme, the club expressed deep concerns over the following:

The growing incidence of obscene language by certain so-called supporters. To these supposed supporters, we must say that many ladies now attend: wives, mothers and daughters. We ask, would they use this language in front of their own dear ones?

Sadly, the answer was likely yes, and the bad language was just a precursor to far worse behaviour to come. The surface had merely been scratched...

The summer arrival of the new management team of Brian Clough and Peter Taylor would surely refocus minds on football. Tim Ward's legacy had been to leave them with five players who would all incredibly go on to become League champions only five years later. Some of the early additions to this inherited spine were inspirational investments like John O'Hare and Roy McFarland, who would both mature into accomplished internationals. Alan Hinton, on the other hand, had been around for years and his career appeared to be stagnating when he was suddenly thrown a lease of life by Clough. The manner of his signing could *never* happen today. In a chat I had with him years later at Radio Derby, Hinton told me that he could so easily have ended up at Eric Morecambe's Luton Town. This was not a comedy sketch; this really did happen:

I made an appointment to see Brian Clough at 10pm at the Baseball Ground. Unknown to me, Alan Brown, manager of Luton, had also made arrangements to sign Ian Buxton from Derby. I was the first to arrive and it was dark, and the second man to arrive was Alan Brown. So he came up to me and said, hello Ian, shall we go and have a chat somewhere? I said, I'm sorry, but I am not Ian Buxton, I am Alan Hinton and I've come to see Brian Clough.

Nowadays, there would have been a posse of minders, agents and a PR team monitoring every move. Clough and Taylor would invariably size up a potential signing by watching him in action away from home – a more accurate guide to his character. Neither would need to go and assess the two men who would go on to transform their team. Looking back, it's amazing how a twist of fate can alter history.

In the summer of 1968, I was employed at the Derby Co-op as a vital cog in their machinery, operating the lift for customers and announcing 'Haberdashery' when we cranked our way up to the second floor. On my first morning, my grateful passenger remarked, "My, your life is all ups and downs." Quite whimsical, I thought, until hearing it for the eighty-third time. When I used to re-emerge into the daylight after clocking out like Steve McQueen coming out of the cooler in *The Great Escape*, I would buy the *Derby Telegraph*, and there would nearly always be a 'RAMS EXCLUSIVE' on the back page. The club were known to be prioritising the signing of an experienced campaigner and one night it was revealed that their top target was Graham Cross of Leicester City. It would be one of those rare occasions when Clough and Taylor didn't get their man and with hindsight, his rejection of the move now looks a bit like Decca Records turning down the Beatles. Instead arrived two soldiers any general would want to go into battle with: the pint-sized Willie Carlin and the barrel-chested Dave Mackay, or David Mackay as Clough would always call him.

The great Tottenham manager Bill Nicholson didn't make too many miscalculations, but he did when he allowed Mackay to prematurely leave White Hart Lane for this reason:

Unfortunately, the age limit in the First Division is lowering all the time. A few years ago, players of thirty-three, thirty-four and thirty-five could last the pace, but these days it seems to have changed.

Mackay was thirty-three, redeployed to play to his strengths by Clough and a year later was in the Derby team that beat Tottenham 5-0. It was worth paying the admission money just to admire his skills in the warm-up. My next-door neighbour, Bill Thomas, once saw him unwinding after one game in the hotel he used as his Derby base. "I have never seen anyone enjoy his first pint of beer quite like that," said Bill, who hadn't exactly led a sheltered existence in a career working as an engineer in the Grand Prix motor racing business.

In Dave Mackay's first season, Derby had a thrilling adventure in the League Cup, winning replays at home to Chelsea and Everton. These were all ticket games, and that meant yours truly bunking off school to join the breakfast-time queues at the Baseball Ground, trying to make sure that I wasn't photographed by the guy from the evening paper. The schoolmates I was also buying tickets for covered for me in my absence and naively, I thought I was getting away with it. On the first occasion that I was late, I explained to the teacher that I had been bothered by a nasty splinter in my foot which had needed to be extracted. Next time, working my way upwards, I reported that because of a stomach pain, I had been to the doctor to check it wasn't appendicitis. Third time unlucky, before I could disclose the stiffness I was experiencing in my neck, I was pre-empted by the teacher's cynicism. "Ah, good morning, Ingham, nice of you to join us, what was it today – brain transplant?" This was the same teacher given a nickname by the pupils relating to his very red face. At a parents' evening, my mum addressed him as Mr Cherry and was never corrected. Mum also, much to my horror, found herself in conversation with the king of the Baseball Ground at a civic reception for Derby County and kept calling him by his surname, Hector. It wasn't intended, just as she meant well when taking her driving test for the first time and, trying to create a good impression, opened the passenger door of her car so that the examiner could get in, only to trap his fingers as she shut it. She had to drive him over to outpatients at the infirmary, so the match was abandoned after thirty seconds. Your mum will always be your mum whatever you go on to do. Much later in life, after one of the few occasions when this 'face for radio' was seen close-up on national television, promoting 5 Live's coverage of the World Cup, I remember asking mum what she thought of it? "Very nice, Michael" she said, "but couldn't you have had a shave?"

Watching the rebirth of Derby County over this period was the stuff of movies. When the Clough and Taylor era was eventually documented in the film *The Damned United*, it made me question the accuracy of other biopics I'd seen. My knowledge on this subject enabled me to see all the numerous flaws. Michael Sheen and Timothy Spall were compelling to watch in the central roles as Clough and Taylor, but I would need fingers on at least a dozen hands to count the factual errors. The whole premise of the story lacked credibility from the moment Clough is shown being snubbed on arrival by the Leeds manager Don Revie before an FA Cup tie at the Baseball Ground. In the movie, this visit from Leeds was such a big deal for Clough that he rolled out the red carpet on the day and was waiting to shake Revie's hands when he got off the bus, only to be ignored. I was at that third-round tie and unfortunately for the filmmakers, I can confirm that it actually took place in Leeds. That imagined humiliation for Clough in his own backyard is then portrayed as underpinning his obsession with getting even, the essence of the whole story. This mistake cannot be dismissed as poetic licence.

When I look back at that visit to the Baseball Ground from Best, Law and Charlton, who had appeared to be on a different football planet, it would have been unthinkable that by the end of the decade the same three players would return to the stadium and be comprehensibly beaten. However, I hadn't legislated for the arrival of the mercurial Clough and Taylor. One of their great skills was the art of knowing when to replace the seemingly irreplaceable members of the team. Colin Todd for Mackay, Archie Gemmill for Carlin being the best two examples and had the management pair not left the club so unexpectedly, Hector's eventual successor would surely have been Trevor Francis. It was a disgrace that Kevin Hector's reward for his two League championships and all of his European goals were just a miserly two England caps amounting to twenty minutes as a substitute. For any Derby County fan who saw him in his pomp at Hector's House, he will always have a special place in their hearts. He gave me the best sixteenth birthday present I could have ever wished for.

Too Much Monkey Business

As David Hepworth so rightly says in his absorbing book, *1971 – Never a Dull Moment*, being born in 1950 for a music fan was being given 'the winning ticket in the lottery of life'. It meant that your teenage albums began with *Please Please Me* and ended with *Abbey Road*. As for singles, the sixties began with 'Apache' and end with 'Honky Tonk Women'. It was a cellar full of treasures.

In the early sixties, my weekend entertainment seemed to be dominated by Brian Matthew. He was the host for *Saturday Club* and *Easy Beat* on the radio, as well as *Thank Your Lucky Stars* on TV. At night time with a transistor radio smuggled into my pillow, I tuned in to Radio Luxembourg's Jimmy Savile presenting his *Under the Bedclothes Club*. This sadly has now taken on an altogether more sinister meaning. Brian Matthew was a broadcasting pioneer, and I admired everything about his style. His doctrine was, 'Treat the audience as your friend'. He always seemed to be undervalued by the BBC. When Radio 1 began in 1967, Brian was informed by management that at thirty-nine he was considered to be too old for the new network. I found that deeply patronising to the audience and an early indication that unless someone like Mike Raven or John Peel were hosts, the music content was going to be of secondary importance.

If John Peel liked a record on *Top Gear*, then that was usually good enough for me. I used to record his Sunday show and wish that I had kept all my old reel-to-reel tapes of sessions with bands like Skip Bifferty and The Idle Race. Long before he famously played 'Teenage Kicks' back to back, I remember him rewinding Love Sculpture's studio version of 'Sabre Dance' and playing that again also. He was his own man, even when occasionally lines of consistency could become blurred. He might enthuse about a rather grandiose rendition of a classical music masterpiece by The Nice and then summarily dismiss an artist who would go on to make a longer-lasting and more significant contribution to music like Sly Stone. I'll never forget Peel joking in one show that he had intended to play a Sly and the Family Stone record, however, as he'd just found out that the second cousin of the drummer had received a traffic citation three years ago, it was out of the question.

For me, the sound of the sixties was the Hammond organ. Nothing transports me back to that time more than 'Green Onions', one of my Desert Island Discs. Just imagine what it must have felt like to have been in that Memphis studio on the day those two minutes and fifty-two seconds were first recorded. Sometimes when you hear a record too many times, familiarity can end up breeding contempt, but never in the case of 'Green Onions'. I hear it and am instantly back in Milford, Derbyshire at the Strutt Arms. An establishment that had nothing to do with Strutt School, although on a Saturday night most of the pupils seemed to be there. For some reason, this pub had a connection with the famous Marquee Club in London, and many of the bands who were regulars in Wardour Street also found themselves in this unlikely venue by the bridge over the River Derwent.

After watching *The Munsters*, I would stuff my shoes with cotton wool to be tall enough to order a drink at the bar and head off into the night. The evening, though, was less about the underage beer and much more the music. It all happened upstairs in a smoke-infested room with a floor that bounced like the Preservation Hall in New Orleans. Whatever the official capacity was supposed to be for the licence was at least trebled. The stage was tiny but on it, though we didn't realise at the time, were members of some bands who would go on to become rock royalty. Keith Emerson played with Gary Farr and the T-Bones, Deep Purple's Jon Lord was then in The Artwoods, and amongst the members of The Graham Bond Organisation were Ginger Baker and Jack Bruce.

Apart from Tea Leaf Tex, aka Brian Dunkley, I had two new partners in crime from school to share these experiences with who would become friends for life. Simon Groom, a farmer's boy armed with an almanac of agricultural jokes that were guaranteed to break the ice at any party. When I watched him years later as one of *Blue Peter's* longest-serving presenters introducing a film for his young audience about Durham Cathedral, after a close-up of the holy door knockers, in an aside to camera he quipped, "What a beautiful pair of knockers." *Yes*, I thought, *that's the Simon that I grew up with.*

The only benefit to us at school from being joined by an 'Express Group' of clever dicks was the arrival into our midst of Steve Cooper, who was better than me at just about everything, especially chatting up girls. When these two budding English scholars were asked to produce the house play for the drama competition, their first instinct was to simply recreate the shower scene from *Psycho* on stage. They were forced to compromise and instead switched to Harold Pinter's *The Birthday Party.*

Simon's appeal as a mate increased when he passed his driving test and bought an old van which somehow managed to find its way to Kempton Park in the summer of 1968 for the National Jazz and Blues Festival. Over the weekend we saw the original Fairport Convention with Sandy Denny, the Jeff Beck Group with Rod Stewart but most memorably of all, an unshaven man in a shabby coat standing on one leg and playing the flute in a group called Jethro Tull. I remember asking Steve Cooper if he fancied leaving the main stage arena for half an hour and popping into a marquee where lesser-known acts were playing to watch a band that I heard were worth a listen. On they came, attired in psychedelic satin and frills, mainly churning out cover versions of pop standards. There was something about Deep Purple, even pre-Ian Gillan that made you think that their days performing in tents would be short-lived.

The following summer, I hitchhiked to the Bath Festival. When the lifts dried up, I had to walk the last ten miles to the Recreation Ground. As I neared my destination, the sounds from the stage became more distinct, and my entry into the Cathedral City was accompanied by the climax to the *Valentyne Suite* by Colosseum featuring the chilling saxophone of Dick Heckstall-Smith. My everlasting memory of that day was the first sighting in this Roman City of a Greek God, Robert Plant of Led Zeppelin.

Later on, in Bryan Adams's summer of '69, Simon and Steve signed up as honorary Boy Scouts for a couple of weeks so that they could accompany me and the rest of the official troop to northern Spain. Under the guidance of our leaders and mentors, Phil Orme and Vic Hoad, we headed to that capital of culture in the Costa Brava, Lloret de Mar. Steve must have had a sixth sense because, in one of those sliding doors moments, he went to a disco and bumped into his future wife, Jill. They were meant for each other, but not until after Steve had finished being an eternal student and that was going to take some time. He and Simon were both reading English in Birmingham and so, I tagged along to the same city and studied law at the College of Commerce.

I was the only person on the course that didn't want to pursue a legal career but wanted to do something different from school. My parents approved, and we had a great day out when I received my degree from the Queen Mother. Looking back now over those three years, it really was more about obtaining an education in life. My studies involved churning out, parrot-fashion, volumes of case law which was then quickly forgotten. Though, in the case of one of the questions I had to answer for my law of tort paper in 1971, to quote Monty Python – no parrots were involved:

Mrs Beastfriend, accompanied by her spaniel dog and a pet monkey, hail a taxi driven by Fred and asks to be taken to the train station. Fred, in spite of his suspicion of the animals, agrees. The monkey is secured by a chain, which Mrs Beastfriend holds securely; the dog is on a lead. Suddenly, the monkey jumps on to Fred's shoulder. The taxi driver swerves and hits a road sign. Fred is injured. The dog immediately jumps out of the open rear window, runs across the road and causes a cyclist [Person A] to fall and suffer injuries. Mrs Beastfriend opens the door and runs to the rescue of the dog. The monkey takes the opportunity to leave the taxi. An old man [Person B], seeing the monkey, falls as he tries to run away.

ADVISE FRED, PERSON A AND B.

I have no idea what I wrote – nearly fifty years later my answers would probably be:

- To Fred: one monkey don't stop no show.
- To A: you should have been cycling on the pavement like everyone else does now.
- To B: didn't you know that its 'softly softly catchee monkey'?

Actually, it seems like, "Everybody's got something to hide, except me and my monkey."

Birmingham was less than an hour's journey from the Baseball Ground, and there was great music in the city. I saw my first Beatle live on stage without realising it. Attracted by Eric Clapton's appearance alongside Delaney and Bonnie at the Town Hall, I failed to identify the self-effacing figure jigging about in the background as George Harrison. On another occasion, we sat on the floor in a Bull Ring ballroom called the Mayfair Suite, inches away from the band on stage, Led Zeppelin.

In the home, or rather slum, that Steve and I shared with three more dear friends, Martin Heiron, Mike Batt and his future wife Shirley, there were elements of our lifestyle that could have been a forerunner to that vintage TV comedy *The Young Ones*. Martin, for example, unable to trust himself to concentrate and do any serious revision for his chemical engineering exams, demanded that we tied him to the chair in his room to stop him from going walkabout. Most of his preparation for his subject, appeared to centre around burning the elements of his frying pan every morning at breakfast time to such an extent that you couldn't see through the smoke to get to the bathroom salubriously placed just past the oven. Our record collection was procured from the Diskery in Hurst Street and every Saturday teatime, we would recreate our own version of *Juke Box Jury*, assessing each other's most recent purchases. In one never-to-be-forgotten session, Martin unveiled the first side of *Abraxas* by Santana, which was met with universal approval. The same applied to Steve's offering of *Teaser and the Firecat* by Cat Stevens and my no-risks-attached selection of *After the Gold Rush* by Neil Young. The problem for the fourth member of our quartet was that Mike never seemed to come back with the LP he had originally intended buying. Having set off in pursuit of *On the Boards* by Taste, he returned with the soundtrack of *2001: A Space Odyssey*. We hovered around the turntable in masochistic anticipation of his reaction. Up triumphantly went his thumb after the opening Apollo mission fanfare of 'Also Sprach Zarathustra', which lasted all of ninety seconds, followed by much uneasy shuffling around in his seat as the music morphed into prolonged monotone monkey sounds that might work well with pictures but don't transfer to the ear. "Not so keen on this bit," said a crestfallen Mike. 'This bit' would actually turn out to be the next fifteen minutes; I've still got the bruises from pinching myself trying not to laugh. 'Space Oddity', on the other hand, was a revelation. Steve and I, without knowing what to expect, got tickets for the afternoon matinée at the Town Hall, starring David Bowie as Ziggy Stardust. It was from another planet and the highlight of our five years in Birmingham. We just made it in the nick of time. He retired the character eleven days later.

Steve was a professional postgraduate, and because I wasn't ready to face a proper job yet, we remained in Birmingham and rented two more salubrious establishments. The first adjoined a bookmakers. Every dawn would break with all the day's runners and riders being declared through our paper-thin walls. It turned me off racing for life. On our first day at the next flat, Steve's amply-built father, Tom, decided to jump up and down to test for dry rot and disappeared through the floorboards. To pay for my rent, I responded to an advert in the *Evening Mail* for a glass collector at a Birmingham nightclub.

The club, located alongside the canal in Gas Street, rather like the Strutt Arms seemed to have great musical connections. It played host to some of the best jazz and blues artists in the business. While I was there, I saw Jimmy Witherspoon, Stéphane Grappelli and Cannonball Adderley, with his brother Nat. The club was next-door to the old ATV studios and attracted regular well-known faces like Chris Tarrant, who was then a TV reporter, and Noele Gordon, the star of *Crossroads*. In the evening under the subdued illumination, it was a beguiling Aladdin's cave, but in the day, it was rather like walking into the ghost train at the fairground when all the lights have been switched on. I have three things to thank this nightclub for. Firstly, it gave me the chance to talk into a microphone for the first time in my life, introducing bands and playing music for the diners. I was encouraged to do so by the resident disc jockey Frank, who wanted to focus more on a management career, and I am grateful that my future career benefited from his ambition. He introduced me to a novel way of making sure that at the end of the evening any would-be hangers-on were dissuaded from breaking the curfew. Last-minute desperate chat-up lines were drowned out by the playing of a disc that was inappropriately released on the 'Music for Pleasure' label. It was entitled *The Exciting Racing Sounds of Grand Prix* and began with the start of the Monaco Grand Prix aboard Graham Hill's car. It did the trick every time.

Secondly, it made me vow that I was never going to allow myself to be bullied by any future employer and thankfully I never was. The club owner rarely made an appearance unless there was a big name in town to entertain. I don't doubt for one moment his entrepreneurial skills, but I'm afraid man-management passed him by. Front of house, with his David Frost patter, he was a charmer but backstage, a very different operator. I vividly recall seeing him reduce one of his hard-working waiters to tears. After breaking off from hosting local dignitaries in his restaurant, he swept through the curtain into the kitchen, grabbed the member of staff and ordered, "SERVE THE F***ING WINE." The waiter attempted to explain that as it was red, he was trying to let it breathe for a moment. The follow-up was an even more threatening eyeball-to-eyeball hiss, "SERVE THE F***ING WINE," after which he painted the smile back on and returned to his guests. He had one face for Des O'Connor, Sid James or any of the other stars who came into his kingdom, quite another, though, for his servants.

Whether or not he was aware of it – and I'm prepared to give him the benefit of the doubt – this owner also presided over the most shocking violence I have ever seen perpetrated by doormen, allegedly there to keep the peace. Some of this was administered in the protected darkness of the canal towpath and was psychopathic. For one of the bouncers, intent on justifying his presence, it became a nauseating badge of honour. Overreacting very often to the most innocuous of transgressions, it might only take someone who had had one too many accidentally bumping into him for his fist to clench. I saw him once after one of his physical triumphs, with his chest puffed out and his face still contorted with venomous self-gratification, secure in the knowledge that in these shadowy days before CCTV, he had been merely acting in self-defence!

The third indirect benefit I received from doing my night shift was to be clear of any daytime obligations and so free to walk to nearby Edgbaston to watch first-class cricket. One sunny afternoon during the tea interval, there was a public address appeal for anyone interested in helping out the local hospital's radio network with their sports commentaries. I wrote a letter expressing an interest and on July 16th, 1973, was invited by David Wigley to do some commentary with him at the upcoming Warwickshire match against Kent. These guys are the real radio sports heroes, doing it all voluntarily for the love of the game. I owe David so much.

I remember reading how Johnny Cash would walk on his own as a youngster, performing songs to an imaginary crowd; it had been the same for me with sports commentary, but now there was going to be a real audience.

White Punks On Dope

Pilot of the airwaves, here is my request
You don't have to play it, but I hope you'll do your best
I've been listening to your show on the radio and you seem like
a friend to me.

"Pilot Of The Airwaves"

Words and Music by Charlie Dore

Black Ink Music Ltd (NS)

All rights administered by Warner Chappell Music Ltd

NOVEMBER, 1973. I WAS TEN MINUTES INTO MY GUIDED TOUR of the former car showrooms that had become BBC Radio Derby. After being introduced to one of the front-line presenters as the new station assistant, I was met with the response, "Oh, I didn't think we needed one." I was feeling not so much like a fish out of water, more a tadpole drained from a pond. It got even better when I was invited to accompany some of my new colleagues for what would turn out to be the traditional two-hour lunch break in the pub. I was joined by one of the main programme producers, a man who would go on to become a senior regional figure at the corporation. "What you need to know is that the management here is crap," he said. I would end up having much more respect for them than for this guy stabbing them in the back. All in all, quite an induction for an impressionable twenty-three-year-old, just given a short-term contract by that so-called 'crap' management.

Whenever I have been asked about how you get into radio, I have had to reply that mine was not a conventional pathway, because it was pure opportunistic luck. All that I had in my locker when I decided to grab the bull by the horns and knock on Radio Derby's front door was that brief contribution to the Birmingham Hospital Radio Network. Timing, though, turned out to be everything. My knock coincided with the radio station having just agreed to let one of its station assistants take an attachment, which is a bit like a footballer going out on loan. There was a temporary vacancy to fill and I would become the surprised beneficiary. I had already been rejected by local radio stations in Birmingham, Sheffield and Southampton, so was not unaware of just how fortunate I was to be given this break.

The five years I spent at Radio Derby were the happiest in my career. For a start, if I had not been there, I would not have bumped into a young lady named Lorna Dickinson, who was learning to make a radio programme at night school, and I am so pleased to have been able to offer her a spot of extra tuition! These were my foundation blocks, working in the sort of community that local radio was made for, alongside an eclectic mix of talented characters. It was very much like the *Drop the Dead Donkey* TV sitcom. At times, it felt like a large dysfunctional family in need of, not so much a board of governors, but a panel of either marriage guidance counsellors or psychiatrists to keep them in check. Initially, the job felt more like training to be a pilot than a broadcaster. I had to come to terms with operating a studio control panel more akin to a Second World War relic from Bletchley Park than equipment Sir George Martin might have used. It didn't take long, though, for me to be issued with a tape recorder, which felt like carrying a microwave oven over your shoulder, and released onto the streets very often to do one of those 'Dead Donkey' features for the end of the bulletin.

The Radio Derby newsroom was mainly recruited from the formidable Roland Orton Agency in Leicester and led by Barrie Eccleston, a considerable presence with a sharp editorial mind, who also doubled up as the Derby County commentator and correspondent. He set the tone with his 'work hard, play hard' principles. Most days were split into four shifts: morning, pub, afternoon and, finally, back at the pub. Whenever the whistle blew, though, and it was time to get down to some serious journalism, they would never go missing. Barrie's voice was associated with the glory years at the Baseball Ground. The respect that he commanded in the community was never better demonstrated than at the end of one of the most dramatic days in the history of Derby County in 1977, after Brian Clough's last-minute rejection of an offer to return as manager. I was sitting next to Barrie in the Radio Derby newsroom late at night when he telephoned Clough and made one last desperate attempt on behalf of the club to get him to reconsider. They spoke cordially for at least twenty minutes, with Barrie even offering inducements like money being made available to buy Trevor Francis from Birmingham City, but Clough could not be tempted.

Barrie's team of news reporters would often regale me in The Greyhound pub with classic stories from days of yore. One of my favourites was when one of their number was supposed to be doing a radio feature on the famous Flying Scotsman steam engine passing through a local village. However, after a liquid lunch, he forgot all about it. He raced back in panic to the studio and cobbled together a vivid eyewitness report using a sound effects record of a train. After this item was broadcast, the phone lines were jammed. The Scotsman's flying visit had actually been postponed for twenty-four hours. When the phone lines were not exactly alive and kicking for the late-night Derby phone-in, one of us would often have to call in ourselves from another studio and be introduced as either Vi or Vic from Spondon to kickstart the debate.

Nothing, though, compared to the fun and frolics to be had working on that Radio Derby institution: 'Spin a Winner'. The listener was invited to pick 'a big one or a little one' choosing either a single, with a number from one to 4,000, or an album, numbered from one to 2,500. If this was not located within thirty seconds down below in the gram library, where there was a buzzer by the turntable, then you won a star prize. When my pal, Richard Faulkner, and I were on duty in pursuit of these selections, we had already predetermined what we wanted to hear. We would wait for twenty-nine seconds and then press the buzzer. "Oh, you were so close," said the presenter. "Better luck next time; now, let's find out what record 2,011 sounds like." On would come something like 'White Punks on Dope' by The Tubes, or Frank Zappa's 'Willie the Pimp', which would then be quickly faded. This certainly made a change from the usual playlist of 'The Old Rugged Cross' or 'Amazing Grace'. We weren't completely heartless and always allowed at least one listener to win.

When I eventually became a BBC member of staff on January 8th, 1975, at a salary of £2,022 a year, I was informed in a letter from London:

If, when they are received, your references are not of the standard required by the BBC, as you have already started work, your employment may be brought to an end immediately without compensation.

They obviously did not get a reference from my mate the bus conductor in Plymouth, and so I was free to carry on performing duties, like recording the daily diary for the Derby area, which was jam-packed with exciting and unmissable attractions like this:

The next meeting of the Derby Electrical Society is tonight at the College of Further Education. The lecture is entitled 'People Protection and High Sensitivity Current Operated ELCB's' will start at six o' clock.

There was also much amusement one evening at the talent show being recorded for future broadcast from the Derbyshire village of Shottle. The judges were so taken by one of the acts on the night they completely forgot about the endgame and voted for this particular entertainer to be given a place in the next round. Unfortunately, this would result in three minutes of silence when the show was aired, as the performer had been a mime artist. Some things just do not transfer to radio, and the sport of darts is one of them. When I attempted to do live commentary on this in the days before electronic calculation, so feeble was my maths that by the time I had worked out what the target was, the winning arrow had already hit the spot.

Local radio's greatest achievement has been to involve, discover and nurture talent from the area that otherwise might never have come to the surface. The best example of this in the history of Radio Derby is the late Deric Longden, one of the most engaging people that I ever had the good fortune to get to know. When producer Roger Mortimore decided to launch a short story competition, Deric entered and won. He repeated the trick the following year, and when it became obvious that he was destined to hold an Ant and Dec-type grip on this annual award, Roger suggested, that in order to give someone else a chance, he would offer him a weekly slot on his show. Deric went on to contribute to Radio Derby for about thirty years. He was the sort of guy who brightened your everyday and put any perceived problem you might have thought you had into perspective. Much of his inspiration for writing in those days stemmed from his way of life, nursing his chronically ill first wife, Diana. After her death, he documented her story, and his book was eventually made into a BBC drama, with Julie Walters playing the part of Diana and Deric portrayed by Jim Broadbent. Dame Thora Hird was cast as Deric's mum, Annie, who reprised this role in the film *Lost for Words*, based on the sequel story written by Deric about living with his mum's dementia. Thora Hird won a BAFTA and Deric an Emmy. Deric was able to find happiness with his second wife, Aileen Armitage, who, in spite of losing her sight, was also a prolific novelist. He was a master of the understated one-liner. Before he died from cancer, we would get an annual Christmas card from him, usually with a message like, "Round robin… er! Nothing much happened, actually." This couldn't have been further from the truth. Deric made every minute and every word count.

Although I was being steered towards producing sports coverage, I made the most of any opportunity to indulge my other passion. It was to be the golden age of record reps. In return for their promotional goodies, Stewart White and I reciprocated by doing interviews with artists who had new releases to plug. Stewart went on to become the long-serving BBC regional TV presenter of *Look East*. I fondly remember him doing a favour for one rep by agreeing to interview an unknown band on his label. When they came in, there were three of them and had to squeeze into a tiny cubicle of a studio to talk about what was their first album. It was *Outlandos d'Amour* by The Police. On another occasion in a Birmingham hotel, before he could chat about his solo album *Ride a Rock Horse*, Roger Daltrey the front man of a band who specialized in destroying equipment, painstakingly mended my BBC microphone which should have been handed back to Noah on the Ark.

Sir Cliff Richard had nothing to plug but could not have afforded me more time when he agreed to have a chat at the Derby Midland Hotel. What was so impressive about him that day was that even though he had given hundreds of interviews over the years, he treated this one as if it was his first. One of his most thought-provoking answers was to my question about how much responsibility he personally felt as a pop star in the '70s towards today's 'young ones':

Anybody who's got that kind of influence has got to realise that they have a responsibility, particularly when the music business appeals to such young people. I've never been to a Bowie concert, but my manager's daughter went when she was fourteen, and the things that were happening both on stage and in the audience were unbelievable. I don't have first-hand experience of one of his concerts, but I feel that a brilliant guy like that – and there's no doubt that he is brilliant, because nobody could make that kind of music and have conceived such a fake act and make it so presentable without being very clever. He obviously doesn't have any idea of responsibility. All the things I go through today will influence my thoughts and my feelings tomorrow. So when

Dad & Mum July 2nd 1947

Me & my Policeman
Poppa Fearick

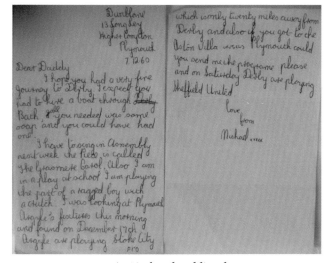

At 10 already addicted

Long Row Junior School Belper 1961, Peter Wight front row centre stage

The Strutts School Cricket Team – and the "Purple Haze Hair" that prevented me from getting my school colours. Steve Cooper is to the left of me and Brian Dunkley's younger brother Andrew is standing just behind Steve

Simon Groom & Steve Cooper 1971

Brian Dunkley auditioning for Lawrence of Arabia

Dad telling Brian Clough and Sir Alf Ramsey
where they are going wrong

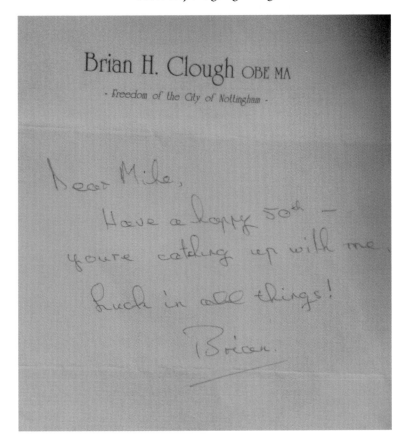

Brian H. Clough OBE MA

· Freedom of the City of Nottingham ·

Dear Mike,

Have a happy 50th –
you're catching up with me.

Luck in all things!

Brian.

Tommy Docherty and Charlie George with a Jason King look alike

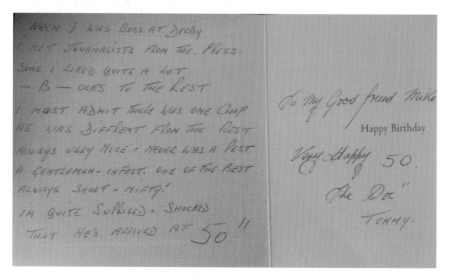

The Poetic Doc

Iain Thomas had rota problems this Saturday. The Sports Room's Gill Pulsford, Garry Richardson, Emily McMahon, Ian Darke, Peter and Jan Brackley at our 1983 wedding in Derbyshire.

Celebrating 50 years of Sports Report with Cliff Morgan, Harry Carpenter, Jon Champion, Jim Rosenthal, Alan Parry, Desmond Lynam, Audrey Adams, James Alexander Gordon, Christopher Martin-Jenkins, Renton Laidlaw, Tony Adamson, Bob Burrows & Pat Murphy

My favourite fictional Uncle

*Peter Lorenzo & Andy Peebles musical
differences but united in sport*

*Penny, Debbie and Frances of Radio Sport
get to the head of the queue to meet "The Greatest"*

The Heartbreak Kid

*My treasured invitation
from Bill Ross*

Radio Times 1980 in distinguished company ▼

▲ *Presenting Sport on Two 1981 with Bryan Tremble*

◄ *Brian Johnston's dedication in Chatterboxes*

▲ *Wimbledon on Radio 2 with: David Lloyd, Richard Evans, Norman Cuddeford, Bob Howe, Joyce Hume, Fred Perry, Christine Janes, Max Robertson, Peter Jones and Tony Adamson*

Sir Trevor & BB Mexico 1985

Flying with the Eagle, Calgary 1988

Jimmy Hill unsure about the 11 he's about to manage: Brian Woolnough, Alex Montgomery, Colin Gibson, Bob Driscoll, Bob Harris, Harry Harris, Paddy Barclay, Jeff Powell, Steve Curry, Stuart Jones and David Lacey.

Ron Greenwood back in Budapest with my two predecessors Brian Moore and Bryon Butler

you get a kid of twelve seeing some of the things Alice Cooper allegedly does, like chewing off chicken heads on stage, what can it do? If they say in an argument that it doesn't have any effect, then I would say why do it? If you're doing it for no effect at all, then I assume you're wasting your time, but if it does have an effect, I think it is a bad effect.

When I saw Cliff and The Shadows at the Gaumont Derby in 1961, I thought it was the most exciting thing I'd ever seen at that time. Similarly, when I was lucky enough to see David Bowie a decade later, I felt the same emotion. I wouldn't have wanted to miss either.

If the music was a pastime, the sports coverage had become a commitment. When batsman Graham Gooch was selected for England for the first time against Australia, he was playing for Essex at nearby Ilkeston. British Forces Broadcasting asked if I might be able to get an interview with him and we did it before the start of the day's play. It was hard going and not helped by pranksters like teammate Ray East pulling silly faces at him. Gooch then was a man of few words and, on his England debut, few runs. Nearly 9,000 test runs later, he matured into one of his sport's most articulate spokesmen – just like another inspirational cricketer, the South African Eddie Barlow, who almost single-handedly lifted the atmosphere around Derbyshire. He set the agenda in our very first interview:

Winning is something that you have to learn. It is something that you cannot teach people. It is something that you eventually learn how to do as an individual and as a group. I've seen games lost when they should have been won by teams that didn't know how to win when the opportunity was provided for them. They didn't see it, didn't understand it, weren't capable of handling the situation.

That should be pinned up in every dressing room – unless you've already got someone like Francis Lee in your team. Like Barlow, he had a similar galvanising effect on Derby County during the 1975 Championship-winning season, which underpinned our sports coverage. When he was interviewed by the radio station's leading female presenter, Kit Poxon, his impish nature crackled through the airwaves and provoked a Ms Poxon blush unobserved on radio. When she asked him if scoring a goal was the best feeling a man could have, he paused deliberately and then chuckled, "No, it's the second best." Franny clearly had not been briefed beforehand that Kit was married to the Commonwealth Games weightlifting gold medallist Tony Ford. Francis Lee, like many of his British contemporaries at the time, was not averse to taking the odd tumble or two in the penalty area. I had a wry chuckle when I heard Sir Alex Ferguson in later years alleging that he thought diving began in English football when the foreign players started coming into the league. More commonplace perhaps, but there weren't too many Tom Daley impressionists from overseas around when Derek Dougan was doing his party piece for Wolves and punting the ball forward, sandwiching himself in between two centre-backs and then collapsing like a sack of potatoes. That was nearly half a century ago.

Francis Lee was to his Derby manager Dave Mackay what Mackay himself had been as a player to Brian Clough. Mackay, although eventually treated abysmally by Derby, was a class act. After his sacking, he agreed to do an interview with me. We met at the White Hart Pub in Duffield, but he suggested that we went to his assistant Des Anderson's home just down the road and asked if he could have a lift. Of course, I said but, anticipating humiliation, knew that this was going to mean a Mercedes man having to wrap his knees around the dashboard of my mum's little Mini. Like the great guy he was, he could sense my embarrassment and, trying to put me at ease as we drove off, observed, "Nifty little things these, aren't they?" Two words never meant to go together: Mini and Mackay.

Derby County were now in self-destruct, free-fall and were becoming a basket case of a club; one that Brian Clough was certainly not going to return to when that approach was made in early 1977.

His old *bête noir*, Sam Longson, was no longer chairman but still at the club, and the antipathy Clough felt for him still was all too transparent. A couple of months after declining Derby's offer, he went off on a tangent in an interview he was giving me on the eve of bringing his Nottingham Forest side to the Baseball Ground for Kevin Hector's testimonial. This extract was never broadcast:

> *The fact that we are taking a side over there is not only ironic, it's good for Peter [Taylor] and me because we wanted to take a side over for Colin Boulton and were refused. We wanted to help with Alan Hinton and for some reason, we were refused. This is the first time we've had a chance to say thanks to somebody who did us a great service, and it's not a coincidence that Sam Longson is not in the chair – that is an absolute fact. We should have been back for Colin Boulton; we should have been back for Alan Hinton, but we're delighted for Kevin Hector because they all gave us so much loyalty, so much dedication that we were just breaking our necks to repay it and a guy called Sam Longson was stopping it.*

Another adversary of Clough's – Don Revie, when he was England manager – came into our patch one Sunday as the guest of honour at a local Midland League ground. It was for a light-hearted game that had been organised between the two grassroots teams in the country who had conceded the most goals and had the worst records at any level. The sponsors set up an interview with him for me in a Portakabin, and I began with my tongue firmly in my cheek by asking him if he was hoping to spot some talent for his England squad. Don's sense of humour seemed to have deserted him that day. He glared at me and snapped, "No, absolutely not – football is only about winners."

Cloughie would have entered into the spirit of it, and as for Tommy Docherty, he would have been armed to the teeth with suitable one-liners, just as he was every Friday lunchtime entertaining the East Midlands' media and sending them away with at least three or four potential back page headlines. In his time at Derby, though, this was not so much a Doc at work; more a vivisectionist. Under Docherty, the club seemed to buy and sell players almost on a daily basis; great for sports bulletins but not so conducive to team continuity. Tommy had come to the Baseball Ground after being sacked from his dream job at Manchester United and never really got Old Trafford out of his system while he was attempting to dig Derby County out of all the holes they had dug for themselves before he arrived.

I was very fortunate that all of the managers I worked with in Derby were helpful and, even more importantly, appreciative of what we were trying to do. I used to hear horror stories from other local radio producers about managers they had to deal with. Some would turn on the charm when the national media turned up but had a very different demeanour dealing with their local reporters, who relied on their co-operation. Household name managers full of bonhomie in *Sports Report* on a Saturday night would then be awkward and patronising when they returned to their local beat on a Monday morning. I was also lucky to be the only local radio operator in my area; nowadays, I would be just one of a pool of microphones. The only downside about being the sports producer at Radio Derby and working closely with the football club was that as my relationship changed from supporter to reporter, so my eyes became less starry than they had been in the 1960s.

The strangest day in my involvement with the club occurred just before I left the city. One morning, I had torn off from the teleprinter in the newsroom a story which went into comprehensive detail about Derby County finances and details of players who were going to be allowed to appear in the North American League over the summer. Normally I would have treated such a report with more caution before using it, but on this occasion knew that it had been compiled by a local journalist with impeccable sources. Within half an hour of my broadcast, I was summoned by phone to the Baseball Ground and what followed was a bizarre interrogation and attempt to discover where I had got all my information from. My lips remained sealed, and to this day I haven't been able to make much sense of their overreaction, yet evidently, I had inadvertently rattled a cage. All I know is that these were nebulous times when players might routinely be given free transfers from one English club to somewhere like Washington or Tulsa and then return to a different English club, sometimes for a fee, and there would be very little in the way of an international paper trail to follow. Derby County were the subject of a police investigation, and no charges were ever brought.

The European footballers who tended to flourish in the States at the time were the players who embraced the new way of life and were able to modify their game. In 1980, for example, the great Johan Cruyff played in the same Washington team as the less-decorated former Coventry forward Alan Green. While Cruyff simply fulfilled his contract, Green's contribution put him in the shade, scoring forty-two goals in fifty-six games.

My life in the East Midlands was nearly over and the wheel was turning full circle, with Derby County on their way back down to where they had been all those years ago when our family first arrived. To rub salt into the wound, Brian Clough and Peter Taylor, after declining to return to the club, were on the verge of making Nottingham Forest the best side in Europe.

I was joining the BBC Radio Sports department in London on January 22nd, 1979. At a farewell gathering for family and friends, my dad uncharacteristically took centre stage and produced a tape for us to listen to. He had dared to venture where other mere mortals would have been too afraid to tread. Not only that, it was a Sunday morning when he marched up the long drive leading to The Elms in Quarndon to disturb the peace in the Clough family household. He wanted Brian to record a farewell message to me and had this not been a request from a loving dad, the message might well have been limited to two words. On this occasion, Clough, the great family man himself, had seen the bigger picture and, impressed by the fortitude of this patriarch on his doorstep, invited him in, poured a couple of Scotches and said this:

Mike, good luck to you. It's far easier being interviewed by you than by your father. His machine, his headphones and his microphone literally inches from my nose, but as both amateurs and laymen in your industry, we'd like to say simply good luck to you in your new position. I hope it goes well for you. I hope you realise any ambitions that you have buried deep down or even on the surface. You know that, having left Derby, you've left a lot of friends and you've left people that you can always come back to. If a telephone call is made and any – what word can I use – co-operation is required, you know you have a friend at Nottingham Forest.

He remained true to his word, and he *never* forgot my dad.

One day my father – he told me,
"Son, don't let it slip away."
He took me in his arms, I heard him say,
"When you get older – your wild life will live for younger days
Think of me if ever you're afraid."
He said, "One day you'll leave all this behind
So live a life you will remember."

The Stoker

Friday, October 27th, 1978: 5 Portland Place, London, W1A.

IT BEGAN UNPROMISINGLY. "WELL, MIKE, WE ARE A BIT surprised to see you here again today." For the third time, I was about to be interviewed for the post of sports assistant at BBC Radio in London. This was not an opening that I had mentally prepared myself for on the train. Where was this going? I was in need of further elaboration. When it came, though, I was none the wiser. The googly with topspin had been delivered by Bob Burrows, head of sport (or rather, HSOBR) everyone in authority had to have letters after their name and all employees, it seemed in those days, were assistants.

"Well, after your last interview with us, although you didn't get the post, we invited you to come and join us on attachment, and you didn't take up the offer." I had been bowled middle stump by Bob, but the stunned expression on my face must have been enough to convince my inquisitor that there had clearly been another of those inter-departmental cock-ups and the boat was then allowed to sail into less choppy water.

I returned to Derby with a bee in my bonnet and, first thing on Monday morning, called in to see station manager John Bright to find out if he could enlighten me further about the hand grenade that had been tossed into my lap. He looked a bit sheepish and asked me to leave the matter with him, which I did. Before close of play for the day, he tapped me on the shoulder and assured me not to worry about any misunderstanding with London, because he had just been informed that I had got the job. There had, though, been a breach of protocol. Radio Derby had been made aware of the attachment opportunity and had blocked it, which was their prerogative, but they had not kept me in the loop. All this, though, was quickly swept to one side. I had been third time lucky, and Broadcasting House (or rather, BH) was to be my new home.

In those early days, however, it could not have felt further away from home. I was in my late twenties and had already experienced five years away as a student and a drifter, but this was to be much more of a shock to the system. This was, at times, acute loneliness. I had become used to residing only a couple of sets of traffic lights away from my workplace in Derby, around which was built a gregarious social scene that was never going to be replicated in my new surroundings. Lorna was now reading theatre studies at Warwick University, where one of her mature student colleagues was the renowned folk singer Ian Campbell, the father of UB40's Ali and Robin. My little house in a Derbyshire village was being replaced by a one-bedroom flat, the size of a postage stamp, in Stanmore. I was the youngest in the block by forty-five years and was treated every Sunday morning to the greatest hits of Father Abraham and The Smurfs by my closest neighbour. My daily journey into central London was made on autopilot in the company of expressionless commuters who looked wiped out even before they got to work with no mobile phones in those days for them to call imaginary friends to pass the time of day. However, there was one massive ray of light at the end of the underground tunnel: I was joining an Academy of Sports Broadcasting, and many of my new colleagues and eventual friends were going to be voices from my childhood, as well as my youth.

Entering the sports room on the third floor of Broadcasting House for the first time was like that first-day feeling at a new school. Rising above it all and taking it in my stride was not something that came naturally to me, and all of my self-consciousness would have been laid bare for anyone to take advantage of, had they been so inclined. You have to remember that the eyes now being focused on my unease belonged to some of the sharpest observers of human life God ever gave a microphone to: Peter Jones, Bryon Butler, Christopher Martin-Jenkins and Gerald Williams. They were all there on that first morning, occupying what appeared to be pre-assigned desks in that class of '79. One of the editors, Phil King, had worked in Derby, so that should have made me feel more at home, or so I thought. One of my first instructions from him was, "Mike, get on the dog and bone and ask where they got the readies from for the new jam jar." It was straight out of *Minder*. Fortunately, I had one in the shape of the more sensitive Gerald Williams, who was able to interpret that I was being asked to make a phone call to find out who put up the money to finance a new motor racing car. Always one step removed from it all, in his oasis of calm, was the chief producer, Bryan Tremble, with whom I would form an all-too-brief close professional bond and who remains my greatest mentor.

Overseeing the day-to-day running of the operation was Iain Thomas, managing editor and battle-hardened from the newspaper industry. First impressions can sometimes be so misleading. After he had pinned up the weekly rota for us all, comprising shifts of Intro, Late, Prod, Back-Up and the dreaded Overnight, he would hover. If he detected that one of the more junior newcomers might be less than impressed with his schedule, he would lead you over to the window, point towards Regent Street and say, "Dearie, dearie, young Ingham. If you don't like it, son: Barclays bank." I don't know what he had got against them, but he certainly wouldn't have said Bank of Scotland – Iain was a fiercely proud man of Midlothian with a heart of gold. The only error that I can remember him making in this male-dominated environment was to think that it would be a good idea to have a social evening for all the wives and partners to make them feel more part of the sports room family. What a mistake that was, as he found himself pinned in the corner of the room by one good lady berating him for always putting her husband on a late shift every Friday and Saturday. Iain was about to deny all knowledge of this until the penny dropped and the invented alibi was allowed to stand. Generally, though, in those early days, there was not the same social interaction as in Derby. Ships passed one another in the night. You could always – if you were brave enough – go and drink a pint with the real power in the office, statistician Bill Ross, while he consumed four, but that was for much stronger constitutions than mine. Bill was the most interesting character I ever worked with and merits more coverage later.

In those first months, opportunities to broadcast were limited. When I was asked to help out recording the racing results, it was such a breakthrough that I called my mum and dad to make sure they tuned in. Good thing they didn't hear our first attempt. "Farting at Fakenham," was how Tony Adamson began. Nothing more guaranteed than some schoolboy humour to get you rolling around on the floor. Tony, once a country and western DJ when at Radio Oxford, went on to become the best tennis commentator that I ever heard on radio. He was a great raconteur. He returned once from covering a tournament in New York and relived for our benefit the ceremonial moment when the stadium announcer, with the aftershave you could smell from our side of the Atlantic, declared, "Ladies and gentlemen, Madison Square Garden is proud to announce that tonight our national anthem will be sung by the world-famous soprano *Jane Doe*." There was a pause to allow his audience to anticipate this treat, only for the silence to be broken by one very loud voice from the top tier: "*Jane Doe sucks cocks*." The master of ceremonies gathers himself up before proceeding with, "Nevertheless..."

Tennis unwittingly the source of much sports desk amusement when it was revealed that 'Martina Navratilova has beaten Pam Shriver in straight sex' and that 'John McEnroe had overcome Jimmy Connors – six minus four, six minus three and six minus two'. Live broadcasting can be fraught with Freudian slip danger – on one round up of the day it was revealed that 'Nottingham Forest centre-half Larry Lloyd has pissed a fatness test'. Unlike today, the sports desks had to be much more disciplined and ended with you often having to talk up to the pips. One colleague, Gordon Turnbull, once found himself running out of time and in a fluster ended with 'finally, tonight's football results: 0-2, 3-1 and 1-1' with no mention of the teams in question. He went on to become one of the best heads of department I've ever had. Occasionally you could find yourself short of material with still a minute to go. This was where the veteran studio producer Godfrey Dixey, who was not unlike the Godfrey in *Dad's Army*, came into his own. He would stand behind you and suddenly thrust a piece of coloured paper, into your hand, that he'd just ripped off the teleprinter. These were stories from around the world that he liked to use as last minute filler material which he described as *odd*. I was always tempted to say, "Finally, some odd for you," before rounding up the latest news from the Jakarta Hockey league. On one famous occasion it wasn't the ending of the sports desk that proved to be a problem but the start. I fondly remember Christopher Martin-Jenkins arriving breathless in Studio 3H Broadcasting House to introduce the 6.45pm Sportsdesk of the day on Radio 2, having left the first page of his script on his typewriter in the office. "Good Evening" he announced with great authority "*First tonight's* HEADLINES"...gazing in controlled panic at the blank sheet of paper in front of him...a little cough and then "*There aren't any...so on to football*"

A very different-sounding BBC had evolved from the corporation I first fell in love with watching that classic black-and-white film of the 1930s, *Death in Broadcasting House*, with its rabbit warren of studios, do-it-yourself sound effects, presenters in dinner jackets and everyone speaking so frightfully well. In Radio Sport though, the legacy of the founding fathers lived on. Everything that you hear when you tune into sport on the radio these days is an endowment from two people: Angus Mackay and Bob Burrows.

Angus Mackay was to Radio Sport what fellow Scottish pioneers John Logie Baird and Lord Reith were to television and the BBC. He was a former military man who looked a little like the actor Fulton Mackay in *Porridge* and had joined the BBC Radio news department from *The Scotsman* newspaper. In 1948, the year of the London Olympics, he started a Saturday evening round-up programme called *Sports Report*. The show was without a signature tune, until someone from the record library produced some music out of the blue, which just happened to also be called 'Out of the Blue', which became the most evocative theme in the history of British sports broadcasting. Like all great football managers, Angus recruited faultlessly and had as his main presenter the biggest star in radio or TV at the time, Eamonn Andrews. Eammon would painstakingly have to type out in advance three different cues for every football report to cover all eventualities: home win, away win and draw. Heaven help any reporter who then strayed by even one second over the time allocated to them. They could expect a phone call and a last warning from Angus. An iron fist approach that crushed even the great racing commentator Peter Bromley, not exactly renowned as a shrinking violet. Peter remembered how he was once asked to preview the Cheltenham Gold Cup and drifted a bit off-piste to include a mention of the Champion Hurdle, won by an amateur rider for the first time in twenty-five years on a one-eyed horse. He received a terse reprimand from Mackay and Peter countered, making four points:

1. I said I was convinced there was a story.
2. I suggested the twenty seconds before the programme to the producer, who accepted it.
3. I didn't overrun.
4. I did tip the winner of the Gold Cup.

Angus Mackay replied:

1. We weren't.
2. He didn't.
3. You're not expected to.
4. You are expected to.

That memo became one of Peter's most treasured possessions.

Bob Burrows also had a newspaper background, and what he did after succeeding Angus Mackay was to move the department to another level. It always amuses me nowadays when I hear the BBC trot out their two favourite buzz words, 'strategy and vision' as if they are new concepts, because Bob Burrows defined these words over forty years ago. His 'strategy' being for sport to split from news and make better use of outside broadcasts and his 'vision' was to expand Saturday afternoons into *Sport on Two* and beef up the coverage of crown jewel events like Wimbledon. Forty years later, it is so ironic to see Radio Sport dancing to the tune of news again after striving so hard to become independent – but that's 'strategy and vision' for you.

I will forever be grateful to Bob Burrows for appointing me but with hindsight, also for leaving when he did. Unlike Angus Mackay, he could see a future in television and within my first year in the department, left to become controller of sport at Thames Television. In my one and only annual interview with him, he reminded me of our first meeting at Radio Derby when he had watched me beavering around, producing all the sport for the evening bulletin and that was how he saw my role – not as a broadcaster, more of a stoker, as editor Phil King used to describe it. I had so much respect for him and was devastated by this appraisal. Ever since I used to tune into my dad's crystal set in Plymouth, I wanted to be one of the voices coming out of it and had presented and commentated on all of sports' biggest occasions in my dreams. Of course, like all the great coaches, he was quite right to make sure that my feet were kept firmly on the ground and that an apprenticeship was fully served, but my gut instinct tells me that I would not have gone on to experience the career that I did had he remained as my boss.

It was a surprise to be included as a stoker in the radio team for the 1979 Open Golf Championship at Royal Lytham & St Anne's. We were bunkered in the radio car mobile studio for four days. I did manage to get outside once when the Home Secretary, Lord Whitelaw, walked past our window, and Bob Burrows instructed to me to body swerve my way around his security and bring him straight in for an interview. Apart from meeting the right honourable Willie, other memories from my first outside broadcast were a sign above my bedroom in our Blackpool accommodation – "No eating pies in the corridor" – and chatting to Les Dawson who lived nearby after he had appeared on *Sport on Four* with Tony Lewis. I thanked him for getting up so early and talking us to live; his response, with a vintage deadpan expression, was, "It wasn't live, was it!?", before eventually, with immaculate timing, cracking into a mischievous grin.

As the new boy, although I wasn't subjected to the school baptism under the cold shower, I was still the victim of a more sophisticated adult prank. I was made an offer that couldn't be refused to attend the next MDR supper. This involved a cross-section of BBC staff gathering in the governor's dining room to take bread and wine with the managing director of radio. When I disclosed that I was from sport, it turned out to be quite a conversation stopper and shed a little more light on why news bulletins would routinely end with, "Finally, sport!" After receiving this invite (or rather, drawing the short straw) I remember asking the *Sport on Two* presenter, Jim Rosenthal, what the food would be like. "Grade C salad," he replied with a straight face. I was concerned that if I was going to have my tongue loosened by carafes of wine that I had better line my stomach first and went to the canteen for sausage, beans and chips. Half an hour later, after my grade C salad starter, I was staring at a mouth-watering dish of beef wellington with all the trimmings but was already full to the brim with grease.

I used to see Jimmy Savile regularly in the canteen when it reopened after midnight for the graveyard shift. He always seemed to be wearing a blue tracksuit, big cigar in hand whilst very audibly joshing with the female staff. While I had a reason to be there, requiring the rocket fuel of coffee to see me through my overnight, I was never quite sure what his reason was for being there at such an ungodly hour.

The main purpose of the overnight was to introduce two morning sports bulletins on the Radio 4 *Today* programme. This was pitched at a more general audience rather than committed sports enthusiasts and as a result, was a little more bland and superficial. To the programme's producers and editors, usually with far weightier things on their mind, your contributions were viewed as a light relief afterthought, but for our department, it was rightly regarded as one of the most prestigious duties that we had to perform. The *Today* programme was an institution, no longer presented by the legendary Jack de Manio but by two personalities that I admired so much that it was quite intimidating at first being in their presence. The procedure would be to try and slip into the studio quietly when the red light wasn't on, find the nearest seat available opposite Brian Redhead and John Timpson, and sometimes next to a politician like Neil Kinnock or a world leader like President Kaunda of Zambia, who told me off air that he was a Spurs fan! Before I did this shift for the first time, I had to learn the ropes by shadowing others. This looked like it would be even more daunting than coping with the quick-witted Brian Redhead, as my overnight mentor was going to be a man I never dreamt of sharing a studio with, never mind bedroom: the revered football correspondent, Bryon Butler.

Bryon liked to volunteer for overnights in the summer to give him more time to participate in his other sporting love, cricket. Bryon's overnight routine turned out to be the polar opposite of mine. He was ready to retire before midnight and would then be bright-eyed and bushy-tailed after devouring at least six hours sleep. When it was my turn to do the shift, I was still belonging to yesterday, red-eyed from a sleepless night, not just because of the unwelcome starched sheets of the hospital-style bed in The BBC's Langham accommodation, which has since become a luxury hotel, but mainly because of concern that I might make a pig's ear of the script that I must have rewritten fifty times. I'll never forget my first appearance on the *Today* programme. With great nervous relief, I ended my bulletin with Julian Wilson's racing tips. A perfect cue for the avuncular, erudite John Timpson, who back announced me with a Shakespearean, "*There you are, then, Mike Ingham for a horse.*"

One delightful spin-off from being in the sports room alone at the start of the night shift is that very often on the way to his studio with a pile of records, John Peel would pop in to get the football results. He turned out to be everything that I hoped he would be. Unlike one or two other heroes I would meet later in life, John was down to earth, friendly and at times appeared almost as self-conscious as me. I remember him telling me that although he had Kenny Dalglish's phone number, he would never be able to pluck up enough courage to ever call him. It used to be joked that professionally John Peel looked upon Tony Blackburn – the disc jockey who launched Wonderful Radio 1 – as the antichrist. If Peel more than lived up to my expectations, then Blackburn far exceeded them.

I was never a fan of Blackburn's type of show but will never forget the day two of my dear old friends from Plymouth, Gwen and Ted Davis, popped in to see me at Broadcasting House. Rather than giving them a guided tour of tape machines and ribbon microphones, I wanted them to witness a live show being broadcast. Without having arranged anything in advance, we headed off to the studios. It would have been quite enough for Gwen and Ted to simply be allowed to gaze from a distance through the glass for a few minutes, but I had not legislated for the generosity of Tony Blackburn. He beckoned to them to come in, take a seat and have a chat while the records were being played. He did not know me, in fact, it's the only time we ever met, and he didn't have to do it. Rather than feeling affronted by having his space invaded, he oozed genuine class and charm; that's why he became a star and I have never forgotten this gesture.

Back in the world of sport, a little bit like John Peel coming into the office, it was equally unreal to meet Denis Law for the first time when he came down to London to summarise on a game. Charismatic Denis had a sense of humour as dry as the Sahara. There were visits too from other icons of my childhood, like legendary broadcasters Brian Johnston and Max Robertson. Max had come in to plug his latest tennis publication and on seeing the rugby commentator Chris Rea asked, "Oh hello, Chris, have you got a copy of my new book?"

"Err, no I don't," said Chris.

"Would you like one, then?" said Max.

"Yes, thank you very much," said Chris.

"There you are, then, that will be ten pounds," said Max.

There was already a changing of the guard taking place. Bob Burrows and Phil King were off to Thames Television, whilst the main presenter, Jim Rosenthal, was joining London Weekend Television. When it was time for the Olympic Games in the summer of 1980, with half of the department seemingly in Moscow – including all of the potential candidates for presenting a London-based *Sport on Two* – there was almost by default only one man left standing ready to step into the breach. There would be live racing to introduce from Peter Bromley, so it was Hobson's choice, enter the stoker, Mike Ingham, for a horse.

Seems like everyone is out looking for the sun
Singing rain and pain on he who hesitates.
But it will shine when it shines.
You might think I'm wasting time
But I'm just a good old boy that's learned to wait.

Don't Mess with Bill

"SO YOU THINK YOU CAN BROADCAST, DO YOU?" THE QUESTION was swiftly followed by a more than penetrative prod into my midriff. There I was, still basking in reflected glory after making my *Sport on Two* presentation debut which was a bit like how I imagine it must feel for a cricketer to play for the first time at Lord's. There was never any danger, though, of that first cap becoming too small for my expanding head. Another part of my anatomy was now being targeted by Cliff Morgan, son of the Rhondda, one of the greatest Welsh rugby players ever to live and breathe, and a BBC broadcasting legend. He knew a thing or two about living as well, having survived a serious stroke, but it was the breathing that occupied his mind that Monday morning. "You can't broadcast unless you know how to breathe properly. It's like all the great opera singers; you have to stand up and fill your lungs," demanded the great former fly-half. Cliff despised anybody taking broadcasting for granted; for him it was always a privilege. Now in front of a roomful of colleagues, who moments earlier had been patting me on the back, I was being slapped in the solar plexus. "And another thing," he said, "it's picture, not pitcher. A pitcher is something you carry water in," which was what I needed at that moment, dehydrated by humiliation. Managing editor Iain Thomas had observed the whole incident and adopted the role of good cop, assuring me that, "He wouldn't have done that, son, if he didn't care about you." A decade after my dressing-down, I received several letters from Cliff after he had retired as head of BBC TV Sport. In one he wrote, "Your voice is now moving towards the mature state which comes with age and correct breathing." I was certainly able to breathe more easily after that. I look back at his unorthodox guidance with unequivocal gratitude. The BBC, according to founder Lord Reith, had a duty to 'inform, educate and entertain'. In over forty years at the corporation, many entertained me, but Cliff Morgan was one of only a handful of people to inform and educate me professionally.

Another equally dogmatic, but no less effective was the former local radio training officer Robert McLeish. Four weeks spent in his company was worth four years. He made me think more about what I was trying to do. "You can never be early or late; you can only be on time," was one of his pet phrases that I have tried unsuccessfully to impress on my eldest son!

The biggest influence on me was *Sport on Two* producer Bryan Tremble. I'm not sure which creative genius at the BBC had the 'strategy and vision' to introduce the concept of 'Talent', an elite division which I find obnoxious. 'Talent' is defined by the Oxford Dictionary as a 'special aptitude or gift'. Talented people in life often make a difference, for example, the medical profession, scientists, inventors, teachers, artists, musicians and, yes, a handful from the world of sport. In broadcasting, my definition of 'Talent' would be 'irreplaceable' and to be truthful, not many of the performers who are treated by the BBC as members of this exclusive club fall into that category. As a producer, Bryan Tremble most certainly *did* but like so many of the genuinely talented people behind the scenes filming, directing, writing and editing, their ability is often overlooked. Broadcasters can be here today, gone tomorrow, flavours of the month in the ratings game. Craftsmen like Bryan endure, and when they have to be replaced, as he did when he joined the exodus to Thames Television, the loss is immeasurable. He just knew instinctively what sounded right on radio; I am convinced he must have gone to bed with his headphones still on. Often I would bring back an interview lasting up to half an hour, all of which would have been turned around and played in its entirety at Radio Derby. Bryan would listen carefully to it and comment that he should be able to get something out of it and would reduce what I thought was a thirty-minute masterpiece to three. He made you aim higher, got the very best out of you and was an oasis of calmness. When you were in the studio, he communicated with an economy of words no matter what chaos was unfolding around him. While others might have gushed, "Mike, we can't go to West Ham, he's not turned up yet, and the line isn't working at Spurs, so go to Arsenal." Bryan would simply instruct, "Change of plan, Arsenal." I am just so grateful for the limited time we had together. Bryan set the standards and had he been so inclined would have made a wonderful head of Radio Sport.

One of the great joys of introducing *Sport on Two* for four years was to be able to hand over to some of the most mellifluous football reporters of my childhood. Men like Bill Bothwell with a voice straight out of *Whisky Galore*. Bill had also been chairman of Tranmere Rovers and his beat was predominantly the North West. There was one unusual winter Saturday afternoon when nearly all of the major games were south of the Wirral and because of the imbalance, we were experiencing difficulty finding a reporter to cover the match at Ipswich. Bryan Tremble turned to me and asked if it would be impertinent to ask Bill Bothwell in his veteran years if he fancied making a cross country trek for us. "Do you know," said Bill when we called him, "it's the only First Division ground I have never been to, so pencil me in." On match day in very hostile weather, he arrived at Portman Road just in time to hear that the game had been postponed. Now I can think of one or two others in that situation who might have resorted to a two-barrelled verbal offensive. Not Bill, who found a phone box, spoke to a more than mortified Bryan, gave him the news and, before retracing his tortuous journey, joked, "Well, at least I have been to the ground now."

Our head of sport, Bob Burrows, was succeeded by AP Wilkinson, a name I always used to see at the end of the credits for *Grandstand*. After leaving television, he had been working in the BBC appointments department, and the apocryphal story doing the rounds was that he probably appointed himself. Slim Wilkinson, as he was known, was a TV expert now being wired for sound. When he addressed us all for the first time, he confessed that he didn't really think sport worked that well on the radio, which is a bit like saying that a piano is not much use to an orchestra, but we didn't hold it against him because he was impossible to dislike.

Eager to create a strong impression, Slim attempted to stamp his authority before he had come to terms with the geography of Broadcasting House. Our main daily task was to produce a comprehensive round-up of the sports news on Radio 2 at 6:45. Then it would be a quick retreat to either the pub or, for those with a family, the long commute home. In a premeditated strike, Slim had decided that tonight was the night for demonstrating who was boss and so at 7pm precisely ordered his amiable secretary Izzy to, "Get everyone up from the newsroom!"

"The newsroom?" she queried, looking exceptionally puzzled.

"Yes, all of them, before they go home," barked Slim. Without having the foggiest idea of why they were being summoned, in trooped all of the newsroom team, not a sports journalist in sight. Editors, sub-editors, correspondents and secretaries led by their head of department, Larry Hodgson. Slim launched into a scathing condemnation of their work. "That desk was a bloody shambles, what have you been doing all day? Its nowhere near good enough and I'm not going to stand for it." It was as if they had been addressed by an alien from another planet. Not a word of it had been comprehended by some of the nation's finest journalists, until a collective penny dropped. The three 'i's were dotted, the three 't's crossed and out of this game of charades the words *'mistaken identity'* emerged. On realisation, rather than going redder than normal, Slim broke the ice by getting it out of a bucket in his fridge and served everyone with a G&T or three. Under Bob Burrows, Radio Sport had become a sovereign state achieving independence from news; in less than five minutes, Slim had attempted a merger even Rupert Murdoch would have shied away from.

Slim presided over my one and only Wimbledon presentation in 1982, when the usual host, Peter Jones, was at the World Cup in Spain. At the time, it was the wettest tournament on record, meaning there was a lot of sitting around. In Slim's case, idle hands led to some mischievous work and one afternoon he invited everybody to gather around while he phoned the esteemed cricket commentator Don Mosey to tell him that he wasn't going to send him to cover the Ashes tour of Australia. This was going to be a devastating blow to Don and should have been dealt with in private, instead of being turned into a Vaudeville act in front of us all. "Hello, Don, I am afraid that I have some bad news for you." He then withdrew the phone from his ear so that all the assembled could listen in to the inevitable as Don smashed for six the full toss that Slim had just delivered. "Well, I'm sorry you feel like that, Don," said Slim with relish, still playing to his gallery. It was, of course, unprofessional and the height of indiscretion.

It was such an honour to work with the great champion Fred Perry in our Wimbledon team. A self-effacing, sophisticated charmer with a dash of Douglas Fairbanks Jr about him. We would need his help that fortnight to raid the Royal Box for guests for us to interview. He would set off on his mission, return ten minutes later and say, "I've got Tony Bennett for you, will he do?" Bennett was a universal celebrity, unlike the most famous TV personality in the USA, Johnny Carson, who was comparatively unknown in Britain. One day, after drinking too many cups of BBC coffee, I remember relieving myself in one of the All England Club urinals. I finished my labours simultaneously with my neighbour and as we both withdrew, I recognised him as the host of *The Tonight Show*! By his face, I hasten to add... I resisted the temptation of pointing at Percy and shouting out, "Here's Johnny," but did shatter his world of temporary anonymity by inviting him on to our programme. He promised to catch up with me later in the week, but our paths never crossed again. Nature must have called him to an alternative loo.

While we were being saturated at the All England Club, one of my very favourite colleague-related stories occurred at the World Cup in Spain. Ian Darke and I had joined the department almost simultaneously in 1979 and when he eventually left us it was one of Radio Sport's greatest losses to television. Ian was such a naturally gifted, all-round broadcaster and back in '82, still in the embryonic stages of an outstanding career, was in Madrid to present World Cup bulletins.

A couple of days before Brazil's group game with Scotland, Brazilian Radio, just down the corridor from the BBC, were sustaining their usual live twenty-four-hour coverage and were in need of a British voice to enlighten them about the Scots. They pounced on Ian, rushed him into their studio and at the end of another medley by Sérgio Mendes, on came the red light. After a long introduction in Portuguese came the words: "So Darkie, Scotland, how good?" That was Ian's cue to praise the Scots' World Cup pedigree, spirit and passion, as well as highlighting some of their leading players. It was typically articulate and succinct and didn't require a follow-up question, but one was forthcoming. "OK, thank you, Darkie, also, why did you invade the Falklands?" The Falklands War had ended only forty-eight hours earlier.

At the end of that Wimbledon fortnight, our programme was up for discussion at the BBC programme review board. Present on Wednesday, July 7th, 1982 in the Langham Gallery were all of these broadcasting sages…

M.D.R. (in the chair), D.M.D.R., C.R.2, C.R.4, C.A.R.M. (Progs.), Ch. Asst. R.1, A.H.R.L., Ch. Asst. R.2, Ed.Mus. R.3, H.T.D.R., (of course not to be confused with) H.R.T.D., H.R.S.R., H.A.R., H. Inf. S.R., G.M.R.P.R., A.H.D.R., ED. RN, Ed. *Woman's Hour*, Pres. Ed. R.4, Pres. Ed. R.1 and 2, S.E.L.E.R., Acting C.A. to H.C.A.M.P., D.G.M.L.R., Ed. Sp Projects, Mgr Radio WM, C.P.P.O.R., Prog. Ed, R.T. and of course who could forget the Asst. Mgr. Output B.R.D.

I do apologise if I left any abbreviations out…

The best review though arrived in a letter from the Convent of Mercy in Glasgow:

Dear Mr Ingham,

A most sincere thank you to you, your team and all your helpers for a most enjoyable Wimbledon '82. How I enjoyed it! You had so many drawbacks with the very poor weather, yet you all remained so patient and cheerful. As well as the tennis, I love the delightful teamwork. I love the teasing and the family spirit which help to bring the happy atmosphere closer.

You have no idea of the number of prayers I say for my favourites. They are not always answered, but I console myself by saying they would do much worse if I had not been praying. Mr Connors was helped out, but not Mrs Lloyd!

Meantime, I look forward to the remainder of the World Cup. I pray for them as well. The first goal for Scotland, by the way, was scored by a former pupil of mine.

Yours sincerely,
Sister M Ignatius

That first goal for Scotland was scored by a certain Sir Kenny Dalglish.

A year later, when Kenny was elected Footballer of the Year for a second time, the award was presented to him by a surprise guest. Pelé, on a flying visit to London, received a standing ovation when he made a late entry into the Café Royal. Amidst all the euphoria, on his way to the top table, he stopped just once when he recognised one of our BBC Radio colleagues, Peter Lorenzo. The two men embraced and Peter returned to his seat with a tear in his eye. They had remembered one another from the 1970 World Cup and that moment defined Peter. He was a charismatic journalist with one of the best contacts books in the business and not just in sport. Having worked for the Variety Club of Great Britain, Peter knew many entertainment stars. Morecambe and Wise broke off from one of their rehearsals so that Eric could have a chat with me for our Christmas programme. When we walked into their television studio, both men immediately went across to Peter to give him a hug and at the end of the interview – mainly about Luton Town – Eric, with a poker face, asked me, "Is the cheque in the post?"

Peter had been brought in to give the output a sharper editorial edge, and I became very fond of him. Some of his newspaper instincts, though, didn't always cross over into radio production. I remember presenting *Sport on Two* on FA Cup fourth round day when lowly Oxford United won 3-0 away to First Division Birmingham City. In *Sports Report*, we were joined live by an emotional Oxford manager Ian Greaves, who said that he'd just come from the dressing room and there were grown men weeping tears of joy; it had been the greatest day in their football lives. Peter, on the other side of the glass, reached for the talkback: "Mike, ask him if he's going to leave and take the Wolves job." Editorially, of course, he was right, but sensitively that question would not only have rained on their parade, it would have drowned it, so unprofessionally, I confess I ignored the instruction.

Peter Lorenzo, with the matinée idol Victor Mature looks, could have charmed the most venomous snake. A Dorian Gray who never seemed to age, which is why it was such a shock when he passed away at only fifty-nine in 1986, shortly after working at the Edinburgh Commonwealth Games. I have to thank Peter for my first BBC overseas trip in late 1982. An invitation arrived for one radio representative to accompany the Football League on a fact-finding mission to Baltimore to discover more about the indoor six-a-side game in the States, or 'Soccer 6', as it was branded. Peter thought it would be a good experience for me to spend time travelling in the company of senior football writers like Frank Clough, Steve Curry, Harry Miller and Jeff Powell. The visit climaxed at the Baltimore Civic Centre with the opening home game of the season for the local team The Blast against

Pittsburgh. An immediate anomaly that I was struggling to get my head around was that in a former life The Baltimore Blast had been The Houston Summit, even though the distance between Maryland and Texas is 1,500 miles. It would be like West Ham becoming Spartak Moscow. I decided to make a little programme about the evening and recorded some interviews with fans, one of whom declared, "Soccer will overtake football in ten years," leaving me even more confused. The Blast won 7-6, and the winner came with fifteen seconds to go. This was the Major Indoor Soccer League and had about as much to do with our 'football' as a round of crazy golf has to the Ryder Cup. My radio programme was called *Soccer 6, The Way Ahead?*, but sadly it wasn't even the way ahead in the USA. The MISL folded and was replaced by MISL 2, then the National Indoor Soccer League, and then finally Major Arena Soccer League. It has no identity and remains peripheral to the rest of American sport. I am afraid that as long as football is 'soccer', it will never unite the States.

One sport that did cross the great divide, though, was boxing. Bob Burrows built up the coverage of what is a natural radio sport, and there were some epic nights on both sides of the Atlantic. We would go on air before a major title fight with just enough time to set the scene and chat to Henry Cooper. Usually, Radio 2 would allocate one hour of their evening schedule for an event like this, so it all had to operate like clockwork. On one particular night when I was presenting the show live from Wembley Arena, we were more than a little perturbed when an undercard fight scheduled for eight rounds was allowed to begin less than fifteen minutes before we were due to broadcast; we did not want this getting in the way of the main event. Our boxing producer went off in search of promoter Mike Barrett to express concern.

"This fight will not be on when you go on air," Mike said with unreserved conviction.

"Are you sure, Mike?" questioned the BBC producer.

"Read my lips, this fight will have finished," assured Mike, and what a coincidence, it did!

Another combative pugilist, the business tycoon Robert Maxwell, was given a platform on *Sport on Two* to explain why merging his club Oxford United with Reading and calling it Thames Valley Royals was an irresistible idea. In the opposition corner for this debate, speaking on behalf of everyone else in the country that cared about the game, was the Oxford fan and distinguished zoologist Dr. Desmond Morris. In my role as referee, I really should have stepped in after three or four rounds and stopped the contest to save Maxwell from further punishment. Looking back, it's interesting to reflect that I was actually taken to task afterwards by BBC management for being a little too hard on Captain Bob, which was a bit like accusing David of bullying Goliath. In 1978, Dr Morris had published his book *Manwatching: A Field Guide to Human Behaviour* and might have written an entire dissertation on the Oxford United chairman. This same title could equally have applied to one of the most colourful characters I ever worked with at the BBC.

In our third-floor office at Broadcasting House, at one end a haven of tranquillity existed around the calm *Sport on Two* producer, Bryan Tremble. Meanwhile, at the other end resided an inhabitant of a volcanic island, capable of erupting at any time – especially after a good liquid lunch – statistician extraordinaire, Bill Ross. He was perfectly described by Bryon Butler as 'the belt and braces of the sports room for nearly thirty years'. Bill's territory was not so much marked out by molten lava but by ash from homemade cigarettes, which either became secreted in his Captain Birdseye beard or simply dropped onto the navy-blue cardigan which was his daily uniform. Bill painstakingly maintained large blue 'News Cuttings' books, handwriting the records of all league football clubs and county cricket teams, and compiled all the classified results. One of his mannerisms would be to have a conversation with himself. Bill would habitually start a day by asking himself, "Now then, what do you think we should start with?" "Yes, I think that's a good idea."

In our *Sport on Two* studios in the bowels of Broadcasting House where you could hear the Bakerloo line through the floorboards, we were linked to Bill on the third floor through a rather unsophisticated early version of closed-circuit TV known as a dot screen. You always knew what sort of a mood he was in by how quickly he would snatch a racing result away from you sometimes before you had even given the final starting price. For Bill, nothing had happened unless he saw it with his own eyes printed by the Press Association. It didn't matter if there was a TV feed of the BBC's *Match of the Day* in his office, if someone called out to him 'all over at Spurs, Bill, it was 2-2', you would only get a grunt. He wouldn't accept the result until he had read it himself off the teleprinter. He used to have help on a Saturday afternoon from a BBC messenger from the Philippines who he always referred to as the 'China Man'. While we always looked up at the sky apologetically, Chris never made a big deal of it and was happy to indulge Bill's old colonialist instincts.

Bill Ross's area was hallowed turf, and all newcomers would be warned. Occupy his seat behind his Agatha Christie vintage typewriter and you would be facing a court martial. He loathed Fridays, when there were always so many more people in the office preparing for the weekend. One of my most treasured possessions is an invitation he created himself and typed on a piece of yellow paper while he was being driven to distraction by a full house. He presented it to me with a chuckle. It just simply said:

THE SPORTS UNIT... AT HOME...
22ND FEBRUARY... 1400 ONWARDS
...DRESS OPTIONAL.

To this day I am not even sure if Bill actually liked sport, but I know that he got a bit of a glow when we asked him to go to Lancaster Gate in a taxi to bring the FA Cup trophy to us when we were making the draw for the third round live. He clearly didn't watch any television sport. I remember him bumping into the veteran boxing commentator Harry Carpenter, whom he hadn't seen for twenty years, and asking this broadcaster who had been omnipresent in our lives, "Harry, what have you been doing with yourself since I last saw you?" When *Star Wars* came on the television in the office one Saturday evening after *Sports Report*, Bill looked up just in time to see Darth Vader exterminating all of his enemies and observed, "Oh so that's Darth Vader, seems like a reasonable chap to me." On another occasion, when police sirens disturbed his peace, Bill simply reflected, "Good, I am glad to hear that, it means that the f***ers aren't sitting around playing cards in the station." At the end of each shift without fail, Bill would be off to The George, where he could put away four pints to your half, and in between swigs of ale, this highly intelligent man would also quickly polish off *The Times*' crossword of the day.

Just before Lorna and I were married, I was amazed to get the ultimate seal of Bill's approval, when he agreed to come on a night out in London with some of my closest colleagues. Bill tagged along to the posh nightclub of choice that Garry Richardson and Ian Darke had fixed up. It was surreal to watch him make small talk with the bouncers on the door, with a *Daily Telegraph* still rolled up under his arm. Fortunately for Bill, he retired in 1984 and never lived to see Radio Sport leave London for Salford. Had he still been around, he would have been like one of those Wild West pioneers protecting his covered wagon. I would give anything to see him now trying to find somewhere to sit at the new Broadcasting House, where there is no desk ownership and being told that to use the photocopier, he had to put in his BBC ID.

Lorna and I were married by our favourite clergyman from Radio Derby, the Reverend Noel Vincent, in his parish church. My best man was Italian. Adriano Ferrari was my brother-in-law at the time, being married to my sister, Christine. Adriano spoke a few warm words but was spared the ordeal of making the full traditional 'piss-taking' speech. That duty was shared between Lorna's good friend Sally Ainsworth and my close colleague, football commentator Peter Brackley, one of the best after-dinner speakers on the circuit. He introduced the then fresh-faced Garry Richardson, whose role was to play in a tape as 'the young blond man with the self-inflicted love bites' and finished with

'I only hope that you get off to a better start in marriage than my wife and I. After three weeks she ran off with my best friend. God, I miss him'. And now I am missing Peter so much, following his premature death in 2018. At the start of that year, after suffering a second heart attack, he had written to me to say that he had now decided to call it a day, as far as live performing was concerned. I replied and reminded him that I still had the archive material from our wedding day that proved that he had been one of the best in the business and that the legend would live on. Peter wrote back in his characteristic style: "Many thanks for your kind words, Mike, my memory doesn't seem to have been affected by my fall. I can't say I recall you instantly. Was I at school or ballet classes with you or something?"

On our honeymoon, Lorna and I went to visit my old school chum, Tea Leaf Tex, Brian Dunkley, now living in Australia with his first wife, Dawn. We flew all the way to the other side of what turned out to be a very small world, as after arriving in Melbourne, I bumped into Harry Miller of the *Daily Mirror*, followed by Don Howe and the Arsenal squad on a stop-over in Indonesia.

Lorna was starting out at London Weekend Television, an industry I would never experience. When introducing *Sport on Two*, I was told that I would never get a job on TV because I blinked!

So there you are, the two golden rules of broadcasting: breathe, but don't blink.

Fourth Exit Second Roundabout

"Thank you for evoking memories, particularly of days gone by." Apparently I said that, and as a result, a gentleman named David Smith won himself a fiver after submitting it to 'Colemanballs' in *Private Eye*. Alongside me in that edition were Bill McLaren, Don Mosey, and Dr Roy Strong, so I looked upon it as a compliment. I can't recall whom I was thanking. It could have been any one of a number of guests during my four years presenting programmes, which provided me with a scrapbook full of memories. I'd like to share with you ten of the most notable encounters, and I'm going to relive them chronologically, starting with the BBC Sports Personality of the Century.

It was just another uneventful January day in 1981. We were in the office working on ideas for the next *Sport on Two*. Producer Bryan Tremble had just popped out for a sandwich, and somebody on the phone wanted to talk to us about Saturday's programme, so I took the call. It was from a press officer promoting a film and offering an interview with one of its stars. The film was called *Freedom Road*, and the star who was prepared to come in and chat to us was the most famous sportsman in the world: Muhammad Ali. Sometimes when you get a call like this, your first instinct is to assume it is being made by a wind-up merchant like Peter Brackley or Garry Richardson, so you tread carefully. But this was for real, and after biting the caller's hand off, I attempted to stay cool when Bryan returned before telling him, "By the way, Muhammed Ali will be coming in tomorrow." You only truly believe that something like this is going to happen when it does, and it did. Ali, with not much of an entourage, duly reported on time at Broadcasting House's reception. I got a call to inform me that my guests had arrived and was asked if I wanted them to be escorted to our studio 3H. I quite liked the idea of walking through the newsroom with this particular visitor and said that I would be coming down to collect them. It was fascinating to observe the delayed reaction from many seasoned correspondents sitting at their typewriters as our party passed through. "That looked like... no, it couldn't be." But it was. There was a capacity crowd in the sports room that afternoon to witness it all, apart from Bill Ross, who couldn't understand what all the fuss was about and concentrated on the 2:30 at Lingfield Park.

Ali had recently been badly beaten by Larry Holmes, and many were urging him to call it a day. His speech was noticeably more restrained, and he could not have been less animated when I started in what I thought was the politically correct way by asking him a couple of questions about his film. Ali's mumbling replies were barely audible, and the sense of anticlimax was excruciating. A last desperate throw of the dice was to put the gloves back on, talk boxing and plead with him on behalf of everyone who cared about him to retire. The bait was irresistible, and after floating innocuously like a butterfly, we were treated to the full verbal bee sting of defiance. This was great for us on the day but would sadly propel him towards another disastrous fight later in the year. That red rag question to a raging bull salvaged the interview, and when it was all over, instead of making a quick exit, he shadowboxed his way through the sports room, milking the applause from everyone apart from Bill Ross, who was now preoccupied with the 3 o' clock at Kempton Park. He left us all with one final reminder of why he had such an aura and a special place in our hearts. Nobody asked for an autograph, and only one group photograph was taken for posterity while I was still coming back down to earth.

Later that year, I presented a programme for the International Assignment series on Radio 4 which attempted to discover the X factor ingredient possessed by all sporting superstars. Muhammad Ali was naturally featured and profiled by Desmond Lynam. This particular edition was produced by the late and much respected journalist Adam Raphael who in the 1960's had been a news correspondent in Vietnam. I was required to do a couple of interviews with two more of the BBC's most cherished broadcasters, and the first required a short flight to the Channel Islands. Waiting to greet me on the island of Alderney was a man I had never met before but who had been the sound of summer on my radio ever since I first became aware of full tosses and maidens. John Arlott was now in retirement. His final major commentary had been the England v Australia centenary test at Lord's in 1980, so had missed out on describing Sir Ian Botham's Ashes heroics in the summer of '81. He always used to say that the art of commentary was to say as little as possible and his final words on *Test Match Special* were simply, 'after Trevor Bailey it will be Christopher Martin-Jenkins', which said so much about his character. Not only did he not expect me to make my own way to his home for our interview, he didn't want me to visit without a personal guided tour. It was another one of those experiences when you expect to wake up suddenly from a dream. John Arlott in his own inimitable style, driving his car around Alderney, drawing my attention to old Napoleonic forts and spinning tales of Second World War German occupation of his island. He really did not have to do this for me, and it was a masterclass in hospitality. Fortunately, we did our interview before lunch, sitting in the library at his home called 'The Vines'; the rest of the afternoon would be a red-and-white blur. When I asked John, first of all, to identify a superstar of cricket, without any notes in front of him his answer was spontaneously eloquent and vintage Arlott:

As far as cricket is concerned, one man stands out completely on his own and this is WG Grace for a number of reasons. First of all, he was a great player; that's obvious. He reshaped the technique of batting and was such a master that he forced the bowlers to change their technique as well. The setting in which he was in made him greater than any modern cricketer can hope to be. You see, soccer was only in its infancy, tennis didn't matter as a sport on those days, and horse racing and boxing were looked upon by the Victorians as a little bit shabby. Cricket really was the national game followed from one end of the country to another, and it was the first major spectator sport. Grace dominated it. He happened to be a striking, huge man with a great black beard and domineering manner, and everything was in his favour. Although he was registered as an amateur, everybody knew that he got more money out of the game than anybody else had ever done and relatively speaking, I would say that he probably made more money out of cricket than any other Englishman has ever made out of any game and my word, he earned it.

We adjourned to the dining room and were joined by John's neighbour Max Robertson, the radio voice of Wimbledon. During the meal, assorted wine from Bulgaria to South Africa had to be reviewed for a magazine and notes were taken by John's wife. I've never been able to drink at lunchtime, and by the time my taxi for the airport arrived, I must have done more than a passable impression of Bambi on ice. I don't remember much more about the day, certainly not the short return flight or checking into the accommodation, which had been pre-booked with a premonition that I was unlikely to be in a fit state for the M3. I had my tape but more importantly, when I was back in the land of the living the next morning, I had my memory of time spent with a great man.

The only radio broadcast comparable with a John Arlott cricket commentary, apart from a report by Bryon Butler, would be Alistair Cooke's *Letter from America*. He was the master of speaking words from a script and then making it all sound as if it was neither written nor being read. It was a remarkable skill from a man who after emigrating presented his celebrated stateside epistle for over fifty years. As a listener, I became addicted to it, even on the rare occasion when the subject matter didn't necessarily interest me, such was his power of communication. I didn't need to travel to America to talk to him for our programme. He agreed to make a contribution on a rare visit to Broadcasting House. Alistair Cooke's sporting passion was golf. The dividing line between success and failure for an individual can be so slender in this game. Doug Sanders missed a one-yard putt by an inch, which would have given him victory in the 1970 Open, and the next day lost in a play-off with Jack Nicklaus. Nicklaus was Alistair Cooke's superstar of golf, but he had never forgotten an earlier defining moment in his career. Like John Arlott, he spoke to me completely off the cuff:

> I remember the Piccadilly Match Play at Wentworth in 1966; Nicklaus was given what he thought was an unfair ruling and he threw his club. The referee, Major Tony Duncan, a very austere soldier, went to Nicklaus and said, "Mr Nicklaus, you will play the ball as it lies." Nicklaus fumed, played the ball very badly and then threw the club. As they walked to the next tee, Nicklaus said, "That was a bum decision you made." I think it was the last time Nicklaus ever said such a thing. Duncan said sarcastically, "Mr Nicklaus, would you like a new referee?", and he said yes. The whole tournament was suspended. It was an awful thing in golf, because that doesn't happen. I mean, we don't have McEnroes in golf, and we couldn't have because they would be suspended for a year or life. I took this up with Nicklaus six years later. He said, "That was the most stupid thing I've ever done."

The footballer we highlighted in that *International Assignment* programme for Radio 4, was Pelé, but it could have just as easily been George Best. What made him so unique, apart from prodigious skill, was his animal magnetism. When he was on the pitch, you simply could not take your eyes off him. He had been playing in America and was looking tanned and fit when he came in with wife Angie to see us on *Sport on Two* to promote his book *Where Do I Go from Here?* Looking back at that interview now, it was both poignant – as he was then convinced he had beaten alcoholism – and prescient – as he faced up to the prospect of not being able to play one day. It had always affected him badly in the past whenever a game had finished and he was no longer centre stage:

> *I got so depressed when I got home whether we'd won or lost, because it had been taken away from me. If I've been playing well, I wanted it to continue. It's been taken away from me at the end of the game. That loneliness of not having thousands of people screaming every time you do something good or being with the boys. You walk away from it, and it's a lonely time. It sounds very depressing, but it's not because you know the next one will come. Maybe that's when I'll have a bigger struggle when I know I can't do it anymore. At the moment, I feel like I can play for another couple of years. I don't know if I could handle finishing if I'd still had the problem with alcohol, but that's out of the way now so I feel like I can handle the situation. Every day is better. I can taste my food again and can get up and go for a run. I've only just started enjoying life after a long time when I was just surviving.*

George Best's Northern Ireland international days were sadly behind him when his countrymen beat the hosts Spain at the 1982 World Cup. After that tournament, England turned to a new manager, and on a day when he was starting to clear his office, I popped over to Ipswich to chat with Sir Bobby Robson for *Sport on Two*.

When I look back at what was our first meeting, it's not so much the interview I remember, but what happened afterwards. I got my first insight into this infectious football man who became so loved throughout the game. When the interview finished, he asked me if I was going straight back to London. I told him that I was, in fact, going up to Derby to see my mum and dad. "Right," he said, "the best route…" And he proceeded to talk me through every traffic light and roundabout out of town. "Better still," he said, "I'll draw you a little map," which he did, and then went over the directions again, only this time using his diagram. I thanked him for being so helpful, wished him well for the new job and headed off to the car park. I was just manoeuvring my way out of Portman Road with his little map on my dashboard when I was halted by some persistent tapping on the passenger window, and there was the new England manager again. "All right, son," he said. "Don't forget, fourth exit, second roundabout, not the third." That is what you call attention to detail.

I don't recall what cassette I listened to heading north. It might have even been one of those great driving tracks by Deep Purple, one of the bands that was hardly ever off our student turntable in Birmingham. Imagine my thrill when Radio 1 presenter Andy Peebles rang me to let me know that their singer, Ian Gillan, was coming on to his show that Friday night to promote his latest solo work. Andy wondered if I might like to interview him as well for *Sport on Two*, as Gillan at the time was fronting a campaign to buy Reading Football Club. I thought it was a great idea and he duly came up to our third-floor studio for the recording. What happened next could have been a scene *from This is Spinal Tap*. Gillan, complete with bandana, unbuttoned shirt and two female adornments attached either side, began the conversation encouragingly enough, talking about his love for football and how he'd always closely followed the game. My follow-up question might have been phrased better, but it was transparently obvious what I meant. "So far you've been talking to me as a fan, but what makes you now want to become even more involved at Reading?" The singer saw an open goal and fully exploited it. "Well, yes," he said and then, making sure that his two female sidekicks were going to devour his every word, "obviously I have been a fan of yours for a very long time." Cue high-pitched hysterics. Never meet your heroes, they say, but I had met Muhammad Ali and George Best, and they had lived up to all of my expectations. Gillan remains a superb rock singer, his vocal on *Child in Time* was gut-wrenchingly iconic. I'm quite sure all these years later that he has left all that nonsense behind. Needless to say, the Reading takeover never happened.

Men behaving badly was top of the news agenda on the morning of Monday January 24th, 1983, following violence over the weekend at the Derby v Leeds game. It was becoming apparent that some poisonous seeds were being sown on the terraces at this time and an FA Commission was being set up to investigate this growing problem. Ted Croker, who was secretary by title but chief executive in reality at the FA, made himself available to me that lunchtime to discuss this mounting crisis:

It's like law and order generally throughout the country, whether it is in bars at night, discotheques or anywhere else, there is a certain lack of respect for law and order, and that's not a product of football, that's a problem of society. So I don't think anyone has suggested that we've cured this problem any more than we've cured any other types of crime in this country. The problem always with FA Commissions of this sort is that they are faced with an almost impossible task. I mean it's like me asking you how we solve this problem. You're asking me. You tell me, because you are a member of the public. The public knows as much about it as we do. We have no hidden knowledge on this. The clubs themselves don't want it. The last thing Leeds want are these particular individuals; they're not giving support to the club because it is killing the club.

Interestingly Ted Croker referred to 'clubs', and they would eventually be banned from playing in Europe. Yet what should have been a source for greater embarrassment to the FA, England, remained free to travel even though hooligans blighted almost every international game the team played in Europe at that time. Croker, remember, was the man who quite pointedly told Prime Minister Margaret Thatcher after the Heysel tragedy in 1985 that 'they are not our hooligans but yours'. He was right, and over two years before that Brussels disaster, as you can see, he had been saying pretty much the same thing. Sadly, Ted Croker died on Christmas Day 1992 and so never lived to see any significant improvement.

At least the devaluation of the FA Cup didn't occur on Ted Croker's watch; on the contrary, 'the first voice you will hear' was always his, whenever a draw was made live on radio. In that year of 1983, the two semi-finals were still being played simultaneously on a Saturday afternoon at neutral grounds and when Brighton clinched a place in the final against Manchester United, their manager Jimmy Melia was linked up live in *Sports Report* with United's Ron Atkinson and said, "We want to get into Europe."

"Then write a song," joked Ron. Sir Rod Stewart wrote a few of those and loves his football. Two days before that Wembley '83 Cup final, he previewed the game with me, eventually...

It was one of those 'come and meet Rod Stewart' media bunfights in a London club. The sort of function satirised in those scenes involving Julia Roberts and Hugh Grant in *Notting Hill*. Rod was there with wife Alana talking to all and sundry about his new album and a forthcoming world tour. Running the show was PR to the stars, Bernard Doherty. When I introduced myself to him and requested a short interview with Rod about football, he said that he didn't think he would want to be bothered by that. I replied that if Bernard didn't mind, I would hang around and take my chances. "Suit yourself, but I am making no promises," said a browbeaten Bernard. So I did hang around for about five hours. Everyone on the day, including probably *Horse & Hounds* magazine, appeared to be granted an audience, until finally Rod came my way and I managed to direct two words in his direction: 'interview' and 'football'. The second word did the trick. "Thank God for that," said Rod with mighty relief, and away he went with his memories of Cup final day as a kid, the community singing with the man in the white suit and his analysis of how he thought this year's game would go. It proved to be a welcome release for him. He had enjoyed it and was happy, so naturally now was his PR guru. "Oh, you should have told me who you were," he said, to which I simply replied, "I did." It was my first exposure to the sort of show business nonsense that Lorna would have to deal with throughout her career.

Brian Clough was more of a Frank Sinatra man. When I left Derby, in the farewell message that he recorded for my dad, he had said that if I ever made a phone call to the city ground requesting 'co-operation' that 'I would have a friend at Nottingham Forest'. Four years had passed, and it was time to put that friendship to the test. Clough, no longer assisted by Peter Taylor, agreed to be interviewed for Saturday's *Sport on Two*, after a routine home win over FC Vorwärts of East Germany in the UEFA Cup. He was so media savvy that whenever he referred back to that game that had just finished, because he knew the interview was for the weekend, he automatically said 'last Wednesday night'. He liked to think that he knew as much about our industry as we did and had a tendency to end an interview for you, not because he was bored but because he had liked his last answer and thought it would be a good ending. I'll never forget the Derby-based journalist Mike Carey going to see him to ghost his weekly column in a local newspaper and being told on arrival, "Morning, Michael, I've got your intro for you. I want you to write, 'What a week it's been for saying bugger me!'"

On this particular night, after first asking me how my dad was, then telling me to 'get on with it man', he talked about the rebuilding job he was doing at Forest, the pleasure he was getting from managing his children's team on a Sunday and finally, prophetically, bearing in mind how his glorious career ended, discussed how much more pressurised the job had become:

I find football management now more demanding than ever before, and I feel sorry for young managers coming into the game who possibly think it's not too bad a job to have. The demands on managers today are greater than ever before.

That begged the question from me that if that was the case, what was it that still motivated him?

Me personally, oh, well, I played the East Germans on Wednesday. I came across from Derby to Nottingham. I came on to the Trent. The sun was shining, parked my car, walked down, and walked along the Trent not on it. The trees were there, and the sun was beautiful, took part in the training session, and I was lucky enough to get a good result that night, and people say to me, what's the incentive? If that doesn't give people a boost working in our industry, I don't know what does.

Finally from one BC to another: Buck Cannon. When Brian Clough rode into town as the new sheriff of Derby County in 1967, a television series was starting up which was to become cult viewing at our school. *The High Chaparral*, in colour, opened up new frontiers in every sense, featuring the life of a nineteenth-century family of pioneering settlers in Arizona. It broke the mould, and for the first time, the storytelling redressed some of the balance and treated the Apache Indian with dignity and respect. There was more depth to the main characters than in other Westerns and though I enjoyed them all, Cameron Mitchell as the enigmatic, wayward Uncle Buck, stole every scene he was in. I became so used to seeing him coated in prairie dust and nursing a black eye that it was so incongruous when he turned up at Moor Park in golfing attire for the Bob Hope celebrity event. There may have been better-known celebrities in attendance, but he was the only one I wanted to meet and on the practice greens of Hertfordshire, he transported me to the ranch, the saguaro cactus, and the Sonoran Desert:

On a mystic late afternoon, you could feel the spirit of Cochise and the Apache Indians. That's why the show was so popular. Some of the atmosphere was transferred because it really happened there. To the best of my knowledge, it's the only TV show that was ever shot where it really happened, and the grandson of Cochise was our technical advisor. He died at 107. He got married at ninety-four to a young woman of thirty. In the pilot, he played the real Cochise, and through the years we had fine actors playing Cochise, but none of them had what he had. He had such quiet, stoic dignity. He just sat on the horse, and he was Cochise.

I will forever be grateful for having had the opportunity to meet so many of my heroes through working for BBC Radio Sport.

George Orwell's year of 1984 turned out to be the most significant in my career. After having been considered as the main sports presenter for four years introducing from events like Wimbledon, the Open Golf and the Grand National, it was not unreasonable to assume that I would be in the team for the Olympic Games that summer. In the event, I was told that there wouldn't be a role for me, not even introducing the sports desks. I didn't handle the news well, and at nearly thirty-four, it made me question the direction in which I was going. Lorna and I decided that we were still young enough to consider the escapist route of emigration. She was working with Clive James at the time, who told her in no uncertain terms that we would be bonkers to think about moving Down Under. However, I did pop around the corner from the BBC in Portland Place to the European office of the Australian Broadcasting Corporation, handing in an audition tape and a letter of application which they kindly posted on to the head office in Sydney. I did not have to wait long for a reply and was informed that there were no positions available for which I would be a suitable candidate. For the next thirty years, I would be thanking my lucky stars that they came to that decision.

Nessun Dorma (None Shall Sleep)

My life changed in thirty seconds. That was how long it took BBC Radio Sport editor Mike Lewis to deliver the news. Ten seconds to inform me that he was just about to board a flight to the Los Angeles Olympics and twenty seconds to tell me that next season he wanted me to exchange roles with Peter Jones. Peter would present *Sport on Two* and I would try my hand at football commentary. That was the most significant phone call of my career and I received it, of all places, at my spiritual home of Radio Derby where I was spending a week of annual leave working on a documentary about the history of Derby County.

Mike knew how upset I had been when I was left out of the Olympics team. I didn't disguise it or handle it very well. Evidently, this had given him some food for thought, and it was no coincidence either that our new head of sport also had strong views about broadcasters, even though her background had been from a very different walk of life as an officer in the Wrens. Up until taking over from Slim Wilkinson, Patricia Ewing in a low-profile, but tremendously effective way had taken care of the administration of the department. I didn't think that she liked me very much, but was wrong. Her sense of detachment was nothing more than shyness. Pat, like Bryan Tremble, had the sharpest of ears for radio and her opinion about programme presentation was that this ought to be a job for seasoned campaigners who had earned their stripes in the field. She was right; Deep Purple's Ian Gillan wouldn't have taken such liberties with a Harry Carpenter or a Cliff Morgan. I understand her thinking now but was still stunned when Mike announced that it was time for 'a little less conversation, a little more action'. How could I seriously swap roles with Peter Jones at anything, never mind football commentary? He was one of my heroes and still is. To this day I am still very conscious of my good fortune to have had such an unexpected silver spoon placed in my mouth without any meaningful audition. I had effectively just been allowed to cut a massive corner without really earning that right. This was a management decision presumably taken for the future, because nothing in the past or present justified it. Peter had presented the first ever *Sport on Two* in 1970 and would be able to do the programme standing on his head. I hadn't even been a football commentator at Radio Derby.

The deal was that Peter would still carry on doing all his midweek games. However, Saturday afternoons were his fix, and this enforced switch was going to change his life. It must have been torture for him handing over to me and George Hamilton on that first Saturday of the new season, for Manchester United against Watford at Old Trafford. George, a wonderfully versatile commentator, was a great encouragement to me in those early days. Two days later on August bank holiday Monday, we were together at St James' Park for Newcastle against Sheffield Wednesday.

The only recollection I have of my second ever commentary was hearing my car registration number being read out over the public address system shortly before kick-off. I had filled up my vehicle just before arriving at the ground; however, after parking on an incline, petrol was now leaking from the car onto a concourse that is nowadays in an area strictly reserved for VIPs, not humble radio reporters. I had to dash from my seat to attend to this messy situation and ended up doing the commentary stinking of fuel. I know that I made numerous errors that day, but management were still being supportive. They had made their beds, and we were all going to have to lie in them, but not for long. George Hamilton was heading off to pastures new, Peter Jones was duly released from his cell and we became a commentary team.

Peter had been a former schoolmaster but although he must have quickly spotted raw flaws in my work, only offered guidance if requested and then would briefly advise 'bit more light and shade' or 'plenty of colour'. Peter never commentated in black and white. We did both of the Wembley Cup finals together that season, and I had to come off the substitute's bench at the last minute to join correspondent Bryon Butler in Rotterdam for the Cup Winners' Cup final between Everton and Rapid Vienna. Peter was unable to make the trip as he was suffering from persistent nosebleeds, which when I look back now, might have been an early warning sign for him. We were reunited for what should have been the highlight of my first season but turned out to be the lowest point of my career, the 1985 European Cup final between Liverpool and Juventus in Brussels.

It is important, first of all, to put this fixture into historical context. There had been trouble in Brussels at the 1982 European Cup semi-final between Anderlecht and Aston Villa and in 1984, more disorder in the city when Tottenham appeared in the UEFA Cup final. There had also been reports of attacks on Liverpool supporters at the previous European Cup final in Rome. In the build-up to Heysel, Millwall hooligans did their best to destroy Luton Town's ground, riot police and horses were needed on the pitch at Chelsea, a Leeds fan lost his life at Birmingham, and there were some deeply disturbing scenes before and after Liverpool's FA Cup semi-final replay with Manchester United. That was the prevailing climate.

Football correspondent Bryon Butler had already flown to Mexico for England's summer tour, and so I was in a BBC Radio team of only three sent to Belgium with Peter Jones and our summariser, the former Liverpool captain Emlyn Hughes. We assembled the day before the game to fly with the club from Speke Airport. In the departure area, a number of local journalists with great contacts at Anfield were hinting that not only could this be manager Joe Fagan's last game before retiring but that he was going to be replaced by a player. Not just any old player either: Kenny Dalglish. I discussed this rumour on the flight with Peter and Emlyn, and we all noticed – or maybe wanted to notice – that the potential manager-in-waiting, Kenny, was being much more active than usual walking up and down the aisles chatting to all and sundry but still no official comment. The national newspaper writer with one of the closest relationships with Liverpool at the time was Bob Harris, and on that Tuesday night after arrival in the Belgian capital, Bob and I tried to move the story on. He had a good idea where club secretary Peter Robinson might be dining, and we were able to track him down at his meal table. "Not now, please, Bob," said Peter gently, but the question hadn't taken him by surprise and the story wasn't denied. During the course of a cloudless match day, it was eventually confirmed that it was indeed going to be manager Joe Fagan's final game, but Liverpool, typically taking each game as it comes, didn't go public with his successor, though by now it appeared to be an open secret.

What I am going to attempt to do now, rather than make judgmental statements on events that have been well-documented, is simply do my best to try to tell you what it was like to be there on that apocalyptic night.

On our way to the stadium, I was sitting next to Emlyn Hughes, who was the first to start showing some concern. As our media bus approached the ground and had to slow down, this easily identifiable legend was being recognised by passing fans. Some wanted to show their appreciation and began head-butting the window next to where he was sitting. Emlyn looked at me and said ruefully, "I think there might be a bit of bother tonight." Outside the venue, there clearly wasn't such a thing as a designated temperance zone. If your business in Brussels was to sell alcohol for a living, then it seemed you had *carte blanche* to do so that night.

For the fans on arrival, there was the usual exercise in futility of a security check to ensure nothing dangerous was being carried into this decaying tomb of a stadium. Once inside, if you were violently inclined, you would be free to squirrel up enough loose masonry of rocks and stones from the crumbling terraces to underpin a small house. Both Liverpool and Juventus had objected to this ill-suited relic of an arena, which would not have looked out of place alongside the ruins of Pompeii. In the official match programme, UEFA made a number of requests to spectators:

To ensure that the Cup final proceeds in an atmosphere worthy of the occasion, spectators are kindly requested to:

- *refrain from bringing bottles of any kind into the stadium;*
- *not throw any objects;*
- *not encroach upon the interior part of the stadium under any circumstances either before, during or after the match;*
- *keep expressions of joy or disappointment within the limits of normal good sporting behaviour;*
- *help the stadium security officials in carrying out their duties;*
- *prevent an unruly minority from spoiling the enjoyment of the majority who have come to see good football.*

From our three commentary seats, we had one principal commitment before the game. At 6:45 in the UK, half an hour before kick-off, as well as setting the scene from the stadium, there was also a special recorded feature to introduce on the life and times of Joe Fagan. It was never broadcast. About fifteen minutes before our contribution, the first missiles were being launched and away to our left, the pathetic segregation wire being dismantled. I advised producer Dave Gordon in London to drop the feature and just come live to Peter Jones. Dave would go on to make his mark in TV Sport and in this split second revealed his credentials. He might have been labouring for most of the day carefully preparing that recorded package, but any thought of self-interest was put to one side as his instinct told him to trust your people in the field and follow their lead. Once Peter went on air at 6:45, he stayed until midnight.

We were a national radio team of just three, with no spare producer or reporter who could have been employed as extra eyes and ears. Liverpool fans were predominantly to our left and the Juventus followers to our right. Only later did we discover the full ramifications of having a so-called neutral section next to Liverpool occupied by spectators – mainly of the Italian persuasion – who had snapped up tickets on the black market. One of the biggest indictments of football is the need to have segregation in the first place. In a civilised world, that should not be necessary, but this was a sport that had been allowed to degenerate into tribalism, and it was now a bare essential in the staging of any game. I didn't hear much of what Peter and Emlyn said for the next two hours. After the very audible screams from the terraces, and the accompanying panic from the understrength police, it soon became obvious that my role for the evening was going to be as a war correspondent. An aggressive charge by some English fans resulted in an Italian retreat, a stampeding crush and the collapse of an inadequate wall. The result was a sickening loss of life.

I had only ever seen one dead body before in my thirty-four years, when I wanted to say goodbye to my dad's mum and was so upset by that experience that I couldn't bring myself to do the same thing again when my other grandmother died. When you see someone who has been so animated and full of life, the stillness is a terrible shock. I don't know how members of the emergency services cope when dealing with death by unnatural causes. Here I was at a football match, looking at a man built like the wrestler Giant Haystacks, covered by Juventus flags and scarves, purple in the face, having had all of his priceless breath squeezed out of him. Distraught family members and friends were nervously uncovering the faces of the deceased in the most shocking identity parade imaginable. The saddest sight of all was to see one young teenager, about the age that I was when my dad took me to the Wembley Cup final. He might have been a nephew, brother or son crawling on top of a lifeless corpse, beating him on the chest, wailing and trying to wake him up. My thoughts were drifting to northern Italy and my own sister, Christine, living with her Juventus-supporting husband, Adriano, no doubt watching TV in horror as innocent lives were being snuffed out in front of them, bodies being carried helplessly on makeshift stretchers made out of broken railings and advertising boards. Imagine being in one of those families back in Italy in an age before mobile phones, watching and knowing a loved one was at the game.

I had to try and regain some composure and after counting the bodies, climbed the stairs back to our commentary position to report on the latest grotesque news. For Peter and Emlyn, it was a broadcasting *tour de force*. Peter calmly, expansively and always with restraint, did what he was born to do, describing only what he could see. Like me, he had prepared to watch great sport, and this was Armageddon. When the decision was taken, for damage limitation reasons, to start the game nearly ninety minutes late, it was utterly surreal. How could you talk about men running around and kicking a ball after such carnage? I have listened back to a recording of our commentary, and just before kick-off Peter says:

Who would have thought that this match would be edged with black, the black of death? All right, let's just try, let's just try to now report on the European Cup final of 1985 and to start the commentary, my colleague, who's been doing very different things for the last hour: Mike Ingham.

If you listen to the tape, this is followed by a silence for ten to fifteen seconds before I pick up, because Peter has grabbed hold of my arm and is squeezing it tight. I begin with:

This final was billed as the dream final, it is the nightmare final now.

When it was all over, and Juventus had won by a dubious penalty, their elegant captain Gaetano Scirea received the trophy for the first time in the club's history; four years later he would be killed in a horrendous road accident. Thank God his team had this hollow victory in memory of the thirty-nine who perished. Thirty-nine steps along the pathway of life destroyed all in the name of sport. I remember after the game being in the company of Sir Bobby Charlton, a survivor of great tragedy himself. When we received false information that some of the victims might have been children who had played in a special game earlier in the day it was too much for the great man to bear. This had been a ticking time bomb. On several occasions over the season, after witnessing mayhem in stadiums, you could be excused for walking away afterwards and saying that someone is going to get killed one day. On this night, after a hot alcohol-fuelled day in a pitifully ramshackle stadium, with insufficient police and medical resources, chaotic ticketing, inadequate security and two sets of fans that were not exactly bosom buddies, this was the final tipping point. That was the mitigation, but the bottom line is that if there had been no attack by English fans, there would have been no deaths. Imagine if roles had been reversed and fans from Italy had caused the death of thirty-nine from our island, how might we have reacted? In the aftermath of the Heysel disaster, more sensitivity could have been shown to the bereaved.

After visiting an empty bomb site of a stadium the following morning with Liverpool officials, we flew home and inexplicably headed for Anfield for a press conference to unveil Kenny Dalglish as manager. Absolutely the right manager; absolutely the wrong time to be doing it. It was not Kenny's fault as he was adhering to the wishes of the club, but it felt inappropriate at the time, and I feel exactly the same way about it now. There was no need for this business as usual approach on the day when other flights out of Brussels were transporting the coffins of fans back to their heartbroken families.

The response from the Football Association fell short. They pre-empted UEFA's inevitable punishment by removing clubs from the

European tournaments, though quite what Heysel had to do with Norwich City is beyond me. The bigger picture was missed. It was illogical to have a blanket ban only on the clubs, when consistently the very worst incidents of hooliganism abroad over the years had been perpetrated by some of those purporting to support the national team. Presumably, there was too much vested interest at stake. At that time, the FA were in the process of making bids to stage future World Cups and European Championships and didn't do the honourable thing and withdraw the country simultaneously from international competitions. England's hooligans were given the green light to carry on destroying tournaments.

The charge sheet was frightening. At the 1980 European Championship, in Turin of all places, England's match against Belgium resulted in tear gas and a suspension of play. France was mercifully spared an invasion at Euro '84, and on the day England failed to qualify for that tournament, some of their followers took it out on the good folk of Luxembourg. In the fifteen years after Heysel, starting at Euro '88 in West Germany, every tournament played in Europe was sabotaged and wrecked by England's imbecilic so-called minority. Due respect to the grieving Italian nation was unforthcoming at their own 1990 World Cup. Their enchanting island of Sardinia was trashed before the match against The Netherlands. England's lunatic fringe said their thanks to UEFA President Lennart Johansson for inviting our clubs back from exile and granting Euro '96, by urinating all over his native country Sweden's 1992 European Championship. Having managed to escape in '84, France copped it at their World Cup fourteen years later and then the final ignominy. The day after Heysel, there had been an editorial in the Belgian newspaper *La Nouvelle Gazette* of Charleroi. The headline was 'Never again football, never again England'. That fair city was moronically trampled on at Euro 2000.

Withdrawing from international football at this time would have been harsh on the legions of decent football-loving folk who follow England all over the world at great personal expense and give wonderful support. A personal friend of mine, for example, Lee

Basannavar, has never missed an England game home or away for the last twenty years, even though he lives in America. David Beckham always used to say that England had the best fans in the world and most of them like Lee were, but there was also an underbelly of malevolence in pursuit of anarchy. When he founded the World Cup, Jules Rimet had a vision that, "Men will be able to meet in confidence without hatred in their hearts and without an insult on their lips." That message was treated with contempt by England's lager louts.

Heysel may not have been a watershed moment for hooliganism, but it was for football. As a direct result of being starved of European competition for five years, the self-appointed big five clubs, seeking alternative revenue, threatened a TV breakaway and in so doing paved the way for an eventual Premier League. Perversely, England also appeared to prosper from having a Neanderthal element following them around by getting invitations to dress rehearsals for three World Cups so that local security could be given the most searching examination. That's the only conclusion I can reach, because often there was no logical football reason to justify their presence.

The weekend after Heysel, I returned to the North West for a much happier event, when one of my flatmates from Birmingham, Martin Heiron, got married. It was great to be back among friends, but I was troubled by pain down the whole of one side of my body. I can only assume it was a delayed reaction to the events of the midweek. The following Monday, I was on a flight to join Bryon Butler for those England games in Mexico City, which were now irrelevant. Peter Jones was needed at home in the build-up to Wimbledon. I should have not been going, and the team should not have been there, as these were matches that should not have been happening.

Underlining the point that I have tried to make about the FA and facing up to their international responsibilities, was that eight days after Heysel, not only was the country unlike the clubs still free to perform on the overseas stage, guess who they were playing in that opening game in Mexico – Italy! Nowadays I would like to think that such a match would be called off. The giant Azteca Stadium was ninety per cent below capacity for a fixture; even the football-addicted Mexicans didn't want to know. Someone who was there, sitting provocatively in the press seats when we arrived, was a well-known hooligan ringleader from England, who was quickly shown the door. But this had been an act of defiant, in-your-face bravado which made me think that there really was no hope. At least dear old Bobby Robson lightened the mood and put a smile on our faces. On seeing members of the media once again proving that only mad dogs and Englishman go out in the midday sun, he warned us all to: "Be careful of those *ultra ray violets.*"

When I retired, I was invited to present the occasional one-off programme and began by looking at the footballers of the First World War. It was then suggested that I should host a special documentary thirty years on from Heysel and the idea was for me to revisit Brussels with former Liverpool star Mark Lawrenson. I agreed to do this with a heavy heart, realising that it would reopen old wounds, but as the only survivor of our radio team of three, I wanted to pay tribute to Emlyn Hughes and Peter Jones. For preparation, I had listened again to our coverage from a night that I had tried to forget. Weeks went by without me hearing any more about the plans for the programme until I was told without any further explanation, "We've decided we're not doing it now." Heysel, as Mark Lawrenson himself observed in the *Daily Telegraph*, for some unknown reason is still 'the elephant in the room'.

In the January 1956 edition of Charles Buchan's *Football Monthly*, there is a picture of police charging up the terraces in a game that was played overseas, with this attached comment:

Such terrible scenes could not occur in our land. In Britain, partisanship does not descend to bitterness. It reflects our tolerant way of life.

Fever Pitch

For Peter Jones and I, the traumatic pain of Heysel was long-lasting. Bill Shankly would never have wisecracked about football being more important than life and death had he still been alive in 1985. I had grown up sharing Bill's passion for the game but was never going to be able to get as closely involved in it as he did. When you are nine years of age, your life is mapped out. You are going to play football and cricket for England, even though you can barely get into the school team. In reality, I had about as much chance of emulating Denis Compton as Ronnie Biggs had of becoming head of Scotland Yard. How many people can you think of from your school who went on to become sporting superstars? At the time, you might have thought they were destined for fame and fortune as they ran rings around you with a football or smashed your bowling out of sight. Big fish in a little pond, though, unable to make any tangible impact at a professional level which made me appreciate just how high the standard must be at the very top. So what to do if your heart still rules your head and is set on having some sort of connection with sport? You could write or talk about it but would need a few breaks along the way, and in my case, I was given a ladleful of good fortune. Doors seemed to open and close almost as if somebody somewhere off stage was calling the shots.

Broadcasting for me became the next best thing to playing at Wembley. I might never have been able to play with Denis Law, but I got to work with him. I received letters from blind listeners, prisoners and the armed forces. I also regularly heard from students seeking career advice, which made me appreciate how privileged I was. One letter arrived from a lady who loved to listen to a game on the radio, whilst watching the pictures on TV. Our sound was always two or three seconds ahead of the picture, and sometimes we would call a goal before she saw it for herself. She asked me if it might be possible to slow down my commentary a fraction!

You never know who might be listening. I made a complete porridge of things one night at Everton. I thought the number on the scoreboard related to the player who had just headed a goal and then became completely confused when the number changed from 5 to 4 and then down to 3. It was, in fact, the number of minutes left to play. I received a letter of sympathy from the comedian Eddie Large, to tell me that he was having a chuckle and recalled falling into the same trap:

> I went to Luton a few years ago to see Man City, and at three o' clock, the temperature on the scoreboard was 45. After fifteen minutes it was down to 30, and I remarked what a great advantage artificial pitches are when the weather gets cold.

In the back of my mind, I always liked to think that Cliff Morgan might be listening, and this was confirmed when he wrote:

> You appear to be enjoying commentary. It is not the easiest of the duties of a broadcaster. You are in the business of instant journalism. Age also gives the voice and the use of the voice a natural flow during the sustained periods of an OB. Look after your vocal chords. You have a natural and very listenable sound, which if you do not overstretch the range, will be your best friend.

For me, this was the ultimate seal of approval, coming as it did from a man who had to give me such a dressing-down in my early days, from simply learning how to breathe, now he was talking to me about how I could fine tune my voice.

I was reminded of what the game of football meant to people around the world when only a couple of months after my visit to Mexico City, the capital was devastated by an earthquake and yet still somehow managed to host the 1986 World Cup ten months later. It was a tournament that I still believe England should have withdrawn from while clubs were serving a ban from international competitions, although there was never a danger of there being any crowd disorder in Mexico. Most hooligans are essentially cowards, drawing strength from safety in numbers and usually taking three steps forward and four back. They pick and choose the trouble spots. Fear of internment in a Central American or South African jail focuses minds, so instead, they take it out on less draconian Belgium or Sweden. Not for the first time in English football history, there was no joined-up writing between club and country. The clubs were still in exile but the country, like an ostrich with its head in the sand, carried on as a magnet for marauders. The national team eventually perished in that tournament, at the hand of what Diego Maradona described as divine intervention. The Football League then duly reacted to that treachery by inviting him two years later to be one of their guests of honour at their centenary celebrations, playing for a World team against England at Wembley. The leading clubs, or rather the so-called 'big five', joined in with the spirit of the League's centenary by then threatening to break away. The Premier League was now an embryo.

In my rehabilitation after Heysel, I was rediscovering what our coverage meant to people inside and outside of the game. At five o' clock, the *Sports Report* theme would invariably blast out of dressing rooms around the country, though sometimes that could be a double-edged sword. When I approached Portsmouth's manager Alan Ball for an interview after a narrow win at Fulham, he had just heard my report on the game and snarled at me, "Smash and grab!?" Alan couldn't sustain a stern face for a very long time, though, and soon dissolved into mirth. Graham Taylor once hurdled over seats in the main stand at Swindon so that he could be on at the top of the programme on the day Aston Villa were promoted. After his first game as manager at Old Trafford, Alex Ferguson was able to walk a few yards from Manchester United's dressing room into our little studio so that I could talk to him live, straight after a report from Peter Jones. We had superior facilities at all of the major grounds in those days before redevelopment or relocation took place. This was a legacy of the sterling work done by all of the OB producers in the BBC regions. Arsenal's manager George Graham hated us having a studio in the dressing room corridor at Highbury. This was a handy position, though, for interviewing opposition managers as well, especially on the day Nottingham Forest won an FA Cup quarter-final there, and Brian Clough wiggled his finger around the door to invite me in.

Over the years, Pat Murphy gained more access to this unpredictable genius than anybody else in the department. One of the reasons for this was that Pat was never intimidated by anyone; he knew that Clough would sometimes playfully spar with you for the first couple of questions and only then, if he was still engaged, were you allowed to carry on. I'll never forget Tony Gubba once interviewing him for *Match of the Day* and starting with, "Brian, can I say first of all what flowing, inventive football you played today." To which Clough replied, "Hold it right there. I'm just going to go straight to our dressing room to tell my players that Tony Gubba thought we played flowing, inventive football." And he was gone, never to return. The danger of making an opinionated statement to a man who defined that adjective. Brian Clough would eventually hand over the mantle of Britain's Best Manager to Sir Alex Ferguson. While he was still at Aberdeen, Ferguson also assisted the Scotland manager Jock Stein, but when the great Celtic legend so sadly passed away, Ferguson agreed to lead his country to the 1986 Mexico World Cup.

It had been decided that I was going to cover Scotland's three group games in Mexico and in order for me to meet Ferguson for the first time, I travelled up to Aberdeen to commentate on their European tie against the Swiss team Servette. I also went to see one of

Scotland's opponents, Uruguay, play Wales in the mud at Wrexham. My colleague Ron Jones introduced me to the Welsh manager Mike England at the team hotel in Llangollen. Mike had been one of BBC Radio's first football summarisers and joked that as our names sounded a little similar to listeners, he would often get letters sent to him complaining about my broadcasts!

I will always be able to say that I commentated at a World Cup with Peter Jones. In what turned out to be his last tournament, we were together for the opening game in Mexico City between Bulgaria and the holders Italy. Scotland without Alan Hansen and Kenny Dalglish, who had both just won the double at Liverpool, soon returned home and so did I. Apart from working with Peter, the other highlight was being in the company of our Scotland summariser, Denis Law. On the way into the ground for the second game against Germany, he was warmly embraced by someone who was obviously an old friend. Denis then casually revealed that it had been Alfredo di Stéfano, one of the game's most respected and distinguished players paying him the ultimate compliment. After I had left Mexico and before they returned home, Denis and my commentary colleague Roddy Forsyth had some brief fun in Acapulco. One day when they were both relaxing by the swimming pool and sounding unmistakably British, they were approached by a film company who were shooting scenes for an action movie in their hotel and were offered a couple of cameo roles. Denis asked for twenty-four hours to think about it and then, the following day, informed the disappointed director that with regret, they would have to decline as they didn't want to get typecast. Had they agreed to take part, it would have been almost as incongruous as when I presented three hours of music live on Radio 1.

I once naively agreed to fill in for Andy Peebles when he had to miss his Friday night music and sport show. Lorna recorded it all for me, and to this day I haven't had the courage to listen back. It was just a technical minefield, as I was expected to play the discs and operate all of the equipment without having had any real instruction. I was only just starting to get the hang of it when it was all over and time to cue Tommy Vance. At least I got to work with Jeff Griffin, who was to radio music production what Bryan Tremble had been to sport. Jeff held my hand, calmly nursed me through it all and allowed me to choose some of the records. Here I was sitting in John Peel's backyard, so I had to play 'Big Eyed Beans from Venus' by Captain Beefheart.

Another major surreal experience was to be sent to the Winter Olympics in Calgary, with producer Rob Hastie in a BBC Radio team of just two. I'm sure that this was editor Mike Lewis's way of trying to redress the balance after leaving me out of the Los Angeles games. The weather in Canada at the foothills of the Rockies was about sixty degrees cooler than California. At night, if you were foolish enough to go outside, there would be icicles in your nostrils within thirty seconds. We were based with BBC TV in lodgings on the Blackfoot Trail. On the flight from London, it was such a tribute to broadcaster Ron Pickering to see nearly all of the British competitors wanting to come over and shake his hand. I don't remember seeing Michael Edwards on the plane; maybe he used his own wings to fly there. Eddie the Eagle, as he became known, arrived an hour late for his own press conference because he didn't have the right accreditation to get in. After he finally gained entry, he went on to more or less hijack the Games. In Canada, Eddie was the personification of the North American Bald Eagle dream. Never give up against all the odds, even if you don't have a cat in hell's chance of winning. Do not underestimate his courage, though, I stood at the top of that ski jump and at the end of his runway, it would have been like being thrown out of a jet without a parachute. Few athletes have embodied the Olympic spirit quite like Eddie the Eagle, but sadly, too many wanted to then milk his human kindness and have their pound of flesh. He was rampantly exploited with records, T-shirts, nightclub appearances and flown to *The Tonight Show Starring Johnny Carson* in Hollywood. It quickly turned from *Where Eagles Dare* to *A Fistful of Dollars*. Eddie had represented his country and given everything he had as a gallant loser.

England's footballers, on the other hand, and some of their barbaric following, emerged only in disgrace at Euro '88.

Peter Jones was required to host Wimbledon, so I deputised for him, teaming up for commentary in West Germany with correspondent Bryon Butler and the former England manager Ron Greenwood. Before I left, Peter told me that when I got to Stuttgart, I really should meet up with a female acquaintance of his who was a huge fan of BBC Radio Sport. A ship in every port was my first thought but didn't think anything more about his suggestion until the phone rang in my hotel bedroom shortly after I had checked in. The lady in question was already on reception and inviting me for a drink. Bryon and Ron were also discreetly keeping their distance in the same bar and judging by their demeanour, appeared to be one step ahead of me. If there had been a pianist there, I would have approached the keyboards and said *Play Misty for Me*. Peter's friend had a big red book, like the one in *This Is Your Life*. This would be her reference point in our conversation which she started with something like this: "On January 4th, why was Jimmy Armfield and not Larry Canning reporting from Stoke?" A nice easy one for starters. She flicked the page of her desk diary and then wondered why Pat Murphy hadn't been the producer at our commentary game at Wolves and so it went on. Still, I suppose it underlined how much our coverage was valued, even in Germany. At least she didn't get around to asking me about how I prepared for big games. I would have been able to tell her that I always tended to do a little bit more for the biggest occasions like Cup finals but would not have been able to furnish her with the following example of my research. Two days before an FA Cup final at the Footballer of the Year dinner, I was sitting next to a former player who had been a teammate of one of the Wembley captains. I was keen to get a line that I could spontaneously slip into my commentary. This was the only insight he could provide:

Well, I know somebody who's shagged his missus…

You won't find that on Wikipedia.

Ron Greenwood was a delightful avuncular companion. This was the man who had the foresight to involve both Bobby Robson and Terry Venables when he had been England manager. Ron just lived for football and adored talking about it. Just before Euro '88, we were together in Budapest for a warm-up game and so Ron found himself back in the famous Nep Stadium, scene of probably his finest hour as England boss when qualifying for the 1982 World Cup. Ron had been talked out of resigning after losing the previous weekend in Switzerland and faced a pivotal game. The memories came flooding back as we stood on the touchline watching training. He told me that after he had picked his team to play Hungary, he was announcing the line-up to his players in the dressing room and changed his mind at the last second as he was about to confirm Trevor Francis's selection. Ron said that he took one look at Trevor's face and just didn't think his body language looked right. I got the same impression when I looked at the England players fraternising with all of the Republic of Ireland squad before the opening game in that 1988 European Championship. It was just too relaxed and convivial, and then when the match started, England were caught cold and lost. It was a bittersweet triumph for the England World Cup winner Jack Charlton, who was managing Ireland after never even getting a reply to his application years earlier for the England job. Jack, who loved his angling, would have been a fish out of water at the bureaucratic FA.

England manager Bobby Robson's press conference before the second game against The Netherlands was one of his most fractious. He had committed the cardinal sin of giving one of his favoured journalists an exclusive that Glenn Hoddle was going to be recalled. The rest of the media entourage were not amused, and the exchanges were feisty as Robson defended his corner. I watched this tense drama unfold sitting next to Ron Greenwood. As Robson became more and more agitated, Ron whispered in my ear, "I can't believe now that I used to get like that?" It was a pity that Robson's team couldn't show the same spirit and passion against the Dutch, who annihilated them. England were effectively eliminated and in their final academic game, hoisted the white flags in what was an appallingly lethargic loss to the Soviet Union. After this embarrassing defeat, I sat long into the night in the bar of our Frankfurt hotel with Bobby Robson. I was admitted to his inner sanctum only because I was with his predecessor Ron Greenwood and Bobby wanted to pour his heart out to him. He was distraught and very emotional, not so much because of the performance but more from the sound of his players letting their hair down in an adjoining room. I vividly remember him saying:

> *Listen to that Ron; they just don't feel defeat like we do. It just doesn't seem to matter as much these days.*

Ron and I had to return home, leaving Bryon and producer Peter Slater to report on the final. Whether or not we would return to do a full commentary from Munich hinged on the weather forecast for the first Saturday of Wimbledon, which turned out to be benign. This meant that Marco van Basten's wonder goal was never described live on the radio; imagine that happening now?

When the Italia '90 campaign began, there were some weird and wonderful trips. There was a bizarre midweek friendly for commercial reasons in Saudi Arabia. No wonder some clubs were becoming reticent about releasing their top players. In the heat of Riyadh, it was cold turkey for us all. We had to endure three days without booze, although staff at a British embassy reception did assure us that from time to time they were in receipt of 'special cargo'. So what does the press corps do when deprived of alcohol and fun for three days? Obviously, we piled into someone's room and played Trivial Pursuit. That gifted writer Paddy Barclay remembered how Peter Slater and I managed to excel in the pop music section:

> *They turned out to have an almost nerdish knowledge of the subject. It was an absorbing contest and as I recall, we didn't get to our beds until nearly eleven o' clock!*

There was a sandstorm for most of the time we were there. All Western journalism was vetted, and any hint of a page three bikini was airbrushed out. Our city tour included a stop off at the public execution plaza, known locally as 'Chop, Chop Square'. At least I was able to buy a current newspaper there. When we travelled to Albania for a World Cup Qualifier in 1989, I went off in search of a souvenir edition to bring home and was delighted to find a kiosk selling a publication that appeared to be devoted to sport, only for our local guide to tell me that it was two years old. Albania in those days was about as accessible as King Solomon's Mines. There was only one hotel in the main square of Tirana for the England party and media, so everybody had to share a room. That must have been purgatory for Peter Jones, a man much more comfortable in his own space rather than kipping down for two nights with me. In my forty years of working at the BBC, I slept with only two colleagues (in separate beds) Peter Jones and Bryon Butler, and that's not a bad claim to fame.

During Arsenal's title-winning campaign in 1989, Peter Jones and I covered their pivotal victory at Middlesbrough, which features strongly in the film adaptation of Nick Hornby's *Fever Pitch*. Colin Firth's character is listening to the match in his car while his girlfriend is trying to talk to him about buying a house. I did the original radio commentary of the only goal, scored by Martin Hayes, which had been erased from the BBC archive and so was asked to recreate the moment for the scene. The only screenplay not written by Nick Hornby was, therefore, my scripted commentary clip.

This would turn out to be Peter Jones's last full football season, which ended on that dramatic night of League title victory for Arsenal at Anfield, a game that was staged in the aftermath of more unbearable disaster. Only four years on from the Heysel tragedy, Peter once again found himself describing the heartbreaking scenes at Hillsborough and never fully recovered from that second ordeal. Our summariser in Brussels, Emlyn Hughes, was sitting behind Peter at that FA Cup semi-final in Sheffield and left as soon as he saw the horror unfolding; he couldn't bear to watch. Fortunately, I was at the other tie at Villa Park.

When I had to interview Everton's Pat Nevin, the scorer of the only goal, on what should have been one of the biggest days of his career, he rightly said that any talk about football would be utterly superfluous.

When Peter Jones reached his sixtieth birthday in 1990, he was forced to retire from the BBC staff – that was the rule then. However, he still appeared to be young at heart, clearly had so much more to offer and so was automatically given a contract to continue.

Peter had only just started this new life as a freelance when we commentated on Southampton against Manchester United at the Dell. He told me that he couldn't quite believe how much he was now being paid and wished he'd had this arrangement years ago. The following midweek, England had a World Cup warm-up friendly at home to Brazil and the day before the game, I went along to Wembley to watch the South Americans train. I was pleasantly surprised but somewhat taken aback to find Peter there as well; it was the first time that I had ever seen him doing this kind of preparation. Something else happened that was quite unusual. As we stood together on the touchline admiring the skills of Bebeto and Careca, he started to tell me stories that I had never heard before about his time as a schoolmaster, when one of his star pupils was England cricketer Graham Roope. Peter, an essentially private man, rarely opened up in this unprompted way. He was looking back over his life with me, almost as if he knew that this was the final chapter. The next night, he commentated on Gary Lineker's winner for England and that would be the last goal he would ever describe. The following Saturday morning on my way to Nottingham Forest, I tuned in to hear Peter live from the towpath chatting merrily to Tony Lewis on *Sport on Four* about the day's Boat Race, which was just another string to Peter's considerable bow. When I arrived at Forest's City Ground and checked in with the studio, I was asked if Peter's son Stuart, *The Times'* football correspondent, was at the ground as they were desperate to get hold of him. Stuart was elsewhere and eventually would be told the news that his father had collapsed, microphone in hand while broadcasting from the Thames. He never regained consciousness.

Painting pictures with my mind
Making memories using my eyes
Filling up my head with golden stories
Who adds some spice to the rhythm of life.

The Heartbreak Kid

As you look around Hillsborough, you will appreciate why it has been regarded for so long as the perfect venue for all kinds of important matches. It's a stadium that befits such occasions and the large crowds they attract.

Sheffield Wednesday chairman Bert McGee in the match programme
for Liverpool v Nottingham Forest FA Cup semi-final
Saturday April 15th, 1989.

The gymnasium here at Hillsborough is being used as a mortuary for the dead and at this moment stewards, just as they did at the Heysel Stadium, are gathering up the personal belongings of the spectators, some of whom died, some of whom are now seriously injured in nearby hospitals. Red and white scarves of Liverpool, red and white bobble hats of Liverpool, and red and white rosettes of Liverpool. Nothing else out there in the enclosure where all the deaths occurred, and the sun shines now.

Peter Jones at Hillsborough on April 15th, 1989.

LESS THAN A YEAR AFTER THAT BROADCAST, PETER PASSED away. Peter was so deeply scarred by the two disasters he witnessed when he should have been watching sport that he struggled to sleep properly and even considered walking away from a job and a way of life that he adored. In what turned out to be his final football commentary, he described Paul Gascoigne coming on as a late substitute for England against Brazil just a couple of months before Italia '90. Peter had been accredited for that tournament but would never get the chance to observe Gazza's impact or his semi-final tears in Turin. However, many were shed for Peter over that Boat Race weekend, so close to another World Cup. I suppose to die with a microphone in your hand for him, was a bit like the great comedian Tommy Cooper's fatal collapse on stage, when he was doing something that had been the oxygen in his life. Peter had only just turned sixty, and there was every expectation that not only would he be commentating on the World Cup final in Rome, but that Euro '96 at Wembley would have been on his horizon as well, not to mention the Barcelona and Atlanta Olympics.

There have been commentators to equal him in individual sports, like John Arlott and Peter Bromley, who became the radio sound of cricket and horse racing, but nobody matched his all-round versatility. In the Olympic swimming pool, Peter would set the scene, describe the start and then rely heavily on the expertise of summariser Anita Lonsbrough. His, though, was the only voice you wanted to hear at the end to confirm that 'David Wilkie touches now'. Peter's approach to the Boat Race was the same. He would paint pictures for you from the Thames and then, during the race itself, draw on the experience of Dan Topolski, an outstanding oarsman and coach to guide the crews home. That had again been the format in 1990. Peter handled the start and then brought in Dan for his first comment. When Dan passed it back, he noticed that Peter was unable to say anything and before he collapsed, there were tears in his eyes. He had always made his work look so easy. Only he knew how much inner stress had been concealed beneath the surface.

A memorial service was held for him only a month before the World Cup at All Souls Church next door to Broadcasting House. Among the hundreds to attend were the England manager Bobby Robson and Liverpool's Kenny Dalglish, who, like Peter, had been haunted by those two disasters. The music and readings reflected Peter's Welsh pride and included verse from Dylan Thomas in memory of this Swansea boy who won a Cambridge University Blue for football and went on to become a modern language master for thirteen years at Bradfield College in Berkshire.

Peter Jones didn't enter the world of broadcasting until October 1965. Even for someone of his calibre, chance meetings and sliding doors played a part in engineering that move. At Bradfield, he became friendly with the BBC football commentator Maurice Edelston, who lived nearby in Reading and used to come to the college to do some coaching. Maurice had been a considerable footballer himself and had played for England during the war. Peter went along to watch him do a commentary at Southampton and in a conversation afterwards with the producer Tony Smith, confessed that he would love to report on a match one day. Tony invited him to cover a game at Aldershot and head of sport Angus Mackay was so impressed with his contribution that he offered him a job. To make such a career switch at the age of thirty-five to a lower salary was a brave step at the time for a family man, but it was his calling, and being such a comparative late starter made him value even more every assignment that came his way. Unlike today, when there are so many commentaries, his schedule was not congested, and that meant that every fixture would be something to cherish. He would be personally affronted if his FA Cup tie was not the one selected for second-half commentary on a Saturday afternoon. "Make it sing," he would insist if you were doing the first-half reports alongside him. Infrequently, when his game didn't make the final cut, there would be no recrimination. Personal pride might have been wounded, but there would be no argument. Like the great professional he was, Peter would placidly accept all studio instruction.

During the first year of Peter's new life, England were champions of the world and yet, remarkably, for half of his twenty-four years as a commentator, between 1970 and 1982, they did not qualify for the World Cup, which was another reason why it would have meant so much for him to be in Italy. His commentary style was unique and beyond parody. He blueprinted the goal clip on radio. The build-up, the execution and the pay offline all neatly parcelled in twenty seconds. Occasionally, he commentated in the future, 'Rush will score', and then he did, 'Smith will score', and then famously didn't. He loved the Welsh triad, repetition of words, one magic was never enough, it had to be 'magic, magic, magic'. He was also very cute. On the rare occasion when identification might not be obvious, he bought himself an extra second or two before committing himself to a goalscorer. So you would hear:

And the shot comes in… and the goalkeeper hasn't seen it… and it's there, and…

By now, unless he has taken his shirt off, the scorer would have revealed himself.

Peter never resorted to lazy vocabulary or had to rely on the sanctuary of research. He never went anywhere without a book, was a prodigious reader and his choice of language in commentary reflected that pastime. He would have had another adjective up his sleeve as an alternative to the over-used 'sublime'. No 'wicked deflections', 'gilt-edged chances' or 'stonewall penalties' passed through his lips. He lived, breathed and understood the game being played in front of him, so didn't need to fall back on the crutch of tedious statistics. The author Sir Walter Hamilton Moberly once wrote, "For God's sake, stop researching for a while and begin to think." He would have approved of Peter.

Peter relished his troubadour life. He was a creature of habit, nearly always travelled in the UK by rail and stuck to his favourite hotels. His tipple was Scotch and water, and in a restaurant, I could have ordered for him in advance: "Onion soup, followed by medium rare steak." Paradoxically, his immaculate, not-a-hair-out-of-place, old-spice appearance was not matched by reliable timekeeping. Ask him to do a fifty-second report on the radio and he would be like clockwork. Arrange a time to meet for lunch, then book the table for at least forty-five minutes later. He would finally show up after 'never having seen so much traffic in all of my life', but then, as Cliff Morgan so fondly remembered, 'he would grab you by the arm and make you feel that for him life had been a desert since he last saw you'. You were happy to indulge such idiosyncrasies and tolerate, even, some of his more maverick eccentricity.

Peter was in every sense 'the commentator', portrayed in verse by Wynford Vaughan-Thomas as:

Napoleon of the talking trade, stern guardian of the spoken word.
For him the whole truth is heard – the honest truth?
Well let's admit, you've got to hot it up a bit.
And then with cunning adjectival skill, he gilds the lily and coats
the pill.

There was no better example of that than when he was supposed to be in position at Wembley Arena ahead of a World Title fight. Peter was due to do a live preview from the Arena but instead burst into the studio at Broadcasting House and told presenter Garry Richardson to still cue him in as normal. He sat opposite Garry and when introduced, closed his eyes and began:

Good evening, welcome to Wembley, where the arena around
me is quiet and dark at this moment, but in just over an hour,
there will be a kaleidoscope of colour when little Charlie Magri
steps into the ring above me and bids to become the champion of
the whole world.

Peter was more than just a sports broadcaster. His ability to make you feel that you were there sitting alongside him meant that he was always one of the first names on the team sheet for the grandest of state occasions. When the procession approached his vantage point on the Strand at the Royal Wedding in 1981, he was just about to launch into his usual purple prose on seeing the Household Cavalry in their scarlet and gold livery. Suddenly and dramatically, he was cut short by co-commentator Lorraine Chase, an actress with an undertone of Chas & Dave, who boomed:

'ERE, LOOK AT THEM GEEZERS IN RED.

At the opening ceremony of the 1982 World Cup in Spain, it wasn't a Cockney Sparrow that wrong-footed him. Peter, in full pageantry overdrive, had anticipated that a giant football on the rostrum was about to be sliced in half and opened by a small boy. This time, just for once in his life, the lily would not be gilded, and when this piece of theatre reached its climax, Peter declared, "And out comes... a pigeon." His producer in London reached for the talk-back and whispered compassionately, "Peter, it's a dove." A rare mistake by a man normally very well-up on his birds.

Peter Jones gave so much pleasure to so many listeners and yet treasured his own public anonymity. He was at his most relaxed in familiar surroundings with a small circle of friends. A nightmare scenario for him would be a long journey in company that might test his levels of tolerance. He told me that after one game at Newcastle, after boarding his train back to London, he lay down on the floor of his compartment to ensure there was no eye contact with any unwelcome companion who might invade his space. I can't imagine what that must have looked like to fellow travellers, but rest assured, Peter would have come up with a very plausible and charming explanation. That is why it was such an honour to be allowed to travel with him by taxi nearly every day from central London to the All England Club when I was helping out at Wimbledon. It was on that journey that I got an unexpected insight into his sense of humour. Peter didn't strike me as a man who made a regular habit of sitting down at night to watch TV, but it just so happened that one evening and coincidentally, we had both enjoyed the same film. It was the original version of Neil Simon's *The Heartbreak Kid* starring Charles Grodin as the hapless Leonard and Cybill Shepherd as the nubile Kelly. Tears were streaming down Peter's face as we both relived the two classic confrontational scenes involving Kelly's ultra-protective father played by Eddie Albert. Peter seemed to know the words off by heart; on paper, the script probably doesn't convey the side-splitting hilarity of the moment, but what makes it all so hysterically funny is Eddie Albert's dramatic timing. That is probably why it appealed so much to Peter, who was a master of this art himself until he so sadly and prematurely left us.

Peter Jones died four months before the start of BBC Radio 5, a new national station with more airtime for sport. When it was first conceived, it was taken for granted that he would play an integral part in the coverage. I am only too aware of ostensibly benefitting from what was a cruel twist of fate. After his death, before I was really ready for it, opportunities came my way professionally that would not have been forthcoming had he still been with us. On a personal level, though, I missed his guiding hand and influence. He always made me try and up my game whenever I was with him. It was an overwhelming loss for the department and the profession. Yet he never completely left us. On any Cup final day, you will still hear his voice from an archive of treasures. I never attended a big game without thinking of him. How much he would have loved to have seen a Cup final in Cardiff and would have also relished watching players like Messi, Ronaldo, Bergkamp, Gerrard and Henry. For those of us who followed in his footsteps, it was impossible to *keep up with this Jones.* He set all the standards, and the monumental challenge was simply to try and maintain, preserve and uphold his legacy.

My candle burns at both ends;
It will not last the night.;
But ah, my foes, and oh, my friends—
It gives a lovely light!

'First Fig' Edna St Vincent Millay, 1920

Goodbye Yellow Brick Road

IT WAS HELD APPROPRIATELY ON ST GEORGE'S DAY 1990 AT the Bank of Sardinia Convention Centre in Cagliari. '*Arrivano gli Inglesi*' – '*The English are Coming*' was a one-day conference aimed at reassuring local dignitaries that all England supporters about to visit their tranquil community would be coming in peace. Bobby Robson's squad would be based on this island for the whole of the World Cup group stage and one member of the English delegation invited to put a positive spin on the imminent arrival of so many fans was that eminent ambassador for his country, Sir Tom Finney. It proved to be an exercise in futility.

Less than a fortnight after that peacekeeping mission, Leeds United hooligans celebrated promotion by creating carnage at Bournemouth. When I returned to my car after covering the game, the roof had been jumped on and had caved in, but when I look back at that day, my temporary inconvenience pales into insignificance. Before the match, I had collected my ticket as usual from Bournemouth's managing director Brian Tiler, who had been a fine player himself but more important was just a thoroughly nice guy. It was Bournemouth's last home game of the season, and in the match programme, Brian's message to supporters was, "Have a nice summer, and I hope we will see you all next season." That hope was extinguished a month later when he was killed in a horrific road accident while attending the

World Cup in Italy with his manager and friend Harry Redknapp; such a tragic loss.

Looking back at Italia '90, I remember Peter Jones being in my thoughts daily. It had only been two months since his death. Peter would have adored being at a tournament that was being held in a passionate, vibrant footballing country, home at the time to all three of the current European trophy holders. At my final World Cup as England correspondent, twenty-four years later in Brazil, I described only seven games at four different venues and hadn't seen Argentina play before the final. In Italy with only commentary responsibilities, I covered fourteen games at nine different venues and saw Argentina play three times before the final. It was a very different experience, and it was also the last major football coverage on Radio 2.

For England in 1990, it was a slow burner of a World Cup. In a turgid opening group and, contrary to all the propaganda handed out to the citizens of Cagliari, there was the inevitable tear gas mayhem in the streets before the Holland game. Straight after that match, I found myself on a flight to Palermo to watch the Republic of Ireland play there the next day. In what felt like a giant floating orange balloon of an airship surrounded by Dutch fans returning to their Sicily base, our small party was outnumbered forty to one, and yet we found ourselves bouncing up and down and joining in with all of their drinking songs. It was like one big glorious scene from *The Muppet Show*, with not an ounce of hostility towards us from supporters who just loved their football and were intoxicated not with hatred but happiness.

In the last sixteen game in Bologna, having ridden their luck a bit against Belgium, England were seconds away from what would have been their first ever penalty shootout. In the commentary, I was already speculating with Ray Clemence about whom the five England spot kick takers might be, then suddenly, all that became academic:

England have got a free kick, Waddle and Gascoigne stand left and right of the ball. Gascoigne trots forward and chips looking for Platt... AND PLATT HAS SCORED FOR ENGLAND ON

THE VOLLEY. A fantastic goal by David Platt of Aston Villa, his first ever goal for England, one of the most important he'll ever score in his life, and it's England 1, Belgium 0.

The final whistle went ninety seconds later, and one of the first people I remember seeing in his TV commentary seat was a beaming Bobby Charlton. I thought again of Peter Jones and tried to imagine how he would have captured that moment.

For Bobby Robson, there would be no more siege mentality press conferences. I fondly remember him with the media occasionally straight batting a question by saying, "I'm not getting into that," but then, like a dog with a bone, he would keep gnawing at it, returning to it and by the end would have more than comprehensively answered it. After Gary Lineker's two penalties in Naples to get England over the line against Cameroon in the quarter-final, I was denied access by security officials to the area where he was waiting to do our radio interview. Gary could see that there was a problem and came over so that I could push my microphone through the barbed wire fence to record his words for posterity – even in those days here was a man with considerable media awareness.

In the semi-final, watching West Germany navigate their way through a penalty shootout against England had such an air of inevitability about it. It didn't occur to me then that this was going to be as good as it would get for this commentator watching the national side. Six more World Cups, but nothing else matched it; talk about peaking too soon. All I ever wanted was to see an England team playing to its potential and doing themselves justice. That night in Turin, they did.

The defeat on penalties by West Germany left us all in the commentary box emotionally drained, not to mention knackered, having been in Naples the night before watching the other semi-final also go to extra time and penalties. Our genial summariser and travelling companion Ray Clemence had just witnessed his friend and former goalkeeping rival Peter Shilton attempting in vain to save laser-precision spot kicks. We now had to rely on Ray's safe hands to drive us 100 miles from Turin to a hotel logically booked by the BBC for us in Milan. As usual, he had no problem maintaining his concentration, but correspondent Bryon Butler, who had been working around the clock, drifted off to sleep in the back of the car. As you entered the outskirts of Milan, there were endless traffic lights, and at every stop, it seemed in the early hours of this particular morning, there was a lady of the night proffering personal services. One was being particularly persistent and was giving the roof of our stationary vehicle an unremitting pounding. Ray had been forced to lower his driver's window to prevent it from steaming up but retained his focus on the road ahead. The thumping, though, had woken Bryon from his slumber, just in time to glimpse the backside of our relentless kerbside vendor being pushed through the open window for closer inspection. This scene was not exactly an everyday occurrence for our correspondent in leafy Surrey. He opened one eye, like they used to in the old Westerns, and observed, "Well you could pick up a pimple or two around here," and then nodded off again. He had just seen England flirt with a place in the World Cup final and was only semi-conscious but still managed to deliver a memorable one-liner. The final in Rome, won by a West German penalty against Argentina, was a colossal anticlimax.

After the World Cup, football commentary moved to BBC Radio 5, a new home for sport and education and described by managing director of radio David Hatch as a network for the healthy mind and healthy body. It provided an eclectic mix of programmes, ranging from children's stories with Andrew Sachs to the cultish *Hit the North* with Mark Radcliffe. In the very first show on 5, presented by Bruno Brookes, the guest was the man of the moment, Paul Gascoigne. When you look back at what a revelation he had been at Italia '90, it does make you wonder why he had been kept in mothballs for so long. Gascoigne was twenty-three at that World Cup and had only just broken into the full national team. Compare that to more recent times, when England debuts were given to Wayne Rooney and Raheem Sterling at just seventeen. Gascoigne's free kick in the 1991 FA Cup semi-final against Arsenal turned out to be his watershed moment playing for Tottenham on what was a retrograde day for the world's most famous cup competition. Semi-finals have no business being played at Wembley. This should not be about finance but about preserving the tradition of the tournament and the sanctity of Wembley. What used to be a once-in-a-lifetime dream for many players, to reach a Wembley Cup final has become increasingly devalued, not just by the staging of semi-finals there but also by rewriting the League rulebook. Sometimes a team finishing seventh can climb the steps to the Royal Box and receive a trophy for winning a Play-off final that very often makes a mockery of a ten-month season. There seems to be more limelight and kudos attached to winning this game than actually being the champion.

Paul Gascoigne's life of extremes was encapsulated a month after bludgeoning that free kick past David Seaman when a self-inflicted injury in the final cut him down in his prime. When judgments are made about Graham Taylor's time as England manager, it should never be forgotten that for half of his forty months in charge, he was unable to call on the services of his most talented player. Bobby Robson's successor was approaching the first anniversary of his appointment when a dossier from his employers landed on his desk at Lancaster Gate; it wasn't exactly bedtime reading. This was a blueprint of 120 pages outlining the benefits of having a Football Association Premier League of eighteen clubs in place for 1992–93. Its primary objective:

Establishing the England team at the apex of the pyramid of playing excellence. For the game to prosper in England, we need a successful England team, which means the Football League should occupy a subordinate position to that of the England team.

In other words, it was as much about the flexing of muscle as football. All twenty-two of the First Division clubs at that time signed up to the idea, including Notts County, Luton, Coventry and Oldham, a penny for their thoughts now. There was to be a revolution, but not in the way it was first envisaged by the FA.

After twenty-three years of noble service, the baton of football correspondent was being passed on to me by Bryon Butler. This appointment, for which I will be eternally grateful, was made by head of sport Mike Lewis. For my first few months in the post, there was more of a need to be consulting my old legal textbooks rather than Charles Buchan's *Football Monthly*, as the FA went to court to establish sovereignty and jurisdiction over the League to administer reform. Before everything was finally approved, most of the bitter wrangling was about finance and not football. England manager Graham Taylor read his blueprint and concluded that there was no advantage in it for him. He was right. Bryon Butler must have seen all this coming when he stepped aside! In all seriousness, he just wanted to have more time to devote to his writing, focus on his family and beloved Merrow Cricket Club. He might also have read the runes and seen how the extra demands of Radio 5 were going to make it harder for him to achieve that balance. Shortly after being appointed as his successor, I received a letter from him, in which he wrote:

> *There may be odd times when you'll wish you were doing something simpler, less demanding like Chancellor of the Exchequer, but for much the most part it will provide a perfect platform for you. I know you will get as much pleasure and reward from the job as I did.*

It was such an honour to be given this new responsibility, although it would be a bit like being a doctor on call, with that call very often coming while I was negotiating Spaghetti Junction or gridlocked on the M25. The football correspondent's most important role is to be the first point of contact for all international matters. So it follows that your relationship with the England manager becomes very important, and I began with Graham Taylor. I had first met him when he was Watford manager at their training ground in Stanmore. I had been given permission to talk to his full-back Wilf Rostron about the prospect of him facing his former club Arsenal. Graham met me and took me over to where the training session was still taking place. He introduced me to Wilf and then suggested somewhere quieter where we could have our chat. That was the kind of guy he was.

In those formative years at Vicarage Road when Graham was starting to make a name for himself, he never forgot receiving a phone call from Brian Clough. Cloughie rang him late at night to try and get him to persuade his Watford chairman Sir Elton John to perform at his testimonial function. In exchange for securing Elton, Clough told Graham that he would give him two tickets for Forest's next reserve team game and that he would be able to sign any three players that he wanted. This was one of Graham's favourite stories, and he related it in Dave Armitage's engaging collection of Clough anecdotes: "150 BC." The only thing he left out was the moment when he asked Clough what would happen if he picked a player who might not actually want to come to Watford and was told unequivocally, "Oh, he'll come," but Elton didn't…!

Later in life, Graham and I became very good friends, but for now, I will attempt to dispassionately look back over our professional dealings. He would have expected nothing less than that. Compared to his predecessors in the England job, Graham Taylor began as much more of an outsider at the FA. He had been only a modest player and, though impressive as a club manager, had limited international experience. His appointment was not universally applauded. The style gurus were apprehensive about his perceived penchant for a long ball game, conveniently forgetting that the most famous goal in the history of English football resulted from the longest of balls out of defence.

I can understand why he did it, but looking back, possibly Taylor's first miscalculation was to want his own support team around him. He dispensed immediately with Don Howe, a coach who had no personal ambition or agenda and either side of Graham's reign, was the perfect assistant to Bobby Robson and Terry Venables. Don would have provided the more senior players with some continuity during this transition. Having lost the services of Peter Shilton and Terry Butcher though retirement, as well as being deprived of Paul Gascoigne through injury, Taylor favoured building his own team and was too quick to move away from other backbone members of the previous squad like Bryan Robson, Peter Beardsley and Chris Waddle. None of their more functional replacements were an improvement.

On one away trip to Turkey, one of the duty-free items being offered for sale on the flight was a cuddly toy with a key ring attached to it. It was a duck dressed as a pilot with the words 'Wing Commander Waddle' on his cap. This purchase could not be resisted and was immediately passed down the plane to the manager, who typically saw the funny side of it. It was, though, a mystery to us that wing commander Chris Waddle, Zidane's favourite player at Marseilles, who became Footballer of the Year on his return to England in 1993, was deemed surplus to the national team's requirements. Andy Sinton, John Salako, Lee Sharpe, Tony Daley and others who were preferred were not in the same class.

Another departure from convention was that Taylor wanted the press and his players to change places, not on the pitch but on the plane, with the FA party sitting at the back and the media at the front. It was a superficial game of musical chairs to prevent the journalists from looking straight at the squad. More of a consequence for the media, and even more of a handicap to some of the FA Committee members, was an alcohol ban on the outward journey. The manager wanted to see everyone walking and not tumbling out of the aircraft on arrival. This, of course, was a red rag to a bull for most of my comrades. There is nothing like a bit of prohibition to increase the thirst for a snifter or two. As a result, out of sheer bloody-mindedness, we probably ended up consuming many more units than would have been the case had it been freely available. All that was required was some duty-free gin purchased at Luton Airport, and when the trolleys came around, copious amounts of tonic were surprisingly ordered, and the crew played along with it all.

Booze ban aside, Graham Taylor could not have been more understanding of our needs. It is ironic that the England manager most vilified in the end by the press had been the most accessible, mainly because of his upbringing as the son of the local reporter covering Scunthorpe United. If he had not had such a fascination and respect for the media, he might not have been tempted into making that injudicious TV documentary that would come back to haunt him. He didn't have anything like the support system of today at the FA to help him prepare for press conferences. Sometimes left to his own devices, he tried too hard to contrive a good back-page headline to keep editors happy.

Taylor made a more than decent start to his job, maintaining momentum after Italia '90 and, unlike Italy, Portugal and Spain, qualified for the 1992 European Championship. He achieved this from a group that was by no means a formality, including the Republic of Ireland and two countries that appeared to be joined at the hip with England in those days, Poland and Turkey. These two would again be lying in wait for Taylor's England after the qualifying draw was made in New York for the 1994 World Cup. One of his great frustrations as an England manager, apart from his disappointment with the attitude of some club managers towards the national side, was what he perceived as an amateurish naivety shown by his employers when it came to the straightforward task of arranging fixtures for the next qualifying campaign. When he arrived at the meeting with all of the other countries in his World Cup group, he was faced with a *fait accompli*. A schedule had already been agreed upon in advance by the other teams, leaving England with four of their last five fixtures away from home. A small detail that would have enormous implications.

Before all of the focus was on Euro '92, thoughts turned briefly to Euro '96 when England were confirmed as the hosts in Lisbon before the Cup Winners' Cup final between Werder Bremen and Arsene Wenger's Monaco. All that I can remember now from making that trip was the journey home. The seat next to me on the plane was unoccupied until just before the doors were closed and then, suddenly and unexpectedly, it was taken by the manager of Manchester United. Up until this moment, I had only spent very brief moments in Alex Ferguson's company conducting short interviews. Now he was going to have to endure me for two and a half hours. He could so easily have buried his head in a book or newspaper and sent out signals that he was not to be disturbed, but that is not his gregarious nature. Ferguson would undoubtedly have sensed my apprehension, but he made it so easy for me to have a relaxed conversation. On our return, he even shared a taxi with me back into central London. His Manchester United team had just lost out to Leeds in the title race, making it a quarter of a century since they were last League Champions. A defining defeat in the run-in would be at Liverpool and one of the banners held aloft at Anfield that day read, 'Have you ever seen United win the League?' Words written by Truman Capote, though, would prove to be more relevant: 'Failure is the condiment that gives success its flavour.' Over the next twenty-five years, Liverpool fans would see United driven on by Ferguson to win the League thirteen times.

Liverpool did win the FA Cup at the end of that season, and when their captain Mark Wright received the trophy from the Duchess of Kent, for the benefit of the worldwide TV audience, he mouthed an expletive. It was heat of the moment emotion, obviously, but I couldn't help remembering Bobby Moore, out of respect, making sure his hands were clean before that other cup was handed over to him in 1966 by the Queen. Mark Wright was going to be a key player for Graham Taylor at the European Championship in Sweden. The England manager wanted him to reprise his World Cup role as a sweeper in a back three and all of the preparatory work was done in Finland at a pre-tournament training camp in Lahti. All of the correspondents attended, and the arrangement was that Graham Taylor would come to our hotel every afternoon to give us a briefing. At the first of these sessions, there was only one topic of conversation.

Yugoslavia were scheduled to be England's first opponents, but because of the ongoing conflict in the Balkans, their participation was looking increasingly unlikely. Taylor's stock answer to all questions about this uncertainty was that until he was told otherwise, all of his plans were being made to face the Yugoslavs. However, when we then sat down shortly after to do our radio interview, he pretty much contradicted everything he had just been saying and told me that his understanding was that there was little chance of Yugoslavia being present and that it was more than likely that their place would be taken by Denmark. Looking back, it was a rather unnecessary bit of mischief to stir up the writers. As I went back to my room to send our interview to the BBC, I could see many of them at their typewriters filing their reports which quite clearly were going to be at odds with our story and so their cards were duly marked. We were all living together and getting on well in our small group, and there would have been nothing to gain from withholding this information. This could not have happened in later years when radio and newspapers were in separate press conference rooms, and rolling TV news would have set the agenda anyway.

All of Graham Taylor's tactical intent disintegrated after the final warm-up game against Finland in Helsinki. An injury to Gary Stevens left him without an authentic right-back for the tournament, and he was also going to have to cope without the services of one of his favourite sons John Barnes. What he didn't realise until it was too late was that Mark Wright, a lynchpin in his strategy, had also picked up an injury and would not only be missing but, because of the delay surrounding his availability, could not be replaced. There was no plan B after losing Wright. Having to revert to a more traditional defensive line-up exposed the absence of a genuine right-back even more. David Batty, such an important member of Leeds United's midfield, agreed to play there in two of the games. His club colleague Tony Dorigo, a left-back by trade, was reluctant to swap flanks, and this was mystifying. Dorigo was always going to have limited international opportunity as deputy to Stuart Pearce, and this was a chance to represent his country at a championship. When he was a player, Graham Taylor was a right-footed full-back who agreed to switch to the left-hand side just to get in the Grimsby Town team. All this should have been clarified before the squad was selected and with hindsight, the more versatile Nigel Winterburn of Arsenal should have been preferred. England came out of this tournament with no credit at all. As usual, the hooligans did their worst in Malmo and after the final elimination losing to the hosts Sweden, Graham Taylor's world would never be the same again. 'Swedes 2 Turnips 1' was an inventive headline and even Taylor acknowledged it went with the territory. However, then portraying Taylor himself with a turnip as his head overstepped the mark. Even Brian Woolnough, *The Sun's* much-missed football writer, admitted that this had crossed a line. It would scar Graham for the rest of his days – but it was only just the start.

Bra Size

In the 1959 *International Football Book for Boys*, *The Times'* correspondent Geoffrey Green wrote:

> *In these islands populated by one of the most inventive races on earth, we strangely continue in an insular dog-eared fashion, stubbornly blind to change, still putting the football cart before the horse. Here the game is geared to the club first and what remains can be eked out by the wretched international team. How much longer is this attitude to continue?*

Thirty-three years, to be precise, because now all this was finally about to change – at least that was the theory. "It's a whole new ball game," boasted Sky Sports as the Football Association Premier League was launched 'to place England at the apex of the pyramid of playing excellence'. "This will be a league of equality," said the Premier League's chief executive Rick Parry. Oh, really? The start of the Premier League also coincided with a major shake-up in Europe. The European Cup, the brainchild of a newspaper, for champions only, was replaced by the misnomer of a 'Champions League', conceived for television and to include non-champions.

Domestically, that white elephant of a competition – the League Cup, with its ever-changing sponsors – trundled on. I fondly remember covering one early-round tie at Chesterfield against Liverpool when the only route to our commentary position involved walking through somebody's home and climbing a ladder at the bottom of their garden. As we made our way through their kitchen, we were offered cups of tea – Derbyshire folk have always been hospitable. On the re-shaped European stage, our refreshment in Stuttgart for two days turned out to be yoghurt. All reporters attending their game with Leeds were issued with a goodie bag of produce from the German club's sponsors Südmilch, and by the end of the trip it was coming out of our ears. Leeds survived that first round but were denied a place in the group stage by Rangers and have never been Champions of Europe. Their best chance disappeared when they handed manager Brian Clough his P45 after only forty-four days. Clough would go on to have the final word, winning those two European cups instead at Nottingham Forest.

All my overseas travel at this time was spent in the company of a group of Fleet Street correspondents who became known as the 'Morris Men'. They specialised in burning the candle at both ends but whenever called upon, would produce work of the highest quality. For some reason, I became an honorary member, and that is something that I will always be grateful for in my formative years as a correspondent. I'm not sure how it happened; it just evolved and although it seriously damaged my liver, proved to be an invaluable learning curve as well as providing great entertainment and camaraderie. Every evening meal was a Sky Sports *Sunday Supplement* all on its own. It was quite normal in those days for the press corps to operate along the lines of a Noah's Ark. You rarely saw Alex Montgomery without Bob Driscoll, Joe Melling without Bob Cass or Brian Woolnough without Nigel Clarke. But this Maypole troupe had five members. The unofficial leader was the *Daily Telegraph's* Colin Gibson, affectionately known as 'Mr Big'. If he hadn't become an accomplished writer, he would have made it as a top travel agent or supplier of sponsored kit. The late and much missed Steve Curry, working then for the *Daily Express* was the Clitheroe Kid with a wealth of experience and great contacts. He was also one of the best raconteurs that I ever met. Stuart Jones of *The Times* was Peter's son, and so I felt a special affinity with him. He didn't have as much to say as the others, but like his father, made every word count. One of his party pieces in any debate would be to round off a statement, so that if somebody, for example, offered an opinion that he was the worst goalkeeper they had ever seen, Stuart would, after an appropriate pause, add, "Oh, by a very long way." Stuart was a talented sportsman but smoked too many cigarettes. Sadly, like his father, he died young from cancer in 2013 but, like his father, was a treasured colleague. The *Daily Mail's* Neil Harman unashamedly supported Southend United and almost uniquely in our industry, as a referee, actually understood the laws of the game. He had transferred from tennis, which is presumably why he was nicknamed 'Hawkeye'. The last of the Mohicans was Harry Harris, headhunted for the *Daily Mirror* by Robert Maxwell. A man with a sixth sense for a story but surplus to requirement when the others were making up a four for golf. Occasionally and playfully, he was used as a punchbag by the rest of the group. Many a conversation would end with 'Harry, don't be silly', a bit like Joyce Grenfell telling off an errant child. In my relationship with Harry, though, he was the teacher and I was the pupil. Had I not been approved by this League of Gentlemen, I would never have been invited to their lunch in London with Alex Ferguson shortly after he had won the 1993 title. I remember Ferguson enthusing about his Manchester United youth team that included Gary Neville, Nicky Butt, David Beckham and Paul Scholes, but was especially struck by his encyclopaedic passion for cinema. *Twelve Angry Men* emerged as one of his favourite films, that epic courtroom drama when one renegade, dissenting juror played by Henry Fonda eventually turns around all the other eleven opinions. You could just imagine Fergie doing the same.

By now the jury was well and truly out on the England manager Graham Taylor. Unlike his predecessor, Bobby Robson, who had enjoyed some World Cup good fortune in Italy to make up for

Mexico, Taylor got very little in his campaign to reach USA '94, especially at Wembley against The Netherlands when Wouters fractured Gascoigne's cheekbone and was allowed to stay on the pitch. Although the away game against the Dutch signalled the end, it was effectively the defeat in Norway that struck the mortal blow. It was such an irony that Graham Taylor, condemned by some for favouring long ball tactics, should be undone by the ultimate exponents of this style. The night before the game in Oslo was memorable for us being in the same Italian restaurant as Bruce Springsteen, though the Morris Men would have been more impressed if it had been Bruce Rioch. The next day, there was a veritable 'darkness on the edge of town' as the Norwegians disposed of England in such a routine way that this time there was no need for any their commentators to ask Henry Cooper or Maggie Thatcher if they were watching. There had been paranoia in the England camp during the build-up about the presence of a former well-known English player who was then based in Norway and had attached himself to the squad. There was a concern that he might have split loyalty, and so Graham Taylor went overboard to try and keep his tactical masterplan secret. The problem was he seemed to have kept it secret from his team as well. In the end, when the line-up was finally revealed and showed Gary Pallister playing at left-back to counter the aerial threat from Jostein Flo, the manager's thinking was explained to us in the hotel lobby by David Teasdale. He was a spin doctor from Whitehall, who had been brought in unsuccessfully by Graham to beef up his PR, another development that further handicapped his relationship with assistant Lawrie McMenemy. After this crushing disappointment, we trudged back into Luton Airport with only Ian Wright; bless him, still trying to look on the bright side of life. "We can still do it," he was insisting at the baggage carousel. What a pity that this character who was such a joy to be around never got to play at a World Cup.

The last thing in the world Graham Taylor and his beleaguered squad needed after Oslo was the *USA Cup*, especially as it was beginning to look as if this dress rehearsal for the 1994 World

Cup might be the only time the team would get to visit Boston, Washington and Detroit, the three venues being used for this mini-tournament. Funnily enough, the other two countries invited to take part with the host nation, Brazil and Italy, would not only return twelve months later but also reach the final. Colin 'Mr Big' Gibson lived up to his name by somehow securing first-class flight upgrades for us all to Boston. Giancarlo Galavotti, the London correspondent of the revered Italian daily sports paper *La Gazzetta dello Sport*, was not a signed-up member of the Morris Men; such an enterprise would have been an anathema to him. However, Colin had also managed to include him on our ticket. There I was for the only time in my life, not wanting a flight to end with more individual space than in my first London flat. Giancarlo was one of my favourite people on the circuit. He had a love-hate relationship with England but was secretly content if they progressed, as that would extend his tournament as well. He was always impeccably attired; never once did I see him in jeans and he reminded me of the actor who comes out of the tank at the end of *Kelly's Heroes* and hands over the keys to the bank to Clint Eastwood. He was, of course, completely fluent in Anglo-Saxon with an obvious Italian lilt and perhaps because of that was able to deliver the very occasional profanity more effectively than anyone else I have ever met. It would be lacerating and hit the bullseye every time. Two hours into our transatlantic flight, he was sitting like a Buddha on his own private island luxuriating in comfort. So I decided to indulge him just to get confirmation that he was appreciating Colin's grand gesture before he converted his seat into a four-poster bed. "Everything all right, Giancarlo?" I enquired – rhetorically, I thought – naively expecting a two thumbs up. He looked up from his napkin and, without changing expression, growled, "Thees cheecken eez sheet." Not a man to be beholden to anyone, Giancarlo, but I greatly valued his company. Sadly, all good things come to an end, and the plane had to land at Logan Airport.

After another defeat in the opening game by the USA, I experienced my one and only falling out with Graham Taylor. It was in Washington, before the meeting with Brazil. I had asked an innocuous question about Nigel Clough's role in the team, and he jumped down my throat. I was taken aback by this sudden change of personality. ITV commentator and former BBC Radio correspondent Brian Moore could see that I had been upset and, typically considerate, came over and reassuringly said to me, "Don't worry, old son, I'm sure it's nothing personal; he doesn't know where he is at the moment." It certainly wasn't personal. Taylor was at his lowest ebb professionally at this time, and yet in the midst of all of his trials and tribulations, he was still thinking of others. As a lover of radio sports broadcasting, Graham took it upon himself that summer to write to the BBC Director-General. He was expressing his concern that when Radio 5 was rebranded and became 5 Live to incorporate news and sport, that coverage of sport might be compromised. Graham had far weightier matters on his mind at this time and didn't need to do this, but he duly received correspondence back from the DG John Birt assuring him that nothing was going to change.

I had far weightier things on my mind as well; seven pounds eight ounces worth on August 7th, 1993 when Lorna gave birth to our first child, born on a Saturday, a good omen. I had joked that if we had a boy, we should name him after whoever scored the winning goal that day in the Charity Shield between Arsenal and Manchester United. That was never going to work. United won after a missed penalty by Seaman. So instead we stuck to our original plan and our son was christened Marshall after his grandfather – second name Quincy after Quincy Jones, who Lorna had recently got to know and greatly admired. Quincy Jones sent Marshall this message:

To Marshall Quincy – This is at least where the second half may have come from. God bless you. The future is all yours, and you have serious stock in your genes. Love you Quincy '93.

England would not feature on the new Radio 5 Live under Graham Taylor's management, as he paid the inevitable price for failing to reach the 1994 World Cup. Looking back at that fateful evening in Rotterdam, I remember taking part in a preview programme the night before. Instead of sitting where he should have been still in the England dugout, Don Howe was in our London studio and was discussing the merits of the man who would be wearing Don's old number 2 shirt, Rob Jones of Liverpool. A telephone caller suddenly stopped us in our tracks. It was from one of Rob's relatives who told us, "I don't know why you are wasting your time talking about Rob. He's just called me to tell me he's injured and not playing."

After England's failure to qualify, Graham Taylor did the honourable thing like the honourable man he was and resigned, along with his assistant Lawrie McMenemy. Their relationship had become strained but in reality, was never likely to work. Lawrie was too strong a personality to be anybody's assistant. He had been a serious candidate himself for the job when his profile had been at its highest a decade earlier. It was only because of Graham's offer that he was given a chance to play a role with his national side and that is why I was disappointed with some of his comments about Graham in his autobiography.

Graham Taylor's England experience left him with deep scar tissue that never healed. I can't ever remember going out for dinner with him or accompanying him on a flight when the nightmare wasn't revisited, and yet on the surface, he always attempted to put on a brave face. This is what he wrote to me on my fiftieth birthday seven years after leaving the England job:

In July 1990, I became the England manager, an event which prompted the BBC to take the approach, 'well, if he can get the job, who can we give our top job to?' and that was how Mike Ingham was appointed chief football correspondent. Naturally, I took pity on him and being the sort of fella I am, wondered how I could make him feel that he had a good relationship with me. I came upon a super idea. Why not let him pick the England teams, it would be impossible to have a better relationship. It is time the truth came out, and this is what happened. He picked the England teams, and I wrote the scripts for him. Outcome: I got the sack, and he is still a top man. One day I hope you will tell me why you picked that team to play Norway. It's been bugging me for a long time.

Bobby Moore had started out covering that ill-fated World Cup campaign for Capital Radio but never lived to see the final outcome. At what turned out to be his final tournament at Euro '92, I had been fortunate enough on a couple of occasions to give him a lift to watch England's training sessions. It was another one of those 'pinch me to prove I'm not dreaming' moments, probably the most careful I've ever been driving a car. Tragically Bobby died of cancer aged only fifty-one, shortly after attending the qualifying game at Wembley against San Marino. I had just popped into Broadcasting House on my way to a match when the sad news broke and was able to record this tribute:

Bobby Moore, indestructible defender, ambassador, unique English footballing figure is no longer around to remind us how the national game at its very best can be a thing of dignity, beauty and integrity. He was the best, Pelé said so, and that has to be the final word. "The greatest defender I ever faced," he said, recalling not only the World Cup of '66 but the legendary meeting four years later between them in Mexico, ending with an exchange of shirts and a deep mutual respect never to be extinguished. At a time when some of our clubs are attempting to withdraw players from an England squad, let the record show that Bobby Moore became England youth captain at seventeen and leader of the senior side at twenty-two. Over twelve years as an international, he won 108 caps and, of course, on July 30th, 1966 received the World Cup at Wembley from Her Majesty the Queen. Not only had he inspired all around him, he'd also provided the passes for Geoff Hurst's first and final immortal last goal. His greatest asset, though, was not so much his passing or his tackling but his brain.

The master reader of the game on the pitch, tactical awareness he strangely was never able to convert into management. He joined West Ham from school, stayed with them for fifteen years before completing his 1,000th and final game with Fulham in 1977. In recent seasons, he became a colleague in the press box, a golfing partner for many of the correspondents – great company, with a delicious dry sense of humour. I last saw him, fittingly, last Wednesday night at Wembley watching England playing in the World Cup. His stadium, his team, his trophy.

I have reproduced that piece for two reasons. Most importantly, as a tribute to a great man, but also because the days were going to be numbered for this sort of scripted, recorded broadcast when you would be given time to collect your thoughts and express your feelings. Soon everything would have to be *live*, and on so many occasions when I found myself being interviewed, I ended up being deeply frustrated after not being given the chance to say what I wanted, having been at the mercy of somebody else's agenda.

Radio 5 Live was now offering more flexibility for getting news on the air quicker, but it could be a double-edged sword. On the day that Terry Venables was unveiled at Wembley as the new England manager in succession to Graham Taylor, I burst out of the stadium to our radio car ready with all the top lines from his first press conference and was patched through immediately to John Inverdale's programme. I regard John as the best radio sports presenter since Desmond Lynam. Like Des, he had such an easygoing yet authoritative style; there was no one better at balancing the light and shade. On this particular day, though, he was having to be more of a light entertainment host and was immersed in conversation with guest Danny Kelly about favourite childhood games like Blow Football and Subbuteo. Nobody in the production team had the foresight to mark my card about the conversation they were having before I was introduced and so when they brought me straight in on the subject, I had no idea what they were talking about. All my thoughts were focused on being first with the Venables quotes, and I was unable to indulge them. The whole impact of what I was supposed to be there for had been thrown away, and it felt as if the real sports news of the day was intruding on the chit chat. If Bryon Butler had been listening, it would have made him feel even more comfortable about having retired.

Unlike Graham Taylor, Terry Venables didn't have to qualify for his tournament, Euro '96, but before all that, there was the little matter of a World Cup. When the final draw for that went ahead without England, it took place at Caesars Palace in the casino city of Las Vegas. That choice of venue tells you all you need to know about the driving force behind USA '94 and leads seamlessly into FIFA's Sepp Blatter, who as usual was the self-appointed master of ceremonies. When it came to picking the balls out of a pot, there was nobody better to ridicule the whole charade than the comedian Robin Williams. Blatter, in full posturing flow, was memorably disarmed by Williams' constant references to him as Sepp Bladder – now that's what I call taking the piss.

The World Cup itself was symbolised by Diana Ross's penalty miss at the opening ceremony. The sun shone, the stadiums were full, much of the football entertained and yet something was still missing. When a country stages a World Cup, it is usually consumed by the event. There is no general unawareness of what is taking place, but that was not the case in the USA. I was based in New York, covering Ireland and the East Coast groups with Mark Lawrenson and Rob Hawthorne. Shortly after arriving and taking a stroll, I was asked for directions by an *All in the Family* Archie Bunker lookalike. When I explained that I was a visitor, he said, like all Americans seem to, "Gee, I love your accent, where are you from?" After confirming that I was from England, my Carroll O'Connor friend responded with, "Oh, we love Europe." I was tempted to say, "Which Europe is that, then?" Berkhamsted Hertfordshire or maybe Bergen Norway or even Bucharest Romania. "Are you on vacation?" was the next question and so I explained that I was in the States for the World Cup. To which his reply was, "The World Cup... wow, what is that, a *bra size*?" I told him that it was a, 'foo— soccer tournament'. "Oh yeah, I heard something about that – I'll tell you who's going to win that," he said, trying to impress me. "ENGLAND…!"

Only two games at that World Cup were shown live on network TV: the first and the final. If there was no ESPN2 in your hotel, then you would miss some of the fixtures. The opening day of the tournament was hijacked by 'breaking news' coverage of the police pursuit of OJ Simpson around the freeways of Los Angeles. From that moment, the World Cup became even more of a national afterthought. Mark Lawrenson and Rob Hawthorne were great company, though by the end of the first week we had to ban Rob from having a starter in a restaurant. He was the world's slowest eater, painstakingly using his cutlery as if he was carefully carving a block of marble with a chisel. Indigestion tablets would never have been on Rob's list of toilet bag essentials.

The Morris Men were in town, and after comparing our schedules, it was agreed that if we were going to have one big night out with a chance to recover afterwards, there was only one date available to meet up. Neil Harman wanted to take us to one of his favourite haunts from his tennis days: a midtown piano bar called Bill's Gay Nineties, a speakeasy that had been around since the days of prohibition and was furnished with boxing and theatre memorabilia. The cabaret was provided by Robert Monet, a crooner from New Orleans who encouraged audience participation as he worked his way through the usual repertoire of standards like 'The Shadow of Your Smile' and 'The Impossible Dream'. I don't recall eating anything. Well, that's my excuse, because all too frequent liquid injections of Napa Valley's best soon had the room spinning like a wheel. By midnight, alcohol level at saturation point, I stumbled back to my barracks near Grand Central Station. I was fortunately still able to remember the route, unlike one veteran reporter years before in Rome who had gone out for a big session on his first night without really registering where he was staying. When it was time to call it a day and pour himself into a taxi, he didn't have a clue where the hotel was or what it was

Italia 90 with BB, Gary Lineker, Ray Clemence
and Gazza

Burning the candle at both ends
with Terry Butcher

Treasured letters from Bryon Butler and Brian Moore

Euro 92, The Morris Men (minus Harry) Steve Curry,
Colin Gibson, Stuart Jones and Neil Harman

With Graham Taylor

Graham's letter blaming it all on me!!

Beijing 1996: Top Row, Neil Harman,
Martin Samuel, Henry Winter, and the
much missed Steve Curry and Rob King,
Kneeling David Lacey, Lee Clayton and
Des Kelly

Brazil 2000 with World Cup icon Jairzinho

From Chuck to his old mate "Musk"   *Billericay Dickie himself Ian Dury*

My son Marshall at 6, teaching James Brown a few moves.

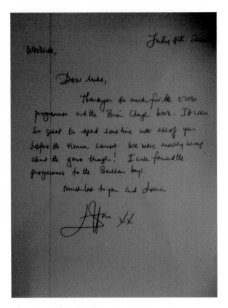

Sir Elton's letter post Vienna 2008   *Elton has an Audience with Lorna*

"Not that one, I want Ringo" – Live 8 2005

"He's what I call a great summariser" Jimmy Armfield Pasadena '94

"The only Law that meant anything to me" Denis full of menace Mexico '86

Lawro didn't want to ruin his hair, Emirates Stadium in the bleak midwinter

How many caps did you win Danny? Danny Mills Ian Dennis Rio 2014

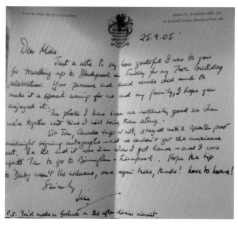

Jimmy's 70th Birthday Celebrations

Charlotte's last England game for 5 LIVE in Montenegro with John Murray, Mark Pougatch Engineer Tom Gilmore, Ian Dennis and Graham Taylor

Hard Hitters in Hard Hats at Wembley: the sadly missed Danny Fullbrook, Shaun Custis, Matt Lawton, Martin Lipton, Matt Dickinson (filing a story), Oliver Holt and Tony Banks

From the Childhood Dream 1959 to

Middle aged reality with Peter Davis

With a great double act, Ian Darke and Garry Richardson

A midfield alliance with Alastair Yeomans and Ian Dennis

2nd July 2007 – Mum and Dad's 60th Wedding Anniversary and six people who wouldn't have been on the planet without them, their grandchildren Nikki, George, Marshall and Robert, my sister Christine and I together with her husband Alan Watkins and Lorna.

A Party at the Palace in 2010

Honorary Master of Derby
University with His Grace
the Duke of Devonshire 2012

THE UNIVERSITY OF DERBY

With Doddy - The Last Happiness Tour

My last England interviewee, the inspirational Steven Gerrard, Rio 2014.

IN SESSION TONIGHT

The ultimate seal of approval from John Peel

Pretending I'm still a teenager with The Undertones

My proudest night receiving The Doug Gardner Award from the SJA Chairman David Walker, with James Lawton, Hugh McIlvanney, Jeff Powell and Patrick Collins 2015

Finally got the England shirt from Roy Hodgson Miami 2014

called. He was in a Roman maze of squares, bridges, monuments and backstreets, and after an hour of aimlessly driving around and with a cab driver losing the will to live, he suddenly had a eureka moment and informed his chauffeur that he was now able to remember the name of the road that they needed: '*senso unico*' (one-way street).

In the hazy, early hours of that Manhattan morning, desperate for the company of my bed pillow and some equilibrium, as I approached my room through blurred vision, I could see a piece of paper underneath my door. It was a handwritten note from Rob Hawthorne and it read 'Diego Maradona has failed a drugs test and the *Today* programme would like you on at 7:25'. *Sod's law*, I thought, *how inconsiderate on our only night out, but still, six hours to sleep it off and then I should be fine*. Then, there was the realisation of the five-hour time difference and the fact that it was already 6:45 in London. Two litres of water from the all-night supermarket later and passably coherent, I scribbled a voice piece which mercifully was recorded and ended with me saying 'what a dope'. Double standards? Without question. Hydrating had helped, but the footballers at that World Cup were illogically prevented from doing the same by FIFA, despite matches being played in oven-like summer temperatures. The final in Pasadena without any overhead cover was the hottest day that I ever experienced watching football, but unlike the players, we were supplied with wet flannels for our heads. If there is one thing that Americans can't abide in sport, it is a draw, especially a low-scoring one and they were rewarded after two hours with Brazil 0 Italy 0 and a penalty shootout; this was never going to be a threat to the Dodgers or Yankees. In the booth next to ours was a crew of three from Sweden and sitting in between the two commentators providing expert analysis was Sven-Göran Eriksson. We said goodbye at the end, little thinking that we would meet up again at two more World Cups in very different circumstances.

Over twenty years later, the true legacy of that American tournament could be measured when German World Cup winner Bastian Schweinsteiger was unveiled as a new signing by Chicago

Fire and at his press conference was asked, "Is it a fair expectation to see a pathway towards the World Cup competition coming out of Chicago?" He was naturally confused, and so the question was rephrased: "Do you think that now you are here, Bastian, that the World Cup for Chicago Fire is a realistic expectation?" A media officer had to intervene and explain, "We as a club don't play for the World Cup, but the MLS Cup."

When World Cups are played, millions of people around the globe take over city centres in Bogota, Zagreb, Cairo and Seoul; they even celebrate in the Antarctic and outer space. No other sport unites the universe in this way. The last time I looked, it is still FIFA, UEFA, FA, FWA, PFA and so on; not an S for soccer in sight. Henry Winter is a chief *football* writer, I used to be a *football* commentator and nobody has ever asked me in over sixty years if I am going to watch the *soccer*. However, if you win a domestic competition in the USA then that seems to entitle you to be hailed as a champion of the world; insularity prevails.

Forty Days and Forty Nights

I'm not lost, for I know where I am. But, however, where I am might be lost.

Winnie-the-Pooh, AA Milne

I was leading a privileged existence with a job that any football fan in the world would have coveted but was out of my depth and struggling to come to terms with the reshaped radio landscape. I was losing the plot, my sense of judgment and falling between two stools. Radio 5 had morphed into 5 Live just before the 1994 World Cup. The seed for this rebranding was sown during the Gulf War of 1991 when Radio 4's FM frequency became a temporary round-the-clock, rolling news service and exposed the need for a more permanent twenty-four-hour radio version of CNN. Helping to sustain this airtime, with similar urgency of tone, would be sports coverage, and as the managing director of radio, Liz Forgan, wrote to Graham Taylor:

> *The new network will have a specific brief to enhance the role of sports journalism on radio so that the excellent existing coverage is supplemented by proper explanation, analysis and debate.*

From now on all news would be 'breaking', all contributions 'hits' and all commentary punctuated by mandatory station identification, but as long as it's *'live'*, then that's all that matters. I did my best to detach myself from any Luddite preconceptions, but every time I looked at my record collection, I struggled to think of too many *'live'* albums that were superior to the original recording. *'Live'* is not necessarily a barometer of quality.

I have often wondered how Peter Jones and Bryon Butler would have handled this transformation. They were such thoroughbreds that they would no doubt have adapted, but the culture shock would have impacted on them both. For Peter on Radio 2, every football commentary had been an event. On 5 Live, it would become an everyday occurrence, and there would have been a danger of him being all talked out before the game had even started. He would have felt like the warm-up artist as well as the star of the show. For Bryon on Radio 2, every correspondent's contribution was a lovingly sculptured work of art. On 5 Live, such a piece would become obsolete. A live soundbite was now more of a priority than carefully considered construction. If my former guiding light Bryan Tremble had still been in charge of production, he would have left behind him a cutting room floor of repetition after using his editing blade to reduce most 5 Live discussions from thirty minutes to a more meaningful three. More airtime does not necessarily lead to more enlightenment. My problem was that the gentlemen that I have just mentioned had been my role models and I had been indoctrinated by them. They had set the standards, and now I would be compromised as I attempted to cover a sport that has no equal in terms of public interest and news value every day of the year.

I have always marvelled at the way newspaper correspondents can deliver words of such quality so quickly on a tight deadline straight after a game. Very often on that same day, they might also have had to file a reaction to an unrelated story. It's a great skill. On radio, there was a different pressure. All contributions had to be *'live'* and not on the phone or via a laptop. Unless you are already in a stadium, a studio or next to your equipment at home, you face the logistical nightmare of suddenly having to track down the nearest BBC studio, which can be tricky when sitting in 'essential' roadworks on the M1.

Such were the increased demands from programme producers who weren't remotely interested in your travel itinerary, that with hindsight, I would have been better off basing myself in Broadcasting House to be at everyone's beck and call. Instead, I took the view that as football correspondent, to have credibility in my subject, I still needed to attend the most significant games and not be bound by geographical limitations. The idea was impractical, and after ten months of 5 Live, things inevitably came to a head.

The forty days and forty nights between January 13th and February 22nd, 1995, even by football's standards, was one of the most toxic periods in the game's history. Dominating this period were the repercussions following Eric Cantona's attack on a spectator at Selhurst Park. This story on its own ran for a month. Then in Dublin, a riot by England fans caused the unprecedented abandonment of a friendly against the Republic of Ireland. There was also serious crowd disorder at Chelsea's FA Cup replay with Millwall. England international Dennis Wise was charged with assaulting a taxi driver. The Arsenal manager George Graham was sacked by the club for receiving an illegal payment and there were also allegations of match-fixing involving prominent players. I attempted to be available 'live' to comment on all of these issues, as well as travelling to thirteen games, nine of which involved round trips to the north of England. I am not ashamed to admit that I found it difficult to cope and can recall out-of-character occasions when I embarrassed myself. However, to put these errors of judgment down to workload is no mitigation.

I clearly overstepped the mark – perhaps because of my legal background – when in one of the endless pieces I did about Cantona, I suggested that his punishment should be community service rather than a custodial sentence. Even though that was the eventual outcome, I was rightly admonished for overstepping my jurisdiction. In a fit of pique, I resigned from a Premier League judging panel when at the end of this torrid time for the game, the Player of the Month award went to Duncan Ferguson of Everton. I felt that because of his history of violence this was sending out the wrong message, but all I succeeded in doing was drawing attention to myself. It was a futile gesture.

That abandoned game in Dublin turned out to be quite a baptism of fire for our new 5 Live presenter in the stadium, Gary Lineker. His day started ominously enough in the breakfast room of our hotel, receiving taunts from Vinnie Jones, who had been sent to cover the match for a Sunday newspaper. The verbal abuse was then followed by pieces of toast being thrown across the room at our World Cup Golden Boot winner, and his assailant didn't even have the decency to cut off the crusts! This turned out to be the prelude to slightly more dangerous pieces of wood from ripped-up seats being thrown indiscriminately by English hooligans at the game. They were unrelated scenes, obviously, but there was a common thread of yobbish absurdity.

When Millwall beat Chelsea on penalties in an FA Cup replay at Stamford Bridge, there were scenes of mayhem and several police officers were injured. If the Belgian police were a little nervous about the prospect of Chelsea's visit to Bruges in the Cup Winners' Cup, then it was hardly surprising. David Mellor MP, host of *Red-hot Soccer Chat* on 5 Live, condemned the Belgian force for using a water cannon on his club's malevolent fringe support at that quarter-final. In the semi-final, these law-abiding citizens duly acknowledged his backing by tearing up seats in Zaragoza and hurling them at the Spanish police. Yet English clubs were back in Europe and not only that, the country had been awarded Euro '96, much of that down to the UEFA President Lennart Johansson. Our FA then showed their appreciation by failing to support him in the FIFA Presidency election after his backing for Germany and not England's bid for the 2006 World Cup. Instead, the FA voted for the eventual winner, Sepp Blatter, and the rest, as they say, is history. I still have my little badge for that 2006 campaign: 'It's got to be England'. Good thing it wasn't; underpinning all of the English lobbying was the prospect of having a brand-new Wembley. In the event, the stadium didn't reopen until a year *after* that World Cup.

Although I hadn't taken any pleasure from watching his England team fail to qualify for the World Cup, I had enjoyed my working relationship with Graham Taylor. Now it was TV on radio, and I was a little more apprehensive about striking up the same rapport with Terry Venables. My anxiety was unnecessary. I first met Terry a decade earlier after he had become manager of Barcelona. Peter Lorenzo, an old friend of his, arranged for me to go and see him in Spain. We recorded our interview sitting high up in an empty Camp Nou stadium; it was like looking down from the top tier of a gigantic wedding cake. Maybe the stunning view distracted him, because the conversation was flat and stilted, and I was disappointed. However, there would be an unexpected retake. Venables and his assistant Alan Harris were heading off to their favourite beach for the afternoon, and as my return flight was not until much later in the day, I was invited to join their party. Here, briefly, I gained an insight into why most footballers warm to this charismatic personality, as a more-relaxed Terry soaked up the rays, charmed the locals with his then pigeon Spanish, handed over some pesetas for a shoe shine and allowed me to switch on my recorder again. This time it was more than I could have hoped for.

Back in England, one of my first assignments as correspondent in the summer of 1991 had been to attend the Terry Venables and Alan Sugar Spurs takeover press conference. I interviewed them together, and Venables was his usual chirpy self. Sugar, coming into football at an opportune time just ahead of the forthcoming Premier League deal with Sky, was unpleasant on that day and has the distinction of being the only person I ever interviewed to give me an impatient hand signal to wind up; not even Robert Maxwell did that when I visited him at 'Maxwell House'. To add insult to injury, he suddenly remembered something he had forgotten to say and asked me to turn my recording machine back on again. I would love to have had the bottle to give him a hand gesture back but was representing the BBC, employers who would later reward such impoliteness by giving Lord Sugar a platform to become a television star.

When Terry Venables became England manager, I was concerned that his ongoing personal conflict with the BBC *Panorama* programme over his business affairs might create some friction. It only surfaced once and was all rather innocuous. On the way to that ill-fated friendly in Dublin, I interviewed him at Luton Airport about the role he was going to give to Southampton's Matt Le Tissier. He was snappy and evasive. When I attempted to extract a bit more, as this was going to be the main sports story of the day, he became exasperated and complained that I kept looking at him as if I didn't believe what he was saying. That reaction might have been more of an indication about how he was feeling about the BBC at the time, or maybe a nerve had been touched. There was clearly some sensitivity about his deployment of Le Tissier, who curiously lost his place in the squad after that Dublin debacle for reasons that I have never really been able to understand. It was always a mystery to me why such a gifted player, who would have been embraced by many other countries, was so overlooked by his own. He would have been worth a place in the '96 and '98 squads if only to come on and take a penalty! I will always remember ringing up Le Tissier's Southampton manager Chris Nicholl to request an interview with the player much earlier in his career. This was declined on the basis that 'he's not one of you London types full of himself; he's just a quiet lad who keeps himself to himself'. It made him sound like a country bumpkin, and I often think about those words when I watch him now as such an entertaining and informative pundit on Sky Sports.

Putting the issue of Le Tissier to one side, Terry Venables was the only England manager I worked with who ticked all of the boxes in terms of team performance, results, selection, tactics, man-management and media relations. There was only one area where the jury would have to remain out, but this was not his fault. Venables didn't have to qualify for his tournament and hardly played any games away from home. However, he could hardly have travelled any further for the final warm-up friendlies before Euro '96 to Hong Kong and China; surely they could have found a dentist's chair nearer to Burnham Beeches! I remember checking in to our Beijing hotel mid-morning after a gruelling journey. Due to the seven-hour time difference from London, I thought I could safely grab a quick nap to recharge my battery before my first commitment. It was wishful thinking. Within seconds of my head hitting the pillow, I got a call: "Is that Mike Ingham? This is 5 Live *Up All Night*."

The international against China was noteworthy for having to describe the whole game on the phone, as the Chinese authorities would not give us access to our commentary box unless we handed over an extra 10,000 US dollars. Graham Kelly, the FA's much-maligned former chief executive, did everything he could on our behalf to find a diplomatic solution. I will always have a soft spot for Graham, mainly for having the balls to turn out and play for a press team that often included the likes of Terry Butcher, Alvin Martin and Trevor Brooking. All that was missing as he marauded down the left wing was the accompanying sound of 'Colonel Hathi's March' from *The Jungle Book*, as for one day only the great mammoth ceased to be extinct, while the opposition became the endangered species. If only the football public could have seen more of this Graham Kelly than the television interviewee on auto-pilot looking as though he had lost all his worldly goods. He was a genuine football man and there aren't too many of those around in the corridors of power. His eventual fall from grace was linked to the flawed attempt to stage the 2006 World Cup, which ended, as expected, in dismal failure.

At Euro '96, Terry Venables defined himself as an England manager before the game against Scotland. After the damp squib of an opening draw with Switzerland, the last thing he needed next was such an emotive fixture. The pressure was intense and yet he was outwardly the most relaxed man in the camp which must have rubbed off on his squad. At one of his press conferences, he was asked by an overseas reporter to talk about the rivalry with the Auld Enemy. The correspondent put it to the England manager that it wasn't really like a war. "Err, how far you want to go back?" chuckled Venables. His tactical masterclass against the Dutch was the most complete performance that I ever saw by an England team, only to have the edge taken off it afterwards when someone at 5 Live had the brainwave to get my wife on the phone to talk to me '*live*', as I had been fortunate to describe all four England goals. It was a crass idea; this was not about me, but it was indicative of the new pre-occupation with the cult of personality and self-projection. I was there to report the story, and not be the story.

Looking back at England's quarter-final with Spain, I recall Venables drawing on his experience from Barcelona beforehand and saying that English players had a tougher mentality. That might have been the case in the late twentieth century, but certainly not in the twenty-first. The señors Puyol, Busquets, Piqué and Ramos are not exactly my idea of shrinking violets. England, and in particular Stuart Pearce, did show mental toughness at the end of that game, winning the only one of eight penalty shootouts I saw them involved in.

The cycle for any England manager should be minimum four years: a European Championship followed by a World Cup, and Terry Venables should have carried on for France '98. That is not meant as a slur on Glenn Hoddle, who would then have been perfect from '98 to 2002. At the final draw ceremony for Euro '96 in Birmingham, there was a live performance of what was supposed to be the official theme song for the tournament, a dirge by Simply Red called 'We're in This Together'. Sadly for Venables, behind the scenes not all of the FA powerbrokers were 'in it together' with him; some were still concerned about his business dealings and so shamefully after the tournament, the lights were taken down from his Christmas tree, and English football lost its best chance of 'coming home'.

Venables and George Graham were kindred spirits. They were good friends with sharp and inventive football minds. Graham's nickname as a player might have been 'stroller', but as a manager, he preached work ethic and discipline. When he lost his job at Arsenal, I had no hesitation in recommending him as a radio summariser. He duly came on board and immediately enhanced our coverage, though I was slightly taken aback once when I recorded an interview with him on the eve of a new season at his Hampstead home. George told me that he thought pound for pound, Newcastle's summer purchase of David Ginola represented better business than Arsenal's signing of Dennis Bergkamp. I can only assume that sitting in surroundings that looked like a shrine to Highbury, he was still pining for what he had lost and that temporarily blurred his judgment. Bergkamp, as I am sure George would now concede, turned out to be one of Arsenal's most influential ever signings. George Graham was great company, so much more outgoing than you might have thought watching some of his rather austere post-match interviews. Among the matches that he covered for us was a European tie in Monaco against Leeds and with time to kill on the day of the game, our producer Charlotte Nicol took him for lunch at her cousin's home in Nice. The cousin was so beside herself afterwards, ringing up friends to tell them, "I've just had Graham George in my home." Sadly, all good things came to an abrupt end and after the publication of his book *The Glory and the Grief*, I was informed while I was covering a Champions League game that he was being dropped from our team. I rang him the following day to say how sorry I was, and he told me that he felt some senior figures at Arsenal might have applied pressure on the BBC, something I have been unable to substantiate. George, though, was not a man to bear a grudge and continued to make valuable contributions to Garry Richardson's Sunday morning show on 5 Live. I was grateful for the short time I was able to spend in his company.

Our dear colleague Jimmy Armfield had again been asked by the FA to headhunt the next England manager and, after his success in nominating Terry Venables, was equally astute in opting for Glenn Hoddle. Jimmy had also admired the credentials of another man with Tottenham connections, Gerry Francis, but told me that when he interviewed him, he felt uneasy because the former England captain didn't look him in the eye and kept staring at his shoes. Jimmy concluded that he might be uncomfortable in the media spotlight. Hoddle, like Venables, had worked abroad and his time in France proved to be the making of him according to his former England manager Ron Greenwood. In that interview of mine with Ron that was never broadcast, he said this about Venables' successor:

> *I gave him his England debut. He was an individualist. I think he grew up when he moved abroad and had a different attitude to the game. He used to run and drag his toe along the ground. I used to call him a toe tripper; it was almost a self-conscious attitude. When he moved abroad, he changed as a player and became a more complete all-rounder. When he came back and took over at Swindon, then you saw him growing up as a manager.*

My first introduction to Hoddle was in the wonderful world of flexi-discs. The first was for the *Match Weekly* magazine in the early '80s when I introduced a quiz called Mastermind of Soccer featuring Hoddle and two European champions, Liverpool's Alan Kennedy and Peter Withe of Aston Villa. The second of these memorable recordings was when Hoddle and Chris Waddle released their pop single 'It's Goodbye', and I interviewed them for the exclusive bonus disc that was attached. If anybody still has any of these treasures, then I suggest you go and seek help immediately!

Glenn Hoddle embarked on his World Cup qualifying campaign, having already been dealt a bum hand from his employers. After what sounded like yet another fixtures meeting carve-up, he was landed with a final game in the group away to Italy. This is something that would have never been sanctioned by more streetwise Associations. As Hoddle bedded down with the national side, his great mentor from Monaco, Arsene Wenger, arrived at Arsenal.

Wenger was a man of mystery from Alsace and, according to one of his first overseas signings, more German in manner than French. In football, though, he combined the very best of both cultures – German organisation with French flamboyance – though none of this would have been possible in those early days without his English inheritance. It remains the 64,000-dollar question. Would Wenger himself have signed any of Seaman, Dixon, Winterburn, Adams, Bould, Wright and Parlour: the foundation for everything that followed? All had their eyes opened during his tactical and nutritional tutorials. Attitudes changed, and so did diets. Chips were castigated as 'balls of fat', so imagine my colleague Charlotte Nicol's chagrin waiting a little longer than she had hoped for Wenger to arrive for an interview and suffering from hunger pangs, as she was expecting her first child. Stomach eventually overruled head, and her mouth was full to the brim of smoky bacon crisps just as the Arsenal supremo emerged from the Highbury tunnel. It was a bit like being caught red-handed smoking behind the bike shed at school. Wenger's impact became a trendsetting blueprint for others to follow, seduced by his allure, mystique and new sophistication.

Homegrown management was now in danger of being looked upon as outdated, unless your name was Martin O'Neill. Martin was a Brian Clough disciple and, like Clough, was taking stepping stones up the League and making waves lower down at Wycombe Wanderers. He also vocalised his talent every time he joined us as a match summariser on 5 Live. It was because of the working relationship I had with him that I was approached after one game at Norwich City in the club's directors' lounge. It was made known to me that as a former Canary himself, O'Neill was being viewed as their next potential manager and would I be able to convey that message to him? It was the only time in my life that I ever found myself in this position but rang Martin and put the ball in his court. His time at Carrow Road, though, was short-lived. The chemistry didn't work with chairman Robert Chase and so Leicester City's gain – not to mention Celtic's – would be Norwich's loss. I did apologise to him many years later for possibly leading him up the garden path but, typically generous, he told me that it had been all part of a valuable learning curve and one of the best things that could have happened to him.

Arsene Wenger's first season in England coincided with Alex Ferguson's first decade at Manchester United. As I had done the radio interview with him after his first ever home game, it was suggested that I should do a tenth-anniversary chat with him. This was arranged for 8am on a Thursday morning at the training ground. There was only one fly in the ointment, or so I feared; the previous evening in preparation for our meeting, I had watched Ferguson's team lose at home to Fenerbahçe in the Champions League, the club's first ever European defeat at Old Trafford On the way to my breakfast time appointment, I was fearful that my interviewee, on this particular morning might be a bear with a very sore head, instead as so very often happens with great managers he was even more animated and forthcoming after defeat. During Eric Cantona's long suspension in 1995, United had failed to repeat their double of '94, but with him back in the side, it was achieved again in '96 and confirmed by his goal in the Cup final against Liverpool.

Liverpool at this time had been recruiting too many players who did not fit the traditional profile of what was expected at such a great institution. The stress and strain was beginning to tell on their management as well. This was exposed in a very raw way after covering one of their games at Nottingham Forest. Five days before, I had seen them, against all odds, beat Newcastle 4-3 for the second season running. After the game at Forest, I was asked to get a Liverpool interview but wasn't prepared for what happened next. In the dressing room corridor, I approached a normally affable manager, Roy Evans, who declined and muttered something under his breath. Within a second his assistant, Doug Livermore, launched into a tirade: "Who's going to do the interview, then, Dominik f***ing Diamond?" I had no idea what he was talking about. I had made it a habit whenever I drove to Nottingham Forest to never listen to the car radio. It brought back too many painful memories of listening to Peter Jones broadcasting live for the last time when I had been en route to the City Ground on that fateful Boat Race day. I was therefore unaware that on his 5 Live show that morning, presenter Dominik Diamond had apparently referred to Liverpool's Stan Collymore as a 'scumbag'. Diamond had been of the opinion that Collymore, who had been left on the bench, didn't appear to celebrate that second 4-3 victory over

Newcastle after having scored the winner himself in the dramatic meeting between the same clubs the previous season. Diamond was entitled to his point of view, but his choice of words was outrageous, and now by association, I was deemed to be vicariously liable. While Terry Venables might have had issues with one arm of the BBC, he never held that against me personally. This was another consequence of working for a network that might be offering more 'explanation, analysis and debate', but freedom of speech for broadcasters without editorial restraint can lead to anarchy.

BBC Radio Sport was now on the verge of being relocated or rather, amalgamated into a monstrosity of an open plan design called Stage 6 at Television Centre at White City. A closely knit and intimate craft shop was being exchanged for the impersonal atmosphere of a factory production line. Togetherness and team spirit was being replaced by ships passing through the night. Godfather of the department, Angus Mackay, would have turned in his grave. There was never a day, working at Broadcasting House and entering what always felt like a holy temple, that I wasn't aware of walking in the shadow of giants as I climbed the staircase to our third-floor home. Moving out of these headquarters was a symbolically dark day in the history of BBC Radio Sport, and it was hard to see it ever again recapturing its lost identity. If that wasn't bad enough, Derby County were leaving the Baseball Ground, or as it had suddenly become known in this world of abbreviations, the BBG, which sounded more like a Roald Dahl story or a rapper. In all the time I spent at the ground in the '60s and '70s, never once did I hear it referred to as the BBG, in the same way that I have never heard a Geordie say he's going to SJP. Derby County were now moving to the more soulless environment of Pride Park, where on the opening night at the *new* stadium, symbolically the lights went out!

There Must Be No Sentimentality

Time is
Too slow for those who wait,
Too swift for those who fear,
Too long for those who grieve,
Too short for those who rejoice,
But for those who love,
Time is eternity.

Henry Van Dyke, 1904

WHEN THE FOOTBALL FIXTURES WERE PUBLISHED FOR THE 1997–98 season, I put a ring around one in particular. Liverpool against Newcastle at the end of August. Surely it couldn't be another 4-3 home win for Liverpool for a third successive season? I did not want to miss this one, and neither did Sky Sports, who instantly claimed it for prime-time Sunday afternoon viewing. Because of my paranoia about getting stuck in traffic, I had a match-day routine whenever I was heading north. I would leave early without disturbing the family and then break the journey for a coffee and sandwich at Corley Services on the M6. It became such a ritual that even the staff in the café were able to pre-empt my order. CDs, and not wireless, would ease me into the day. I would listen to a couple of albums before the

West Midlands; something mellow to start and then a bit more upbeat as I began to wake up. My radio would be silent until the second half of the drive. At my pit stop, I would always buy and then quickly scan a selection of morning papers and intended to do the same on this day. Something in the air, though, was different about this last day of August 1997. Most of the parked vehicles, at the service station, still seemed to be occupied by travellers, whom I then discovered were digesting news that was hard to take in. Diana, Princess of Wales and her partner Dodi Fayed had been killed in the early hours of that morning in a Paris car crash.

It was one of those moments that you never forget where you were as you try to absorb the enormity of what has happened. Someone hardly any of us would have known personally, but who had been omnipresent in our lives, had suddenly gone. Immediately and insignificantly, I rang the office for practical reasons to find out if the match would still go ahead. I was told that this was most unlikely and that a decision was imminent, as many Newcastle fans would soon be starting out on their trip. I was advised to stay where I was and not travel any further north.

In the minutes before the postponement was eventually confirmed, I remember flicking through some of the papers; all had gone to press before the tragedy had occurred. In one there was a forty-page glossy insert of 'Diana and Dodi: A Story of Love' as well as a column in the main section headlined 'Be clever like Camilla and clam up, Di'. The writer observed that 'the Princess, I fear, suffers from the open the gob before brain syndrome, a condition which affects the trivial and the braindead'. This was a snapshot of what she had to endure. Some might say that much of the intrusion into her private life was self-inflicted, but Diana had been a radiant ambassador for her country. It is very difficult now to stand back, rationalise and make sense of the outpouring of public grief that prevailed during that unprecedented week of national mourning. The funeral was covered on Radio 4 and 5 Live, and I was asked to be part of the broadcast.

At a briefing for everyone involved in the coverage, hosted by Radio 4 controller James Boyle, we were instructed that 'there should be no sentimentality'. I had just taken my four-year-old son to see the flowers outside Buckingham Palace in the hope that this might be lodged in his memory bank for a later day. It was going to be difficult not to be affected by the mood. My commentary position was on The Mall opposite Horse Guards Parade, only a few yards from where I had stood sixteen years earlier for the Royal Wedding between Diana and the Prince of Wales. When Jane Garvey handed over to me from the King George VI statue as the funeral procession passed by, I decided to focus on a wreath on the gun carriage. There was a white card that had the word 'Mummy' written on it: a final message from the young Princes William and Harry to their devoted mother as they walked slowly behind her coffin with the eyes of the world on them. That was, for me, the everlasting image of the day. Overall, I know that I did get caught up in the emotion and therefore, failed in my brief. When the cortège made a return journey after the service, I fell back on the crutch of quoting a line of verse associated with another Diana – Ross: "*Reach out and touch somebody's hand, make this world a better place if you can.*" It felt appropriate at the time, but it was corny, and I wish that I hadn't done it.

At this time, my wife, Lorna, was working with Elton John, producing his *An Audience with...* for ITV, a show that he had privately been hoping Diana might attend. Instead, he found himself in another studio before the television recording with Sir George Martin reworking *Candle in the Wind* for his tribute performance at Westminster Abbey.

Football felt insignificant at this time, but England had to play a World Cup qualifier at home to Moldova just four days after the funeral, and though we didn't realise it at the time, Paul Gascoigne scored what would be his last ever goal for his country. The following month, Gazza returned to the stadium where he had played for Lazio and gave a controlled and disciplined performance as England held Italy in Rome to qualify for the 1998 World Cup. Tactically, Glenn

Hoddle was matching Terry Venables' astuteness, employing Gareth Southgate in a back three; possibly significant in this future England manager's football education. Pragmatically, considering the sort of flair player he was, Hoddle had a couple of minders clearing some space for Gascoigne, Batty and Ince. Because of his Inter Milan background, another future England manager, Roy Hodgson, helped out as an interpreter for Hoddle in a press conference the day before the game. He found himself unwittingly translating some of the disinformation being spread about alleged injuries to Southgate and Beckham, in a bid to mislead the opposition. Another man with experience of Italian football, Paul Ince, was captain in Rome and, wearing a bloodstained shirt from a nasty head wound, gave his best ever international display. A few weeks later, Ince was representing his country in a European team playing against the Rest of the World before the final draw for France '98. All the responsibility he'd shown in leadership in Rome appeared to desert him that night in Marseille. After what effectively had just been an exhibition match, our producer Charlotte Nicol waited patiently for him to emerge from the dressing room and requested a short interview. "Nah, you're all right," was his reply as he headed off for the team bus. I remember as a child reading a letter in Charles Buchan's *Football Monthly* from a couple of fans:

> When England were playing Belgium at Wembley in 1952, we went to see them train at Stamford Bridge. Billy Wright, one of the greatest players in the world, asked us to come onto the motor coach to get the autographs of himself and all the other international players. It was a wonderful experience that day; we had no difficulty in getting the autographs of such famous players as Nat Lofthouse, Tom Finney and the rest.

That is how England captains, as ambassadors for their country, behave. Lofthouse, Wright, and Finney were all one-club men with over 200 caps between them and would have walked through a minefield to play any sort of international game, especially just before a World Cup. That was not the case when Chris Sutton of Blackburn was given the opportunity to establish his credentials prior to France '98, only to decline an invitation to represent England B against Chile. Among those who saw the bigger picture and were prepared to appear were Frank Lampard, Emile Heskey, Jamie Carragher, Paul Merson and Kieron Dyer, who all, unlike Sutton, went on to experience being in a World Cup squad.

Sutton was not the only player to shoot himself in the foot at this time. Casablanca, home to that fabled Humphrey Bogart 'gin joint', turned out to be the last chance saloon for Paul Gascoigne, who was humiliatingly and ruthlessly dropped from Hoddle's World Cup squad. Two warm-up friendlies in the North African city against Morocco and Belgium had confirmed the manager's worst fears that the star of Italia '90 was now a busted flush. The writing had been on the wall at another episode of *An Audience with...* produced by Lorna with Rod Stewart. Less than a month before England's opening game of the World Cup, the singer was asked in the show about the night out he had just had with Paul Gascoigne, and he didn't spare the rod. "I think he'd had a couple before he got to me, but I think I put the nail in the coffin," was his answer. You can say that again.

The World Cup in France was going to be my first as a correspondent covering England, and I got a real confidence booster before setting off from an article written about 5 Live by the journalist Michael Henderson, in which I was described as:

The dull-as-ditchwater Mike Ingham, who is football correspondent and yet seems to have no opinions on anything.

The problem is that one man's meat can be another's poison and when I did feel roused to deliver a heartfelt editorial at the end of *Sports Report*, I was described by the 606 phone-in presenter Richard Littlejohn as sounding like an evangelical Billy Graham. It turned out to be the last such 'final word of the day' piece that I ever did, as they were being phased out. It had been motivated by taking my son to one of his first games and being appalled by some of the behaviour around us in what was supposed to be a family enclosure. The network had never had as much airtime available to talk about sporting issues, but the proviso was that it shouldn't be from a script. A rambling two-way was now preferable to offering the sort of platform given in newspapers to skilled columnists like Martin Samuel, Paul Hayward, Oliver Holt and, yes, Michael Henderson. Sports desks stuck religiously to thirty-second reports, whether you were talking about an England groin injury or an England manager's resignation. Actually, that's not strictly accurate; I do remember being allowed forty seconds when Sir Alex Ferguson retired. I'm not saying that every contribution from a correspondent should be in the form of an Alistair Cook monologue. Live *can* be illuminating, but there are occasions when the weight of a story merits more than a superficial two-way. As Peter Jones always used to say about commentary, it's a matter of light and shade. There should be room for both, yet it has gone too far the other way. You may eventually see the light but often need some shade first to process your thoughts.

Glenn Hoddle acquitted himself well at the French World Cup, though his days would soon be numbered. Who knows what might have happened if David Beckham hadn't lost his head against Argentina? Paul Ince and then, fatefully, David Batty might not have had to take and then miss those penalties in the shootout. "Who would wish this moment on David Batty?" I remember saying just before he ominously stepped forward. After Chris Waddle and Gareth Southgate's traumatic experiences in 1990 and 1996, Charlotte Nicol asked Batty afterwards how long the pain might last. "I'm over it already," he said in a typical matter-of-fact way. It had been one of the most dramatic and high-quality games of international football that I ever commentated on. This was Michael Owen's breakthrough night wearing an England shirt, and my son fell in love with Liverpool after watching him score that spine-chilling goal in Saint-Étienne. My most vivid memory now of that long night was the tortuous journey back to our base in Brittany, made bearable only by the company of the late and much-missed journalist Bob Cass, who maintained our spirits in the way only he could. Bob was an infectious, Jimmy Cagney kind of character from the North East, who could have recited the words of a nursery rhyme and make it sound like the most hilarious thing you had ever heard.

I have two other souvenirs from that tournament. Firstly, the night before England's group game in Toulouse against Romania, a guardian angel escorted me through a battlefield back to my hotel. Even though our England summariser Terry Butcher was staying in a different part of the city, he refused to allow me to run the gauntlet on my own. England fans were fighting amongst themselves in the main square; presumably because they had failed to find any hostile Romanians to beat up. Heads were being butted, backsides kicked and it was like walking into the soundtrack of a Batman cartoon. What made it even more surreal was that some of the pugilists would break off when they recognised Terry and would preface their next assault with a cheery: "All right, tel, how do you think we'll do tomorrow?"

There could be no greater contrast between that chaos and the genteel company of Brian Moore. The much-loved television commentator was bowing out after the World Cup final in Paris and in his case, retirement meant retirement. He had been BBC Radio's first football correspondent and was always a joy to be around. Very generously, he would often mark our cards and pass on team news that he had managed to glean. He would whisper 'strictly *entre nous*' and he knew that you would not betray his confidence. On the eve of the final, I interviewed him about his distinguished career, and it was riveting stuff. However, I had been so engrossed that I had forgotten to take the pause button off my tape machine and none of it had recorded. "Not to worry, old son," said Brian, not wanting to exacerbate my shame. "Always better second time around," and he made sure that it was. A class act sorely missed.

Brian Moore's co-commentator at the '98 World Cup had been Kevin Keegan, who would be back in a coaching tracksuit at the next tournament with three Lions on his sleeve as well as his heart.

Keegan, an inspirational player, succeeded Glenn Hoddle as England manager. It was another of those appointments that always seemed to be an antidote to the previous incumbent. If Hoddle had been more detached from his players, then Keegan was going to be a cheerleading buddy but without Hoddle's tactical awareness. Glenn Hoddle's reign was over after a controversial interview in *The Times*, although many of the comments that were published about his views on reincarnation had already been voiced much earlier in his England tenure, during an interview on 5 Live with Brian Alexander. Then the results had been going well; now the mood had changed, and so he was shown the door.

Kevin Keegan was an impulsive and passionate man. He had stunned Newcastle United when he called time so abruptly on his first great adventure there as manager. His team had been one of the most exciting sides never to have won the title. Even though driving to Newcastle from the south felt like undertaking a 24 Hours of Le Mans endurance race, it was always well worth the effort when you finally turned off the A1, approached the Redheugh Bridge, drove over the Tyne and were able to admire a skyline dominated majestically by St James' Park. It is not necessarily the best stadium in the country but certainly the best appointed, in the heart of a community fed for so long on a diet of very little yet with support that was always unconditional, even if constantly being short-changed. It was such a 'carry on' there at times that journalist John Richardson used to refer to the ground as 'Sid James Park' and at times you half expected to turn up and see a back four of Hawtrey, Douglas, Williams and Connor.

I remember travelling to the North East after Keegan had been confirmed in the England job to watch Newcastle, now under Ruud Gullit's management, play the game that meant most to their fans, at home to Sunderland. I was expecting to see their talisman, Alan Shearer, leading the attack as usual, but the England captain was dropped, Newcastle were beaten and that team sheet effectively represented Gullit's P45 as he was duly sacked. That is not my everlasting memory of the night though. Stadium renovation had meant there was no roof or protection from the elements in our commentary seats and on this particular stormy night, my much-missed colleague David Oates and I ended up looking like Eric Morecambe at the end of his *Singing in the Rain* sketch. I had no change of clothing and had to drive back to my overnight stop in the Midlands naked from the waist down. If my image had been captured on camera that night the CCTV film would have been X-rated.

One of the great frustrations for Glenn Hoddle when he lost the England job was that he had taken a young Rio Ferdinand to the World Cup just for the experience and had big plans for him going forward to Euro 2000 as a sweeper in a back three. England returned to a back four under Keegan; Ferdinand missed out on selection and was destined to never play in a European Championship. Rio, though, would instead have a different meaning for English football at the dawn of a new century.

In an act of gross expediency, the FA sacrificed their own crown jewel in a wild goose chase pursuit of staging the 2006 World Cup. FIFA had come up with another one of those Einstein ideas that they seem to specialise in, extending their irrelevant Intercontinental Cup into an even more gratuitous Club World Championship. Not only that, it was to be held in the middle of the European season in Brazil. Among those expected to be there were the 1999 Champions League winners, Manchester United, and there was a veiled threat that if they didn't show up, it would seriously compromise England's bid to stage a World Cup they were never going to get anyway. What this meant in an already congested season, was that something had to give and so United, who were also the holders of the FA Cup, were actively encouraged by the FA not to defend their trophy. United legend Denis Law had always said that in his day, the most important game of the season was always the FA Cup final at Wembley. In more recent times, though, the club's captain in that 1999 FA Cup final, Roy Keane, said in his autobiography that he 'never bought into the Wembley dream' and regarded the competition as a 'consolation prize'. Keane's career, though, might have had a very different look to it if Alex Ferguson hadn't won that 'consolation prize' in 1990. It bought Ferguson some extra breathing space at a time when without trophies, he was starting to come under pressure. Thanks to Keane's superhuman performance in the Champions League semi-final in Turin and David Beckham's set piece delivery in the final itself, United stunned Bayern Munich in Barcelona to win that European crown for a second time on what would have been Sir Matt Busby's ninetieth birthday. One of their dubious rewards for that was an invitation to play the might of Necaxa and South Melbourne thousands of miles away, when they should have been preserving the sanctity of the FA Cup.

I had the pleasure of commentating on the final of this FIFA non-event: an all-Brazilian goalless draw after extra time between Vasco de Gama and Corinthians; the tournament got the showpiece climax it deserved. However, it would be churlish not to feel grateful for being given this chance to visit such a picture perfect location. Our radio accommodation in Rio would have been suitable for *any* visitor to this carnival city. BBC TV's, by way of contrast, was designed for sultans and princes. The Copacabana Palace is one of the grandest hotels in South America. I popped in one night and bumped into Garth Crooks. "Ah, come to see how the other half live," he joked, though I didn't need to seek first-hand confirmation to be aware of the gulf, correction, chasm that existed between television and radio. All one BBC, I think not, this was a typical, unnecessary and extravagant expense.

England had been somewhat fortunate to reach Euro 2000 that summer in Belgium and Holland. Kevin Keegan's squad only qualified for a play-off against Scotland after Sweden, who had already won the group, upheld the integrity of the competition by beating Poland. At England's leafy retreat in Spa, near the Belgian Grand Prix circuit, along with BBC TV, ITV and Capital Radio, we were, as rights holders, entitled to a daily interview with a player in the team hotel and all had rooms on the ground floor for that purpose. For many of the players this was seen as a welcome release from the tedium, but not, it seemed, for Martin Keown. When it was his turn to perform this task, producer Charlotte Nicol tried to explain the procedure to him. He immediately demanded that the two radio interviews be done together in one room. When Charlotte then gently explained that we had *all* paid money for this privilege and were entitled to have our own short recording, he began jabbing his finger at her and shouted, "You're out of order, you're preaching to us." I complained to the FA about the incident but was told by press officer Steve Double, "Oh, that's Martin for you." Indeed it was, and it was his prerogative, but then later in life, in a classic poacher-turned-gamekeeper transformation, he was selected as BBC TV's match summariser for the 2018 World Cup final.

Keown's conduct epitomised England's performance at the Championship. Their game management after being in winning positions was dreadful, and after appearing to make progress in '96 and '98, this was such a backward step. Ironically, they did beat Germany in a group game, but the Germans had the victory they had set their hearts and political expertise on when they were confirmed, as expected, as the hosts for the 2006 World Cup. England's £10 million campaign had cost Graham Kelly his job as FA chief executive, boosted Sepp Blatter's candidacy as FIFA President, dictated some of the fixtures undertaken in the hope of securing backing and undermined the standing of the FA Cup, all for a grand total of two votes in a second-round exit.

Wembley was about to close for the renovation originally designed for that 2006 World Cup, and the final visitors to the old stadium just had to be Germany. On a day of bewildering distraction, with thoughts it seemed more on 1966 than reaching Japan and South Korea, the final international goal in the arena was a German hit and hope, followed by a goalkeeping fumble that dramatically heralded the end of Kevin Keegan. He had taken the FA by surprise when as a caretaker manager he suddenly announced in Budapest that the job was perfect for him. The manner of his departure, with another qualifying game only four days away, was even more of a shock when he decided that he wasn't quite up to it. I had enjoyed working with him, even though his message to me on my fiftieth birthday was, "I have noted that you have one of the best faces for radio in the country!" Our last interview was conducted live on the staircase leading up from the dressing room shortly after he had broken the news of his resignation to the players; not the way the curtain was supposed to come down at the old stadium.

An absent friend on that day was former England manager Graham Taylor, who was on holiday in the USA and in those old-fashioned days when people used to write to each other, he sent me a letter on the day of the Germany game from Boston. Seven years on, he still hadn't got England out of his system:

Dear Mike,

It's about 7:30am here, so I imagine you have either already done or about to do a preview prior to the game against Germany. How I would love to be the England manager, and if we had qualified in 1994 and reached the semi-final; won the European Championship in 1996; qualified and reached the final in France 1998; won the European Championship again in 2000 and were favourites to win the World Cup in 2002, I guess I would be in charge this afternoon, although there would still be some people wanting change!

As it is, Rita and I have spent three days in Washington (Brazil 1 England 1) and four days in Boston (USA 2 England 0). Having updated ourselves on the Battle of Bunker Hill, how the hell did anyone expect any other result?

I think I will be shopping in Macy's when England score the winning goal.

Graham

In the event, it was Germany who scored the winning goal, and in the immediate aftermath of that defeat not a lot of credit was given to temporary manager Howard Wilkinson for steadying the ship and getting what turned out to be a valuable draw away to Finland four days later. The agenda was then set for the next full-time manager when Peter Taylor, in his one and only game in charge, selected David Beckham as captain for the friendly against Italy in Turin. This was a trip that was shrouded in sadness. Rob King, chief football writer for the Press Association, was affectionately known to his colleagues as 'Baldrick'. He was a one-man band who worked tirelessly and shared much of my musical interest. Rob sadly died after returning from that game at the ridiculously young age of forty-six. He had looked to be in some distress in the departure lounge of the airport and even apologised to Charlotte at one point for his barking cough. His condition was then not helped by a seriously delayed flight, but little did I think, going through passport control in the UK with him, that it would be the last time that we would ever see each other.

At his funeral just twelve days after that game in Italy, there was a service sheet in church informing the congregation:

Rob had a great love of music and, aware of his poor health, put together a tape which he requested to be used at his funeral. The three songs which will be played during this service have been taken from that tape.

One of these songs was 'A Glimpse of Heaven' by Strawbs.

The hillside was a patchwork quilt neatly stitched with tidy hedge
*   and crumbling gray stone wall*
The trees were bare but spring was near
To conjure up its endless strings of green magic handkerchiefs
Could you only see what I've seen you would surely know what
*   I mean*
I think I must have caught a glimpse of heaven.

"A Glimpse Of Heaven" Words and Music by David Cousins © Reproduced by
permission of Old School Songs/ Sony/ATV Music Publishing Ltd, London W1F 9LD

His Master's Voice

The story of football over the past 100 years or so is the story of a simple game that has circled the globe. It has created untold interest and excitement, evoked passion and devotion, been the unwitting cause of disaster, made fortunes for many and stored away a million memories.

Bryon Butler, *The Story of Football*, BBC World Service, 1997

I FIND IT IMPOSSIBLE TO READ THOSE WORDS WITHOUT hearing the author's voice. A voice I still hear in my head whenever I need reminding of radio broadcasting perfection. A voice carved from the Cheddar Gorge belonging to my predecessor as BBC football correspondent, Bryon Butler. He had his own unparalleled and distinctive style and wrote sentences for broadcast that just wouldn't have sounded the same read by anyone else. There may have been other equally talented scriptwriters, but none could match His Master's Voice. Bryon's writing for radio shunned hyperbole and pretension. He used simple vocabulary, devoid of cliché and it drew you in, demanded attention and left the listener even wanting a little bit more at the end. It was never prosaic and certainly not contrived. What Bryon wrote he would have said to you in his normal everyday articulate conversation. He was to sports broadcasting what David

Gower was to batting: elegant and fluent, and he was an impossible act to follow. To everyone who knew him he was simply BB.

I've heard him described as a wordsmith and in the same way that a blacksmith can so skilfully and creatively use the tools from that trade, then so he was. There was no verbosity, just the perfect selection of words that he would literally speak on to the pages of his script. He may not have reached academic heights himself but graduated with honours from an education of life through reading, travelling, journalist training and military discipline acquired in the Somerset Light Infantry. His appearance and manner defined his work. Quintessentially British, a mellow St Bruno man with a Jack Hawkins twinkle in the eye. A dress sense that was immaculately smart-casual with not a hair out of place, and handwriting as lush and ornate as any architect. I associated BB with all the endearing qualities that I had grown up admiring about football and the BBC. The history and tradition, spirit and integrity, and when he died aged only sixty-six in April 2001, as well as feeling the loss of an inspirational close colleague, I found myself mourning also the passing of many of the things we had both cherished during a golden era for the game and radio sport.

After leaving the BBC in 1991, Bryon returned to his roots as a freelance journalist. The last time I saw him was in a Surrey churchyard on a dank November day at Rob King's funeral. The following month, I received what would be my final Christmas card from him with this self-effacing message:

Definitely decided to retire more or less at the end of the season. It will nearly complete fifty years in the 'black hole'. Strewth, half a century spouting and scribbling rubbish.

Tongue in cheek, I hope, because deep down inside, I trust he appreciated that nobody on planet football would have concurred with that.

Ewart Bryon Butler was born on June 5th in between the semi-finals and final of the 1934 World Cup in Italy. The last World Cup that he would cover for the BBC would also be in Italy fifty-six years later. His parents christened him Ewart after the distinguished nineteenth-century Prime Minister William Ewart Gladstone. He grew up close to the Taunton County Cricket Ground, and his addiction to the summer sport lasted a lifetime. He entered the world of journalism at sixteen, and his apprenticeship was considerable before transferring to the BBC from the *Daily Telegraph* in 1968 as successor to football correspondent Brian Moore. When I was a student, he made a profound impact on my impressionable ears. Hours were spent listening to his mellifluous tones when I should have been more preoccupied with the judgments of Lord Denning, the Master of the Rolls. Instead, the Master of Ceremony at the FA Cup draw was of far more interest. I was bewitched by Bryon's orchestration of this ritual from the game's headquarters in Lancaster Gate. An enchanting piece of theatrical tension and drama, all memorably packaged from top to tail by BB. There is no better demonstration of radio as an empire of the senses than this broadcast. Imagination working overtime as you waited on edge for your team's number to be pulled out of the blue velvet bag. The ultimate example of 'video killing the radio star' in recent years has been the televising of this made for radio experience. It has been a dog's dinner of a spectacle with fittingly, celebrity chefs on hand sometimes to conduct the draw.

At least on October 31st 2019, a day originally reserved for Brexit, a major draw did return to BBC Radio. It was for the quarter finals of the League Cup with both of the Merseyside and Manchester heavyweight clubs still involved. There was only one anomaly, it was made not on the corporation's home of live sport (5 Live) but on a network that hadn't featured football since Italia 90, Radio Two. There was no build up to it and at a time in the morning when listeners rely on the radio for timekeeping, it started late. While all this was happening 5 Live was concentrating on John Bercow's final day as speaker at the House of Commons.

When Bryon Butler introduced proceedings from FA headquarters, even though the whole charade was a preposterous delusion, we willingly bought into all that melodramatic nonsense about the venerable Challenge Cup committee arriving at the very point in their hectic schedule when the next item on the agenda would be the draw. How convenient was that, just after Bryon had set the scene quietly from an anteroom waiting to be given the sign to enter? I deputised for him on a few occasions, and of course, the reality was that you were calling the shots. The FA committee men were only there to make the draw, and you told them when to start. Why would anyone though want to tamper with all that nostalgic mystique, especially when BB made it sound like this?

"Good afternoon, and with only eight numbers in the blue bag, this is the last draw which will decide home advantage. So luck, that little commodity which can't be won or bought or taught or rehearsed, is all-important. Right, there's the sign that the Challenge Cup committee are all set, so let's move into the Centenary Room here at Lancaster Gate, and the first voice you'll hear is that of the FA Secretary Ted Croker."

Ted Croker's successor at the FA, Graham Kelly, always used to say that when Bryon did the draw you could almost smell the cigar smoke coming out of the radio, not to mention the aroma from the dusty hardbacks of footballing folklore housed in the library where Bryon would adjourn to for his summing up of the ties just announced. One of the reasons why he displayed such a relish for this day was because he believed passionately in the FA Cup. "It is," he said, "part of the fabric of our society. It is as much a part of our way of life as the Sunday roast and a pint at the local. It has the wrinkle of a centenarian and the bloom of a newborn baby. It breathes hope and new spirit into the heart of every winter." Bryon was of the same opinion as Harry Johnston, Blackpool's captain in the legendary Matthews final of 1953, who said, "I just can't think of any other three words in the English language which conjure up so many visions of excitement as *the Cup final*." Nearly half a century later, though, Manchester United's captain Roy Keane had his own three words to sum up Bryon's favourite day in the football calendar: "It was bollocks." BB could see the landscape changing around him and retired from the BBC before the increased demands of the

Premier League and 5 Live. He summed up his decision like this: "From now on, it's going to be will you instead of you will." And so he took on only projects that would not impede on his private life of family, local cricket and other hobbies he listed, such as 'rummaging around in antique shops and avoiding work in the garden'. He had more than earned the right to make that transition.

For many, his name will always be synonymous with Peter Jones; joined at the hip as they were for so many years at the big games. They were not bosom buddies but were an ideal complement to one another and helped to enhance each other's contribution. Bryon, with his preference for the written word, removed the burden of editorial responsibility from Peter's shoulders, allowing him free reign to commentate like only he could. Something that I don't think Peter ever gave Bryon enough credit for. They were two completely different characters. Peter's more bohemian nature had been cultivated during the post-war years at Cambridge University. He loved his life on the road and the spirit of adventure. His sense of timing as a broadcaster was flawless, but his private life was often in disarray. Bryon, by way of contrast, was military precise. At seven o' clock every night in Broadcasting House at the end of his day shift, he would telephone his wife, Barbara (Babs), to confirm that he would be on the usual train to Guildford. A far more tolerable commute in those days when you were not seated next to someone giving phone instructions to a partner trying to find a tin of ratatouille in a supermarket: "It's next to the pickles, directly opposite the toilet rolls!"

Once on that train from Waterloo with his *Evening Standard*, Bryon could feel secure in the knowledge that he was now out of reach. That double-edged sword of technology, the mobile phone, was not yet part of a correspondent's armoury, and so until he reached his landline at home, he was a protected species. He had such high personal and professional standards that he was unprepared to compromise, and so if he felt there was not enough time in a schedule to prepare and do justice to a piece that had been requested, then he would say so. This was wrongly interpreted sometimes as inflexibility. It led, on occasions, to some mimicry behind his back and did not reflect well on the perpetrators who would mockingly tap on an imaginary pipe and say things like 'can't possibly do it, old boy'. Imitation, though, is supposed to be the sincerest form of flattery.

In commentary, Bryon was more intense than Peter. While he would be studiously engrossed in a game, Peter would be observing it all on a broader canvas, feasting off the atmosphere around him. On one occasion when the pair were commentating on an England game in Spain, Bryon was so absorbed in the play he had not spotted or heard a rotund Iberian, Ginger Baker, pulverising an enormous drum in front of their box. BB's producer wrote the words 'mention the drummer' on a card and held it up for him to read. Without missing a beat, Bryon proceeded with, "Now Wilkins square ball to Keegan, who plays it wide to Coppell, mention the drummer and a chance for Woodcock." But you were happy to indulge such idiosyncrasy from a man equally capable before the 1984 European Cup final, having been handed the Roma team to face Liverpool, to suggest that it looked like an 'international sweet trolley of a side'.

Paul Hayward was so right when he described Bryon Butler as an 'enemy of stock phrases and cliché'. In Bryon's commentary, there were never any 'mountains to climb', maybe the odd peak or ridge. 'Deadlocks were never broken,' you didn't get anybody 'firing on all cylinders', 'crossing the white line' or 'scoring goals for fun'. Why would anyone want to score a goal for misery?

Bryon was brought up in an age when Nobby Stiles didn't set out to just win '*the first ball*', he wanted the second, third and fourth; in fact, he wasn't counting. Alan Ball did not just want to '*beat the first defender*', he wanted to beat them all. Bobby Charlton didn't need to get in '*the final third*' to be a threat, and as for big brother Jack, his idea of '*zonal marking*' was simply to make sure he got his head to the ball before anybody else. Bryon recognised 'greatness' but used the term sparingly and with moderation for, as he wrote in an introduction to Ron Greenwood's book *Soccer Choice*:

The great trick when writing about great players is to avoid the word great at all times. It is a word which defies happy definition, invites but complicates selection and provokes the kind of bullish argument which loses friends. The word great is applied with scholarly impartiality to everything from wars and grandparents to dogs and mountains. Perhaps the truth is that the word is damned beyond redemption. Football has played its part; the game's history is bent double beneath the weight of great matches, teams, moments, goals, managers and players. In many cases, all that is meant is memorable or unusual, but to leave it there would be unacceptably easy.

Taking all that on board, Bryon was still a *'great'* broadcaster.

He was always in his element at a World Cup, though had to wait until his last one in 1990 to see England finally do themselves justice again. The World Cup for Bryon was 'the great rolling stone of a tournament, generating passion, excitement, stress, colour, drama, prejudice, controversy, hostility and a pile of money'. Some food for thought for you in these changing times of false economy: if Peter Jones and Bryon Butler had been working for BBC Radio at the 2018 World Cup in Russia then only one of them would have been on the rota for the semi-final between England and Croatia. Think about that for a moment and judge whether that represents broadcasting progress.

On overseas trips, BB would often regale us with tales stockpiled from visiting sixty countries. Some we might have heard before, but, just grateful to be in his company, we hung on every word as he reminisced about one of his first ventures behind the Iron Curtain. An occasion when, in a frantic bid to make the TV in his hotel bedroom transmit an actual picture and not a mosaic of interference, he did what all right-minded Brits abroad would do and thumped the top of the set. Within seconds, he received a call on the house phone: "Mr Butler, this is reception, would you kindly refrain from hitting your television." He was in a Big Brother house years ahead of its time.

Wherever he went everyone – well, almost everyone – treated him with due respect. I remember being with him at Anfield one day and passing Liverpool manager Kenny Dalglish on the stairs who playfully informed our correspondent, "Eh, Bry – Aldo wasne bought to replace Rushie," grinned and moved on. The ultimate seal of approval. The great Sir Kenny had been listening to Bryon's work. Bobby Campbell, on the other hand, had a rather less decorated career as a Liverpool player than Dalglish and when he was manager of Chelsea was interviewed live on *Sport on Two* by Bryon and, in dismissing one of his questions, added disdainfully, "You're just a reporter." There was no need for BB to nibble at the bait. He was content with his usual dignity to confirm that, yes, he had reported on one or two games.

Because he had reported on a 'few games', he was asked by the Football League to write their Centenary Book in 1988 and then in the '90s compiled the official history of both the FA Cup and the Football Association. When he was invited to add his message to a BBC card sent to Lorna and me when we got married, he wrote simply and straight to the point: "Time you both had a bit of production," and we were happy to follow his advice!

Bryon's *pièce de résistance* was his football preview at the start of *Sport on Two*. It was his *Letter from America*. He would usually be allocated around fifteen minutes to set up the afternoon, and there would be at least four inserts, either live or on tape. When I was presenting the programme, I would watch him on a Friday fine-tuning his script, only breaking off to double-check on the phone with a Terry Neill or Ron Atkinson that they would be at the ground in time for their interview. He would slide into the seat next to me in Studio B9 while I was reading the early racing results and this was how he started on Saturday November 17th, 1982.

"Well, what a routine, ordinary old week it's been. Derby County fined £10,000 for piracy, Leeds ordered to close their terraces, Tottenham losing £50,000, Aston Villa up for sale, Tranmere saved by the braces on the edge of a cliff, Brian Clough saying that Justin Fashanu has no talent – which means Forest paid a million pounds just for his smile – Charlton telling their manager he had nothing to worry about and then sacking him in the same doleful breath, another flock of hoolies sent to jail, and Alan Brazil and Frank Worthington joining the queue of players who'd rather like a change of clubs."

One of the many differences between our sports room on the third floor of Broadcasting House and the relocation Bryon never had to endure at TV Centre was that it was roughly, from wicket to wicket, the length of a cricket pitch and often at the close of play before we all headed off to our respective home counties, there was just time for Bryon to get in some net practice in readiness for his Sunday game. A chance to tweak a few tennis ball off spinners towards the litter bin doubling up as the stumps, guaranteed to send Bill Ross off in a huff to the pub after declining our offer to stand as an umpire. Sometimes there would also be a batsman for Bryon to entice as well and I fondly remember him more than meeting his match one Friday, when the former England captain Tony Lewis took time out from his *Sport on Four* preparation to drive one of BB's deliveries that failed to tweak straight through an open window into Regent Street. "Six and out!" appealed Bryon.

When Bryon finally declared his innings at the BBC, instead of retiring to the pavilion, he went back out into the field, only this time on his own terms. When the Premier League began in August 1992, he had traded his microphone for a pen and, working for the *Daily Telegraph*, described Alan Shearer's two goals on his Blackburn debut at Crystal Palace.

"The first was merely very good; a dam buster from just outside the penalty area, but the second was self-evidently brilliant. Shearer pursued the ball like a puppy for thirty yards towards the left, won it easily, manoeuvred it inside for another fifteen yards and then whistled the ball inside the low right corner from twenty-four yards. Speed, determination and high technique in one rich capsule."

As Bryon approached the millennium with more time to devote to family and friends, his new way of life was rudely derailed by cancer. Stoically, he won that first battle and by the turn of the century was able to witness the last Cup final at the old Wembley, a day that for him would have been smeared with mixed emotion. When terminal illness struck him down in the spring of 2001, he died just before the Cup final was played for the first time in Cardiff. An occasion that Peter Jones would have adored and would have been tolerated by Bryon, though it just wouldn't have felt quite the same. At his funeral, I met up again with his predecessor as correspondent, Brian Moore, and sadly that would be the last time that I would see him. On the day Bryon died, I was asked to pay my tribute to him, and all I could think of was that voice – that warm and comforting overcoat in winter.

We both did twenty-three years as correspondent. Forty-six years between us from 1968 to 2014: a period of untold change for the sport. Seven months before he died, he wrote to me on my fiftieth birthday. That letter is the most treasured keepsake from my career:

My dear boy,

One of my warmest convictions when I left the workhouse last century was that you'd pick up the old job's baton with verve, wit, the clearest of eyes and, in a game which wouldn't always deserve it, a degree of loving tolerance. I had no doubts then and having listened to you hundreds of times since with admiration and pleasure, I have absolutely no doubt now, even though the demands on you are infinitely greater than they ever were on me. Especially now that the world is becoming smoke-free. The cigars you smoked were always much classier than mine and by his cigar shall a man be judged.

Congratulations on the first half century, but believe me, the best is yet to be.

Bryon B.

And I can still hear his voice.

Are You Going to
Stand There All Night?

Bryon Butler always felt at home visiting the FA at Lancaster Gate. For all the colonial, diehard intransigence that seeped out of the listed building, when you entered you were conscious of treading in the footsteps of footballing knights, the three Rs: Rous, Ramsey and Robson. You were walking in corridors of history and former global influence, and the day the FA relocated was as significant to me as when the BBC moved Radio Sport to Television Centre. In fact, there are many parallels between the two institutions. Two bureaucratic empires once envied around the world attempting modernisation but in so doing, losing sight of what they were supposed to be there for in the first place: football and broadcasting.

The FA's white elephant equivalent to the BBC's Stage 6 was in Soho Square, where the best things in life are never free, and your neighbours include Sir Paul McCartney's publishing company. No aroma of dusty Charles Buchan annuals here, but an open-plan scent of aftershave and corporate management speak. Spearheading the FA in their new surroundings was an executive from the world of advertising and Adam Crozier had a readymade marketing slogan for his England team: 'The Golden Generation'. This turned out to be not even silver or bronze, but more kryptonite, and the branding didn't end there either. A concept of 'Club England' would evolve at a time when there could hardly have been less international togetherness. 'Clique England' would have been more appropriate as the only 'club' that mattered to many of the players during this era was the one paying their wages and image rights. Imported into this brave new world was England's first overseas manager: the urbane, taciturn and more emotionally detached Swede, Sven-Göran Eriksson.

As a person, Sven was charming, helpful, patient and kind-hearted. As an England manager, though, ultimately he was unable to get the very best out of his resources. His CV revealed a reservoir of club achievement and yet at international level, he was shown to be too rigid in his tactical thinking. Instead of devising a system in the way that either Terry Venables or Glenn Hoddle would have done to enable his very best players to perform, square pegs were squeezed into round holes, when all that was needed was a tweak or two to achieve a better balance. It was no coincidence that Eriksson's best result came comparatively early on in his stewardship when Gerrard and Scholes were both given their normal club roles and partnered in central midfield in a 5-1 away win in Germany. It was simple, uncomplicated and, on the night, devastatingly effective. That surreal evening in Munich was overshadowed, though, by great sadness when news reached us of the death of Brian Moore, who was forever associated on BBC Radio with England against West Germany in 1966. Brian passed away on the day his national team enjoyed their best result against the Germans since that Wembley final.

Only a matter of days after Munich, a city associated with sport through great human tragedy, I found myself in Majorca on Tuesday September 11th, 2001 to watch Arsenal play Real Mallorca in the Champions League. The build-up to the game was spent watching heartbreaking live television pictures from New York and Washington DC of unparalleled disaster and grief. When the match started, similar to the European Cup final at Heysel had been, it was an inconsequential blur and being on a plane at the end of that mournful day returning to London was a melancholy experience. In the early hours of the next morning arriving back home, I did what I am sure every parent in the land must have done that night: looked in on my two sleeping sons and gave them a hug. George Lucas Ingham had been born on July 12th and so was only two months old. He was christened George after Lorna's much-loved uncle and Lucas was added, so I tell him because he's from a galaxy far, far away!

In all of his time as England manager, Sven-Göran Eriksson never got to play at Wembley, but that turned out to be hardly disadvantageous. England didn't lose any of their qualifying games at home while Wembley was being refurbished and the two remaining group matches after Munich against Albania and Greece benefitted from having a more animated atmosphere at St James' Park and Old Trafford. The fixture at Newcastle against Albania stands out because on the night, a BBC Director-General actually went out of his way to find our commentary seats so that he could introduce himself. During my twenty-three years as BBC correspondent DG's frequently attended the big tournaments but Greg Dyke was the only one in that time to pay us a visit and make us feel appreciated.

David Beckham's beat-the-clock free kick against Greece endeared him even more to Eriksson and heading to a World Cup in the Far East, four years on from his naivety in France, his profile was bordering on John, Paul, George and Ringo status. That hysteria was hardly going to be diminished either when his great scriptwriter in the sky spiced up his life by making him a doubt for the tournament after fracturing a metatarsal, the first time I ever knew that such a bone existed.

Of course, Beckham beat that clock again, as we knew he would, thanks to regular briefings from the England doctor John Crane. As broadcasting rights holders, we were billeted in the same hotel as the team on the Japanese island of Awaji and every time the good doctor joined us for a cappuccino, he would indiscreetly give us a full medical update. I don't think he ever worked out who we were but like many of the FA entourage, was in danger of going stir crazy and just welcomed some company. At all times of the day, there were coach parties of Japanese fans camped out in the gardens outside the England base looking up at the bedrooms for a glimpse of Becks. I would delight in doing a Rhys

Ifans impersonation from the film *Notting Hill* and venture out onto my balcony to tease the voyeurs into a moment of orgasmic squeal until their binoculars soon confirmed that my torso was more Trex than Becks. Beckham had his redemption against Argentina with a winning penalty. Remembering the disrespectful aftermath in St Etienne four years before when some of the Argentines had mocked Glenn Hoddle's squad and because the English media just happened to be in the same Sapporo hotel, we gathered on reception the next morning to wish the South Americans '*bon voyage*'. Unfortunately, this caused some confusion and wrong-footed one of our number, the hugely popular Worcestershire Boy John Curtis of the Press Association. John, one of my very favourite travelling companions, came out of the lifts with his bag already packed, saw the team vehicle outside the hotel, assumed it was for our group and followed the exodus of Argentine players, who were avoiding all eye contact as they headed for their transportation. John climbed on board and only realised his mistake when he found himself sitting next to Gabriel Batistuta. "Eh, Gabby, what you doing on our buzz?" was probably his line of enquiry before retreating to a hero's welcome back on reception.

There were some notable individual performances at that World Cup by England players, but collectively the team fell short in what was not a particularly heavyweight competition. Even though Brazil were reduced to ten men for the last half an hour of the quarter-final, they still seemed to outnumber England in midfield, a lesson that was not heeded by Eriksson. Brazil did go on to win the final, but by their very high standards this was not a great side even with Ronaldo, Rivaldo and Ronaldinho in it, but unlike England, they knew how to win tournaments and were afraid of no one. It was a privilege in Japan to sample a culture underpinned by civility and bullet train reliability. The only downside from this once-in-a-lifetime adventure was to miss an irreplaceable moment back home when my second son, George, took his first unaided steps.

England's first game after that World Cup was a friendly at Villa Park against Portugal, who would be hosting the next European Championship.

Leeds United's Alan Smith scored for England in a 1-1 draw. When he was required to model yet another exploitative latest edition of the England kit, Charlotte Nicol drew his attention to the one star on the shirt signifying one World Cup win. "Aye," said Smith. "One World Cup, two world wars." His commitment to the cause got the better of him when he was recklessly sent off in a European qualifying game against Macedonia at Southampton. It had been one of those rare occasions when Eriksson did try something different and began with both full-backs, Ashley Cole and Wayne Bridge, on the left; not that he was able to keep this under wraps. One source of England team news in those days from inside the camp was Gareth Southgate, who was contributing a column to a daily newspaper and would, from time to time, give them an off-the-record steer on what he thought the line-up might be. I wonder what he would make of that now? The newspaper in question generously shared some of those titbits with me. The other memory of that night was having Harry Redknapp with us for the commentary. Harry was not a big fan of his country having a foreign manager and was becoming so disillusioned by what he was witnessing in a disappointing 2-2 draw, that you would have given anything to have had him in the dressing room doing the debriefing. I always found it amusing that Harry and Terry Venables were perceived by some FA powerbrokers as carrying too much extraneous personal baggage to be the England manager and yet when the team travelled to Bratislava, all of the build-up to the qualifying game with Slovakia was taken up interviewing Sven-Göran Eriksson about Ulrika Jonsson's imminent autobiography.

Under Eriksson's management, many of the friendlies became even more gratuitous than normal, as caps were handed out as liberally as vouchers in Boots. It was an insult to some of the great names of yesteryear like Billy Bonds and Howard Kendall, who had been starved of international recognition. It also smacked of too many deals done in advance with the top clubs to secure the release of players for an agreed length of time in a game. All ten of the outfield players were replaced at half-time during a home defeat by Australia, though that did pave the way for the first international appearance of seventeen-year-old Wayne

Rooney. In his teenage years, Rooney was thrust into the spotlight like a man-child in a media jungle. Unsurprisingly, for an essentially shy young man, he found some of those early press conferences quite an ordeal. I remember Mark Lawrenson on behalf of BBC television ringing up Rooney's Everton manager David Moyes, to ask him if he thought his player would be able to cope with making a live appearance and saying, "Thank you," for receiving the Young Sports Personality of the Year Award. "Just about," replied Moyes. However, in my final tournament at the Brazil World Cup in 2014, I was struck by what a difference a decade had made and in my last interview with Rooney, found him engaging, expansive and forthright, though sadly, a bit like me, his best years were now behind him.

Still only seventeen, Rooney treated the big stage a bit like the young Gazza as if he was having a kick around in the local park when he inspired England to a crucial 2-0 win over Turkey in a European Championship qualifier at Sunderland's Stadium of Light. The atmosphere at this game was vile, and at the end of the evening a pack of England fans circled the press box, inanely chanting 'kill all Muslims'. Their evil intent evaporated at the first sight of Terry Butcher, who rose from his seat in such a vigilante manner that he could have been auditioning for Clint Eastwood's role in *Gran Torino*.

In the goalless draw in Turkey that ensured qualification, England gave one of their most resilient performances under Eriksson, following a chaotic build-up when players had threatened to strike as a protest after Rio Ferdinand had been dropped for failing to attend a drugs test at Manchester United. His club colleagues were prime movers in escalating this dispute until common sense prevailed, and I trust they would have been equally vociferous in their support had the disciplinary measure been levied on an England colleague from another club. Ferdinand had been excellent at the 2002 World Cup and would be a major loss in Portugal, but this was a case of strict liability, and the issue for me was perfectly summed up at the time on Sky Sports' *Sunday Supplement* by the late Joe Melling:

The bottom line is this – if you get stopped by the police for a breath test and say look do you mind, I'll come back in forty-eight hours, that's not going to happen, and I don't think the FA are going to back off this for credibility in drug testing.

At Euro 2004, ten years on from my Morris Men night out in New York, it was an odd experience trying to adapt to my new relationship with Colin 'Mr Big' Gibson who was now sitting on the other side of the fence as the FA's head of media in Lisbon. At that championship, until his injury in the quarter-final, Wayne Rooney had been single-handedly threatening to hijack the whole event. Little did we know at the time that this was about as good as it was going to get for him at a tournament. Once again this was not a particularly strong field, underlined by the fact it was won unexpectedly by Greece. If only Eriksson had been able to solve his three into two won't go conundrum in midfield. Frank Lampard had emerged, and all it needed was to slot Gary Neville into a back three, use Beckham and Ashley Cole out wide and allow Scholes to anchor rather than giving him a fish-out-of-water role on the left. I'm not surprised that Scholes called it a day on the international stage after this; it was an insult to a great player.

The recently appointed manager of Chelsea, José Mourinho, had been given permission by the FA to meet his new players who were in the England squad at Euro 2004. That invitation didn't extend to one of the names at the top of his wish list: Steven Gerrard. Another of those 'what-ifs'. If Gerrard had gone to Chelsea, Mourinho would unquestionably have managed to dovetail him with Lampard in a way that England never did. Instead, Gerrard remained at Anfield and in the 2005 Champions League final in Istanbul, was the catalyst for one of the most remarkable comebacks in the history of the competition against AC Milan.

I have several vivid memories from what was an unforgettable experience. The first, twenty years on from the Heysel tragedy, was the insensitive absurdity of the venue, miles from the city centre and approached over a lunar landscape of rocks and debris. Not that UEFA executives, in their chauffeur-driven limos, would have been remotely aware of this logistical nightmare. The second was hearing the Liverpool fans, with their team 0-3 down at half-time and seemingly intent on damage limitation, singing 'You'll Never Walk Alone' even louder than at the end of the game. During that interval on 5 Live, our guest John Toshack gave us an insight into his tactical awareness when he prophetically said:

> I think that Rafa has been railroaded a bit in the Premiership, playing players who are a little bit more offensive. Tonight he's gone against what he felt he should have done. They've been at their best with Alonso and Hamann with Gerrard pushed a little bit further forward. They've been solid and hard to break down. Alonso and Gerrard together, I think, has been too much work for them. The players in front haven't been able to drop back and help them out. The wide players have to come in and it's given space for Milan to attack down the sides. I thought when Kewell got injured Rafa would maybe have seen that and said, hang on a minute, there's ninety minutes here, we'll get Hamann on, move Gerrard further forward and at least we'll just keep it tight for twenty minutes to half an hour and get ourselves back in the game.

As Toshack was identifying the problem, Rafa Benítez was making the changes that he had advocated. Hamann came on to partner Alonso, releasing Gerrard and the game was turned on its head. John's observations had been so astute and yet, despite his credentials, he was a man who had been overlooked as a Liverpool manager when he had appeared to be a prime candidate. Toshack himself thought that he was going to succeed Bob Paisley and has revealed in his own book that he never really got over the disappointment of not getting what he considered to be his dream job. He might not be aware, that perhaps the die was already cast at the first match at Anfield after the death of Bill Shankly. Toshack's in-form Swansea team fittingly provided the opposition, as he had been one of Shankly's protégées and was looking every inch a Liverpool manager in waiting. Just before the one-minute silence prior to the game, Toshack had stood with his Swansea players and removed his tracksuit top, revealing a red Liverpool shirt with his number 10 on the back. Another Welshman, Peter Jones, had described what he felt was an emotional scene for us on radio. Peter was always invited into the Liverpool boardroom after he had commentated on a game. On this particular day, he was sharing a drink with the club chairman Sir John Smith, who asked him what he had made of Toshack's gesture. Peter replied that he had found it very moving. "Oh, did you think so?" said the chairman. "A bit too showy for me; we don't do things like that here," and in that moment Toshack's fate appeared to be sealed.

My third memory from that most dramatic game of club football in Istanbul, was the return journey home. On the flight, I was surrounded by UEFA marketing gurus and all of their conversations were about how successful the perimeter advertising had been; there was not one mention of an epic game.

The old British championship was almost reinstated in the qualifying campaign for the 2006 World Cup. Only Scotland were missing as England were paired with Northern Ireland and Wales, but that's where the domesticity ended. Where there used to be only two international football teams – Yugoslavia and the Soviet Union – there were now eighteen on the new-look map of Europe. One of them, Azerbaijan, was also in this group, necessitating a marathon expedition and a visa for what was always going to be an academic exercise. In an already over-congested season, the biggest indictment of allowing such a team straight in without prequalification is that when FIFA work out the best second-placed finishers, they disregard all of the results against countries like Azerbaijan, who finish bottom of the group. Political expediency is the order of the day, not to mention canvassing for electoral votes. After watching England beat Northern Ireland at Old Trafford, I stayed in the press room to watch Azerbaijan's game in the same group against Poland and was joined by John Dillon of the *Daily Express*. We were not impressed by this uncompetitive non-event and made our feelings known. The former Minister for Sport, Kate Hoey MP, had also been at Old Trafford and was sitting nearby. At no point did she speak to us but reported our conversation in her column in the *Daily Telegraph*:

> *As I waited in the press lounge for my lift back to London from the England v Northern Ireland match at Old Trafford last Saturday, I overheard a conversation between two respected football journalists. The Poland v Azerbaijan match was on in the background and Poland had just scored their fifth goal. "What a load of crap," said one. "It's time these kind of mismatches in the World Cup were scrapped." "Yes," said the other, who was a BBC broadcaster. "The top nations should be seeded and that would stop this waste of time." The remarks were symptomatic of a growing trend among some people who seem to want to write off any club or player who is not premiership material, and any country that is not tipped to win the World Cup. To them, the FA Cup is devalued if the final does not feature Manchester United or Arsenal.*

Funnily enough, United and Arsenal did meet in the FA Cup final a couple of months later, and it was one of the most turgid games that I ever saw... however, back to Kate Hoey:

> *I mentioned their remarks to another distinguished journalist the following day. His response was that I should remember before being too critical that they have to sit through these one-sided matches, and it can get a bit boring. Maybe football journalists have it too easy these days. They don't sit on overnight trains and buses to get to matches. They stay in luxury and don't have to scrimp and save to follow their team.*

For the record, Azerbaijan ended up losing 0-8 to Poland. What disappointed me most of all about that article was that Kate Hoey had sat in silence and made no attempt to engage either of us in conversation or debate the matter. The beauty of football is that it is a game of opinion and I would have had so much more respect for her if we had been able to exchange opinions face-to-face.

It makes me smile whenever I see football ethics and the governance of the game being discussed in Parliament; not much etiquette and protocol was observed that day. Serving up some teams as cannon fodder in world football does not help anybody when the calendar is already at saturation point. If you go to the theatre, you want to be entertained, and your tolerance level is bound to be lowered if you feel you are being short-changed. The thinking, apparently, behind allowing smaller footballing countries to appear on the main stage, without prequalification, is the hope that after accumulating enough experience they will eventually become more competitive. Fourteen years later in June 2019 during a European Championship qualifier in Saransk, San Marino played Russia and lost 0-9. Interestingly, watching Kate Hoey in a BBC TV discussion about Brexit with Victoria Derbyshire, she said, "I'm not so sure these days that anyone trusts anybody in the establishment." She might well be right.

Ten days before the England v Northern Ireland game at Old Trafford, I had interviewed George Best at a health spa in the New Forest; it turned out to be his final appearance on BBC Radio. In England's return fixture with Northern Ireland, two months before George Best died, his fellow countrymen had a famous victory over England in Belfast on a night when, paradoxically, Sven-Göran Eriksson did change his system, but the home side had bigger hearts. I was supposed to be going to the North East the following weekend to watch Michael Owen's debut for Newcastle, but there was a last-minute change of plan when the FA, not wanting the Belfast result to fester, took the unusually proactive step of offering up Eriksson for a live Saturday afternoon interview at TV Centre. Sven, never a man to make a drama out of a crisis, surfed the waves and duly qualified for the 2006 World Cup, which would be his swansong.

In the build-up to the finals in Germany, one friendly with a little more substance to it was against Argentina in Geneva. I will never forget it, but not just because of the football. I was about to enter the lift in our hotel with *No Particular Place to Go* but opted out at the last minute when the previous occupant stepped out. I know it is a nerdy thing to do, but I found myself in the same corridor as the father of all of the music that I cherish: Chuck Berry. I reached for my clipboard in my briefcase and asked him if he would kindly sign a piece of white A4 paper. He was wearing his trademark sailor's cap and the one personal assistant accompanying him ticked him off for having some chocolate on the breast pocket of his jacket and brushed it off before addressing my request. He asked for my name and used my pen. I thanked him profusely and returned to my room to make a closer inspection of this unexpected souvenir. I suppose when you have been blasting out *Johnny B. Goode* for over half a century, it is bound to take a toll on your hearing and this is what I have framed at home: 'TO MUSK – CHUCK BERRY (smiley face)'. It doesn't matter; I may be Mike Ingham to most people who know me, but Chuck was always his own man and Musk Ingham will do nicely.

Before England set off for the World Cup, the squad visited Wembley Stadium, posing for pictures wearing builder's jackets and hard hats. It would be another year before they would play there, so it's a good thing Germany and not England were hosting the 2006 tournament. Sven was going to have to play Sweden again and cope with another metatarsal injury, but he made life more complicated for himself by calling up seventeen-year-old Theo Walcott, who had made only a handful of senior club appearances. The dramatic impact of this selection was lost at a typically extravagant press conference to unveil the squad. BBC TV had been commissioned by the FA to produce a film package to accompany the announcement of each name, and so the identity of all those chosen was known well in advance to us. Walcott's selection was extraordinary bearing in mind the uncertainty over Rooney with his broken toe, and when Owen was injured before the knock-out phase, this compounded the miscalculation. Walcott didn't get on the pitch in Germany. He had been included to give him some experience for the future and yet when the next World Cup came around, he was left out. Jermain Defoe had been involved in the pre-tournament training but had to return home when it was finally confirmed that 'the big man was back in town'.

Being based in the England hotel as a broadcast rights holder was always a double-edged sword. Access was easier to players when it was their turn to leave their Aladdin's cave of a games room to do an interview, but it felt like we had signed the Official Secrets Act when it came to being free to report on events around us. The Wayne Rooney story left us with no other option. His metatarsal had been broken inadvertently but symbolically in a challenge with a Portuguese defender at Chelsea. Manchester United assumed his World Cup was over, but Rooney and England thought differently. He was allowed to travel to Germany, but his club demanded that he returned home for a final scan to determine his fitness, so back he went to Manchester, accompanied by the FA's David Davies. It became clear that he would be returning, as soon as Sky TV pictures captured the Cheshire-cat grins of Davies and Rooney emerging from his examination. Within seconds of seeing those images in the England hotel, our producer Charlotte Nicol fortuitously bumped into Sven-Göran Eriksson. "Everyone looks happy, Sven," said Charlotte. "Yes, I think we will have some good news," said the England manager. We duly reported his comment as this was a major public interest story and immediately got it in the neck from the FA.

Much later in the day, in anticipation of Rooney's return to Baden-Baden, we did what any reporters would do and waited discreetly at the hotel so that we could finally put this story to bed by confirming that the eagle had landed. When Rooney emerged from his transportation, he was greeted on reception by the FA's amiable kit man, who embraced him and declared that 'the big man is back'. Standing just a few feet from the scene, I was able to hear Rooney respond with 'the big man is back in town'. I know that in later years, perhaps through embarrassment, Rooney has distanced himself from having made that comment and in his defence, the words were almost put into his mouth. This was never said in an arrogant way, but it was said. We reported on the incident, but that is not what I remember most from the night. Having accompanied Rooney, David Davies on return had to debrief his manager. More than aware of that, I kept a respectful distance from them both, allowing them their privacy but intended on grabbing a word with the FA Executive before he retired for the night. Davies was himself a former BBC correspondent and had been a reporter in the England camp at other tournaments, and so I was trying to do exactly what he would have done in another era. He observed me hovering in the shadows and called out in front of Sven, "Are you going to stand there all night?" It was a very public demonstration of what working for the games' governing body can do to you. David Davies was not the only former broadcaster working for the FA who occasionally forgot where he'd come from. In the end, the Rooney gang show came back to bite England in the backside, or rather, kick Carvalho in the groin. After the Manchester United man had been sent off, there was another quarter-final exit on penalties and another classic underachievement. There were red eyes the next day on departure, and the most noticeably emotional person was John Terry. His magnificent partnership with Rio Ferdinand throughout that championship is now a watershed mark in England's history. David Beckham resigned the captaincy.

Throughout his decade as an England player, Beckham had been a joy to work with and never flaunted his fame with us. He approached every interview as if it was the first one he'd ever done and I don't ever remember him turning down a request. On the longer trips away from home at tournaments, he would ask us questions about our own children, and as an ambassador for the team, he was a class act. The final memory, as we prepared to wave goodbye, yet again prematurely, to a Three Lions team bus, was when Charlotte Nicol noticed a cardboard cut-out stand of Sven-Göran Eriksson in the hotel lobby. She asked his partner Nancy Dell'Olio if she wanted to take it with her as a keepsake. "No," said Nancy. "I want the real thing." So had we...

Delivering Quality First

We were for centuries, downtrodden and derided
Because we are not one people, because we are divided
Let's be united by one flag, one dream.

'*Il Canto degli Italiani*' (Italian National Anthem),

Mameli / Novalo, 1847,

IF UEFA CARED ABOUT THE MOST IMPORTANT PEOPLE IN THE game, the fans, then in the event of two teams from the same country being in a European final, there would be a contingency plan, and a stadium in that country would be on standby to replace the one originally selected. In that way, supporters would be spared exorbitant travel costs and exploitative hotel surcharges. Making Arsenal and Chelsea supporters journey to Azerbaijan for their Europa League final beggared belief.

A decade earlier, instead of ludicrously having to trek to Russia for the 2008 Champions League final, Manchester United and Chelsea followers should have been at Wembley. In that Moscow final, ten of the outfield players starting the game were English, and yet two and a half weeks later there was no England team at the European Championship. One of the results that had been most damaging in a wretched qualifying campaign had been in that same Moscow Stadium: a 1-2 defeat by Russia on an artificial pitch sanctioned by

UEFA. Not that the new playing surface of grassy divots at the re-opened Wembley in those early days was any more conducive to playing decent football. The last rites were administered there in an apocalyptic defeat by Croatia when only a draw had been required to qualify.

As a member of Sven-Göran Eriksson's coaching staff, Steve McClaren had offered England continuity as a manager, and there had been the usual rhetoric from the players in his early days about spirit in the camp and a new era. However, by the time the squad arrived in Barcelona to play the mighty Andorra, straight after a goalless draw in Israel, a siege mentality had once again set in. It was the only time that I ever had to ask an England manager, to his face, if he was considering resigning. That was not something that I enjoyed doing as McClaren, like all of the other full-time England managers I worked with, was always affable and generous with his time. His case had not been helped from the outset by the FA's knee-jerk pursuit initially of Brazilian Luiz Felipe Scolari, who turned the job down, making McClaren look like the default option. He didn't help his own cause, though, after that unconvincing win over Andorra when he allowed the stress and strain of the job to overwhelm him at a press conference which was brief and to the point:

There's a great determination now to prove a lot of people wrong and gentlemen, if you want to write whatever you want, you can write it because that's all I am going to say – thank you.

Sitting alongside him was the FA's head of media Adrian Bevington, and his face was a picture. He knew from experience that these words might come back to haunt McClaren.

Interestingly, McClaren's team on that Hammer House of Horror night against Croatia contained only two of those ten Englishmen who would go on to play in that Champions League final. Six of the ten not involved all played for their clubs the following weekend. The morning after that abysmal exit, McClaren left, and the FA promised a 'root-and-branch' review into what had gone wrong. They came up with the idea of appointing a manager who lacked fluency in English and belonged to a different football culture, Italian Fabio Capello.

In Italy, there was at least a more enlightened attitude towards women reporting on football than in England. It wasn't a big deal there because it had rightly become the norm. There has been some improvement here, but in 2007 pockets of chauvinism still existed. After Tottenham's League Cup semi-final defeat at Arsenal, Charlotte Nicol interviewed the Spurs manager Martin Jol and asked if he thought Arsenal's Arsene Wenger would continue his policy of playing his youngsters in the final. It was one of the talking points at that time. Jol's response was that she was only asking him that because she was a woman. Charlotte was justifiably shaken, and we expressed our displeasure to the Tottenham press officer. Jol did return, apologised to Charlotte and gave her a Spurs shirt, but the damage had been done. Today's generation of impressive female football reporters owe a lot to the likes of Charlotte, Eleanor Oldroyd, Louise Taylor, Sue Mott, Amy Lawrence and Alyson Rudd for blazing a trail for them to follow, but it would not have been necessary in the first place if an element in the game hadn't still been living in the Dark Ages.

In 2007, we celebrated eighty years of football on the radio, and there was a special one-hour programme on Radio 4 to commemorate this landmark. Even though I was BBC Radio's chief football correspondent, I was not asked to take part. Later in the year when the *Today* programme held a reception to mark its fiftieth birthday, at least this time I was given a reason for not receiving an invitation. The BBC's director of news, Helen Boaden, informed me that even though I had a twenty-eight-year association with the show, I did not meet the criteria drawn up by the BBC events team. I was upset, not because I had been overlooked, but because others in my department who only had a tenuous link with the programme were approved.

Euro 2008 in Austria and Switzerland, like other tournaments held in two countries, was rather soulless, apart from one night in Vienna. Graham Taylor had arranged for us to attend a concert by his former Watford chairman Sir Elton John. There was no band, just Elton performing his classic songs in the way they had been written, sitting at his piano in the home of Johann Strauss. We talked football with him in his dressing room until it was time for him to perform. Our posse followed Elton, guided by torchlight until he went up the steps to the stage and we went through a curtain to our seats. Halfway through the show, he dedicated a song to Graham and told the story of how in his early days at Watford, he had been helped by his manager to confront his addictions and how it forced him to change his way of life. Graham told me that one Sunday morning, in a bid to make his chairman see some light at the end of the tunnel, he had goaded him into shame by putting two very large bottles of alcohol in front of him on his breakfast table. Elton sang 'Someone Saved My Life Tonight'. I was sitting next to Graham and did not need to look at him to gauge his reaction but was aware of him drying his specs at the end.

Later in the year in another European capital, there was a very different emotional experience for the former England manager. We were in Belarus, another of those eighteen football countries that used to be two. Graham always liked to find out a bit more about the place he was visiting, and this was his first trip to Minsk. On the morning of the game against England, he decided to go to the Belarusian Great Patriotic War Museum, a memorial to three million inhabitants who had lost their lives at the Nazi's concentration camps during the Second World War. Graham was naturally in a sombre and reflective mood when he was recognised by two England fans who approached him. It was a scenario that he had become well used to over the years. Instinctively he would feel some uncertainty about how the conversation might develop, but he did what he always did, and held out his hand in his usual jaunty way and said, "OK, fellers?" One of them replied, "It's Graham Taylor, isn't it? I've been waiting for many years for this moment to be able to tell you that *you are a tosser*." It was a snapshot of what this dignified man had to endure for over twenty years, although this personal abuse was even more brutal in a hall of remembrance documenting real human tragedy and not the loss of a football match.

Unlike Graham Taylor and Steve McClaren, Fabio Capello had been a serial winner on the international stage as a player and manager, but unlike them, he had no innate awareness of English football culture. This, coupled with the problems he experienced adapting to a new language, proved to be a handicap. Capello scored the last ever goal against Sir Alf Ramsey for Italy against England in 1973, and there is a black-and-white photo of him from that game on the wall in the referee's dressing room at Wembley. I know that because very often that was where we did our radio interview with him after a squad announcement or training session at the stadium. Like any reporter, out of respect for the interviewee, I would try and have a few questions prepared in advance to ensure there was a structure and that all main talking points were covered. Capello at all times remained friendly and charming, but when I was recording a conversation with him, it felt like being a showjumper on a horse trying to clear fences at Hickstead. The language barrier invariably got in the way, though I was amused to hear Wayne Rooney in later years looking back over his experience, with the Italian pointing out that 'his English *weren't* that good'. When it became obvious that he was finding communication difficult, I did telephone the FA, offering help and suggested doing some mock interviews with Capello. Not for broadcast; just to help him feel more at ease with his adopted vocabulary, but this was never pursued.

After the failure to reach Euro 2008, Capello's first objective was to qualify for the 2010 World Cup. The friendly matches would be ancillary to the main agenda and were difficult to attach too much significance to, especially when even FIFA themselves failed to recognise them as major competitive fixtures. You could win your first cap and play the full ninety minutes in a friendly against Argentina but still be free to switch your allegiance to another country. However, get thrown on for the last thirty seconds of a qualifying game against Andorra and then your nationality was set in stone. Under Capello, England won a friendly in Berlin against an experimental German team, but that would count for nothing when they met at the World Cup.

There was another campaign being waged to stage; this time, the 2018 World Cup in England. A friendly took place away to Trinidad and Tobago to curry favour with that upstanding man from FIFA, Jack Warner. When Qatar controversially won the right to stage the 2022 World Cup, this was described by the former FA Chairman Greg Dyke as 'the worst decision in FIFA history', yet England indirectly had helped to endorse their candidacy by agreeing to play a bizarre fixture there in Doha against Brazil.

The aftermath of a 0-2 defeat in Seville by Spain turned out to be very revealing. The morning after the game at the airport, a number of the Spanish squad, including goalscorer David Villa unescorted by security, were catching domestic flights back to their respective bases. There was no red carpet and private jet for players who were already European Champions and about to win the World Cup. Recently I heard some of the England players from that era bleating about club rivalries impeding on camaraderie in the England camp which, frankly, is feeble piffle. There is no greater rivalry in world football than between Barcelona and Real Madrid and yet when their players turn out for Spain, club issues are temporarily put to one side. Fabio Capello would have experienced that himself when he was manager of Real Madrid as did Sir Bobby Robson during his time at Barcelona. Sir Bobby, alas, finally lost his battle with cancer and I attended a memorial service for him at Durham Cathedral. Observing the outpouring of affection for him made me think about that fly-on-the-wall Channel 4 documentary in the '90s when Orient's beleaguered manager John Sitton revealed, "I'm reading a book about Bobby Robson's eight years at England and he said, 'I'm not in the game to make friends.'" Well, hundreds of friends were there that day to pay their final respects, including Sir Alex Ferguson, who spoke movingly, unscripted and straight from the heart about a much-loved man.

In his limited English, Fabio Capello identified a fear factor in his England team, especially playing at home. The problem was that some of his 'my way or the highway' methods would only succeed in perpetuating the mental fragility diagnosed. Interestingly a decade later, Gareth Southgate who had a greater understanding of the English footballing mentality, embraced the Wembley heritage. The word was that he moved the England dressing room across to the other side of the corridor where you could hear the noise from the crowd better and so the players became more aware of the atmosphere waiting for them outside. At least Capello's England did qualify impressively for the South Africa World Cup and in the process had an avenge-winning double over Croatia, with Theo Walcott scoring a remarkable hat-trick in Zagreb. Just as unexpected was his omission, then, from the final squad, which was chaotically announced to the players in a frenzy of mobile phone calls. This seemed to set the tone for what was to come. The Football Association had been left rudderless following the departures in quick succession of both their chief executive Ian Watmore and chairman Lord David Triesman. There was a vacuum at the top when Fabio Capello negotiated a contract extension before the World Cup, taking him through to 2012. At the end of the usual physically demanding domestic season, the England players had to make two rather unnecessary trips to Austria: the first for altitude training in readiness for Rustenburg and the second for a friendly against Japan, because Wembley Stadium was required for the play-offs.

Before heading off to the World Cup, what appeared to be a letter from the Inland Revenue dropped onto the mat at home. I could not have been more wrong… It had been sent to me at 5 Live and after at least a fortnight navigating its way around the BBC's internal mail system, was eventually readdressed. I thought it had to be a practical joke and had to read it several times. I was being awarded an MBE for services to sports broadcasting and was required to confirm my acceptance by return of post and because of the delay, the deadline had almost passed. The news was made official on the eve of England's opening game in South Africa against the USA and was generously received by colleagues and friends. One of the phone calls which meant the most was from fellow commentator Darren Fletcher, who told me that this would give all the younger guys something to aspire to. The best thing about this totally unexpected honour was that both of my parents were still alive. When I received the award from Her Majesty the Queen at Buckingham Palace, I was able to take Lorna and our two sons with me; there has only been one other occasion in my life when I was more nervous.

If there were any nerves and anxiety in the England squad, then this was hardly alleviated by their isolated garrison of a base camp in South Africa. The omens did not look good when captain Rio Ferdinand was seriously injured in the first training session and ruled out of the campaign. Something seemed to be troubling Wayne Rooney, who even managed to get himself booked in a glorified kickabout against a local team called the Platinum Allstars, this game going ahead after they had cleared all the sheep off the pitch. Rooney has since revealed his unease at seeing Fabio Capello and his Italian backroom staff in the England hotel cheering for Italy whenever one of their games was being screened. You can understand their natural instincts, but it does underline the dilemma of having an overseas coach. Capello went on to steer England to Euro 2012, only to resign before that championship when in the quarter-final the opposition turned out to be Italy! Sir Alex Ferguson always resisted any notion that he could ever manage an England team. As a proud Scot, he felt he would be emotionally compromised.

Steven Gerrard, and not John Terry, was appointed as the replacement England captain. There were clear divisions in the camp, and these surfaced after Terry had spoken passionately at a press conference about the depressingly inadequate start made by his team. He was condemned unfairly in some quarters for overstepping his authority, and I was shown an indiscreet text message by one senior player which said, "John Terry is a… we're all behind Fabio." Capello himself then inadvertently fanned the flames by suggesting that in speaking so forthrightly, Terry had made a 'very big mistake'. Whatever he really thought must have been lost in translation, because it didn't stop the England manager reinstating Terry as captain after the World Cup and then resigning when the armband was taken away from him by the FA, after he'd been accused of racially abusing Anton

Ferdinand. The only line that had been crossed by Terry was when he had called for Joe Cole to be in the team, but the whole overblown episode exposed all the factions and cliques in a troubled squad. I remember bumping into the considerable presence of actor Ray Winstone in the England media centre; if only he could have banged a few heads together. It was all heading in one direction, and a game with Germany in Bloemfontein was the last thing England needed. On the way to that match, in a land that time forgot, we asked our taxi driver who he wanted to win. "Germany," he said, "because I like Adolf Hitler." The disallowed Frank Lampard goal provided Capello with a morsel of mitigation but camouflaged the reality that England had been systematically outclassed.

The World Cup embarrassment on the pitch was more than matched off it later in the year when the campaign to be hosts in 2018 ended in another humiliation. Notwithstanding FIFA dodgy dealings, there had once again been a complacent sense of entitlement underpinning the English bid epitomised on one overseas trip when one of the FA's delegation told me, "I think we'll be all right on the night as soon as the Prime Minister, Prince William and David Beckham show up." More recently, Martin Glenn at the FA upheld this grand tradition of issuing statements that left you asking 'did he really say that?'. For example, when asked about the possibility of Chelsea being allowed to play at Wembley, if their ground was closed for renovation he said, "If we can help the 'football family' then that's what we are here to do." Pardon me, which 'football family' is that, then? Certainly not the one that Chelsea belong to. Families support one another and don't greedily demand a larger slice of overseas television money than the fellow members of their League. A league is supposed to mean an alliance, a working together in partnership and what makes the Premier League so marketable overseas is the competitive nature of all of its games. Sepp Blatter always liked to talk about his 'football family' as well, but always made it sound like something John Gotti might have said.

At Euro 2012, Roy Hodgson, with little time to prepare after replacing Fabio Capello, didn't lose any of his games but went out predictably in the quarter-final on penalties to Italy. In that match, I thought fatigue caught up with an England team that had stuck with Capello's plan of being based in the Polish city Krakow and flying to all of their matches in Ukraine, a distance further than travelling back to London. Italy went on to play the holders Spain in the final, and there was a moment in this game that played a big part in convincing me to retire in 2014. I have never commentated off a TV monitor and didn't make use of one in this final, even though the far side of the stadium in Kiev was as distant as the Milky Way. I committed myself too early and credited a Spanish goal to Fabregas when it should have been Alba. In such an important game, there is no excuse. When eyesight is not as sharp as it used to be, even if the vocal chords are still belting out a decent tune, then it is time to heed that wake-up call.

Before Roy Hodgson had taken charge of England, Stuart Pearce stood in as caretaker manager for a friendly against The Netherlands. After all the controversy surrounding John Terry's loss of the captaincy, Pearce made a left-field call to appoint Scott Parker and not Steven Gerrard as leader. Parker was an outstanding professional, but this was disrespectful to Gerrard. Unless there were reasons that I am unaware of, equally mystifying was Pearce's decision to deny David Beckham one of the three places for over-21 players in the Great Britain Olympics football squad, despite having gone over to see him in California and included him in his provisional list. Whatever you may think of Beckham and his penchant for self-promotion, no ambassador did more to help London get their Olympic bid over the line. To play in the Games would have meant more to him than it clearly did to some of those selected for a squad that was as authentic as a Robbie Williams Eleven at Old Trafford. Having a British team at this Olympics to please the IOC was a bit like when FIFA pressurised Manchester United into attending their World Club Championship. Beckham might have injected a bit of passion into what turned out to be a cosmetic waste of time. GB went out in the quarter-finals, naturally on penalties, but here are a couple of quiz questions: can you remember who they lost to and who eventually went on to win the gold medal? I had always wanted to work on a Summer Olympics for the BBC, but the football was so peripheral that the matches were quite rightly only seen on TV and hardly heard on the radio.

It should be obvious to anyone that there is a substantial difference between watching sport on television and listening to it on the radio. Nobody should be more aware of the distinction between sound and vision than the BBC. Yet as predictably as rain falling on the first day of the school holiday, it was decided to end the 'historic mismatch', as *The Guardian* described it, between TV and radio football coverage by dispensing with a second commentator on 5 Live. The use of two commentators was seen as an anachronism. "There is no reason why one person cannot commentate for the whole game," said a Radio 5 Live source. "If they can do it on TV, why not on radio?" was becoming a widely held view in the corridors of power. However, in television football commentary, the voice is not the focal point of the coverage and should be used only to adorn the pictures. David Coleman was the master of this art: "Bobby Charlton with the corner, Bobby – Jack 1-0." Magical simplicity that would not be enough on radio where pictures have to be created. On radio, the voice is pre-eminent and over ninety minutes – plus, often, extra time and penalties – one voice, no matter how mellifluous, can be a hard listen. *Test Match Special* would never dream of having just one cricket commentator for the whole of a two-hour session. These changes were made in line with the BBC's '*delivering quality first*' manifesto, which in this instance had nothing to do with quality but all about financial cutbacks and amounted, in my view, to false economy. A more practical method of putting the licence fee to better use would have been to prevent duplication of resources and to make one BBC Radio commentary available to all outlets, instead of having two or three local radio stations turning up to broadcast the same game. Whatever money was allegedly saved by scrapping the second commentator was then ploughed straight back into having a presenter at virtually every game. Axing a second commentator was the justification for the pruning of staff and the price paid for making these changes would be a heavy one.

Invitations were sent out to all staff football commentators to consider voluntary redundancy, and if there were no takers, then management would make the final cull. In order to be able to back up their decision, reports were compiled on us all and marks awarded in various categories. One particular priority was the cross-trailing of other programmes and identifying 5 Live as much as possible during commentary; Peter Jones would not have passed this test! I was briefly shown my report, and the only thing that I can now remember from it was that apparently, I had a tendency 'to growl'. Feedback is always welcome but should have been part of everyday communication. At the end of this frankly obscene procedure, two valued colleagues lost their jobs. Nigel Adderley had been a pleasure to work with at Euro 2004 and thankfully was able to become more appreciated at talkSPORT. David Oates had worked for the corporation for over a quarter of a century and was now deemed to be surplus to requirement, even though as a talented all-rounder there were many other roles he could have performed. Broadcasting ability is often best judged when you find yourself having to react to an unexpected event like Jon Champion had to when Eric Cantona jumped into the crowd at Selhurst Park. For David Oates, his defining moment as an eyewitness was at White Hart Lane when Fabrice Muamba suffered a cardiac arrest on the pitch. David handled it all so sensitively and professionally. Less than a year later, and just sixteen weeks after finally severing his links with the BBC, David died aged only fifty, after being struck down by a virus that attacked his heart. It was a devastating loss to us but more importantly to his wife, my football producer of ten years, Charlotte Nicol and their young girls, Imogen and Kate. At his funeral, there was a message of sympathy from Sir Alex Ferguson recalling his association with David when he had been at Radio Manchester. In later years, when he was in dispute with the BBC, Fergie had to apologise to David for not being able to grant him an interview. "Sorry, David, it's nothing personal. I just don't like some of the people you work with." "Don't worry," said David, "there's one or two I'm not keen on either."

Not only did Charlotte have to rebuild her life without her husband but without the BBC career she had worked so hard and against so many obstacles to secure. When the BBC decided to uproot the sports department to Salford just in time for an Olympic Games in London, it informed all staff that they had to make the permanent move to the north or resign. An easy decision for someone who is young and unattached, but there were a host of skilled producers like Charlotte who had a life with their families in London that was difficult to leave. Forcing such valuable members of staff like her and head of radio sport, Gordon Turnbull, to choose between keeping their jobs or moving over 200 miles away and making it clear there would be no half measures, meant that BBC Radio Sport lost a generation of experience and knowledge that would be so difficult to replace.

I chose to end my career at the BBC for many reasons and to finish at the Brazilian World Cup. A month before that, my last commentary memory from an FA Cup final was describing a winning goal for Arsenal, scored fittingly by a player called Ramsey at Wembley. My last goal would be the one from Götze that confirmed Germany as World Champions in the Maracanã; not a bad way to bow out. England, though, had yet again crashed and burned. In Rio, we always knew when the squad were about to arrive back at their hotel after training because we could see the helicopters in the sky and an increased naval presence in the ocean. Over the hill would come the Three Lions coach in a convoy of more military might than would have been needed to protect a G8 conference. When the draw had been made and placed England with Uruguay and Italy, FA chairman, Greg Dyke, had made that 'group of death' sign. England did lose to them both, but the group was won by Costa Rica! The last interview I did with an England player was with captain Steven Gerrard in the team hotel. When it was over, I thanked him for his help over the years and wanted to tell him that he had been an inspiration to my son Marshall. We then went through the usual ritual of alerting the BBC that we had just interviewed Steven Gerrard and this was always the patter…

Us: "We've done Steven Gerrard."

BBC: "What does he say?"

Us: "Well, we'll play the tape down to you, and you can put it out in a few minutes."

BBC: "No, we'll come to Mike, and he can talk about it *live*."

And so, rather than listening to the recorded interview, I had to talk about it live and afterwards as we prepared to leave our little studio, there was a knock on the door. The England captain, without any FA minders, had returned with one of his shirts for my son. In the maelstrom of Premier League cynicism and self-interest, this was a moment to treasure that took me back to all those working-class heroes of my childhood who had fostered my love for the great game. If only Steven Gerrard could have been cloned.

There were some embarrassingly complimentary words written about me when I retired, and I was so pleased that both my parents had been able to read them. I telephoned them as soon as I arrived home from Brazil and my dad told me that the only thing they had missed out in the tributes was to call me 'fatty sonkin', the name he had given me when I was in nappies. He had been able to hear my last commentary, and he died three weeks later. Mum passed away in March 2019.

He's What I Call

On December 27ᵗʰ, 1980, I was invited to be the studio guest on BBC Radio 2's Sport on Two programme. During the afternoon, the presenter Mike Ingham suggested that I might like to try out his job and cue over to the commentators at various sporting events around the country. I did not do it very well, but I thoroughly enjoyed myself because I found that I knew all of them personally. So I thought it would be fun to look back and recall the characters and techniques of some of my colleagues. This book will be just an appreciation of my friends, the commentators

Chatterboxes, Brian Johnston, 1983

AND SO, TAKING A LEAF OUT OF BRIAN'S BOOK, HERE IS A personal appreciation of 'my friends' the summarisers: *Chatterboxes 2.*

The role of a summariser in radio commentary is considerably underestimated. It does not follow that if you played a good game, then you are bound to be able to talk one as well. The list is far-reaching of accomplished footballers doing what came naturally to them on the pitch, who then found it more challenging to articulate their thoughts concisely on a match. Mastering the art of summarising is a far more demanding discipline than commentating. Instead of just describing what you can see, you have to explain succinctly why what you have just witnessed happened. The job calls for the following qualities:

1. An instinctive understanding of the rhythm of a radio football commentary.
2. An appreciation of knowing when to come in and then ensure that your interjection is justified by contributing something incisive with an economy of words.
3. To have an entertaining and enlightening style and be able to add something to the broadcast that only an experienced eye might observe.
4. To do it for love and not money or self-projection and be a team player.

The summariser is the expert; the commentator is not, and those who excel are not only natural broadcasters but dovetail seamlessly into the ebb and flow of the coverage. At its best, it operates like a well-oiled clockwork machine, like a partnership between two centre-halves, with one holding back to sweep up all the loose ends. The perfect combinations are often the result of years of building up an understanding and when it works, there is no need for a dig in the ribs or any eye contact. There will be no discernible pause as the summariser telepathically, and without being prompted, steps in and illuminates.

Becoming a radio summariser after a successful career in the game will require readjustment. There will be no luxury travel or accommodation. You will have to make your own way to the ground, engage with fans and integrate with all sections of the media. You will not earn a fortune either. One well-known former player, who had earned millions playing abroad, after being told what his match fee would be, replied that he 'wouldn't cross the road for that'. Over the years I worked with a vast array of summarisers, some more regularly than others, and my personal favourites, boasting over 500 caps between them would have made a formidable team on the pitch – not to mention around the dinner table – and here it is in a 4-3-3 formation.

Ray Clemence

Danny Mills   Mark Lawrenson   Terry Butcher   Jimmy Armfield (Capt.)

Martin O'Neill   Jan Molby   Trevor Brooking

Chris Waddle   Denis Law   Stan Collymore

Director of football: David Pleat

Manager: Graham Taylor.

RAY CLEMENCE

In their halcyon years, the Liverpool dressing room specialised in closing ranks and revealing 'nowt' for public consumption and yet the club spawned many consummate communicators; Ray was a shining example. He was one of English football's great keepers but always preferred to strut his stuff for the press team as an outfield player and in so doing demonstrated why it had been a sensible career decision to go in goal. He was blessed with the constitution of an ox. At Italia '90, after the first semi-final in Naples had gone to extra time and penalties, there was barely time for sleep before we were up at the crack of dawn for our journey to Turin via Milan for the second semi-final. Ray somehow still managed to be bright-eyed and bushy-tailed and as the cocks were crowing greeted us with his customary: "Great to be alive, chaps." If he was shattered, he certainly wasn't going to show it. He has needed all that strength of character in later years during a brave personal battle with cancer.

DANNY MILLS

How misleading can first impressions be? We met at the 2002 World Cup in Japan, when it was his turn on the players' rota to be interviewed. He fixed me with an intimidating 'I don't really want to be here' stare and conveyed all the cordiality on this particular day of a serial killer. A decade later, as a valued colleague, Danny was generous and warm-hearted and also occasionally managed to get us the England line-up in advance from his contacts.

When we were discussing Gary Cahill's commendable defending after an England game in Ukraine, I made the comment that Terry Butcher had always said that you needed to win twenty caps before you felt at home in the international side and that Cahill was now starting to look the part. At the time, it may well have sounded like a set-up, but I can assure you it wasn't. "Cheers, Mike," said Danny. "Why, how many caps did you win then, Danny?" I wondered. "Nineteen," was his reply.

MARK LAWRENSON

Never once did he play the 'been there, seen that, done that card'. I remember him being asked once by one of our presenters how many League titles he had won. "Five," he casually replied in his typically deadpan, self-effacing way. He wore the red of Liverpool with great distinction, but the colour came to symbolise danger whenever he was part of the commentary. He adored tossing you a hand grenade and seemed to take masochistic pleasure watching you attempting to detonate it. Rather than helping you to dig your way out of a hole, he would toss in a few more buckets of soil. It was a joy being in his company at the 1994 World Cup in the USA. We shared the same cynicism towards the rigidity and intransigence that can exist in the so-called 'land of the free'. Everything in the States is great until you have a problem or a question to ask. As long as you wake up each morning with the attitude that life is *awesome* then you are guaranteed to 'have a nice day'. However, in a country where it seems whatever authority that comes with a job will be maximised to the full, largely through insecurity, more often than not the simplest of requests will be met with 'the computer says no'. In the month that

Mark and I spent together on the East Coast in 1994, this scenario was acted out countless times checking in at hotels and airports, though never in restaurants where the dollar talks and helpfulness is the prerequisite for any tip. Mark could spot potential inflexibility from a distance, and as we approached it, he would whisper in my ear, "Android alert." When it came to christening his son, though, he could not have been bearing any deep-rooted issues with America. One day he will be known in his family as 'Uncle Sam'.

Mark unsurprisingly graduated into television but never turned his back on radio, probably because we were prepared to tolerate his corny jokes. He brought the Anfield dressing room banter into our commentary box and as a professional shrinking violet myself, it made me realise that I would not have lasted five minutes in the company of Hansen, Lawrenson and Dalglish.

TERRY BUTCHER

Like Danny Mills, another character whose fearsome demeanour as a player and famed dressing room rabble-rousing was at odds with the kind and considerate companion that I got to know. Terry lived life to the full and only had a bad word for you if you retired to bed before he did, when you were then accused of letting the side down. He had the stamina of Forrest Gump, although I do remember one early morning in Turin having to prise open his eyelids as he was threatening to drift off to sleep at the very moment the *Today* programme were coming across to him for a live interview. On another occasion in Lisbon, rather like one of those battle-scarred scenes in a punishing World Title fight, it required the face flannel and a '*look into my eyes*' demand before he was given the all-clear to be seen by the nation on *Football Focus*. Terry played for the press team with as much determination as if he was still captaining his country in a World Cup semi-final. He used his natural strength to help our engineer Mike Burgess carry very heavy equipment and teased him by always calling him Spielberg, having given him that nickname the very first time they met, but it was Butcher who was the BFG. He used to prepare for the commentaries by meticulously keeping up to date a captain's logbook of impeccable handwritten notes. Never one to cash in on his name or status in the game, although I do recall him on one occasion having the temerity to ask the FA if there might be any chance of a ticket for an England game. The voice on the other end of the phone felt the need to ask him a quick question before granting his request. "How many caps did you win?" "Seventy-seven," said Terry. "Does that qualify?"

JIMMY ARMFIELD

The best right-back at the 1962 World Cup but prepared to wear the number 3 shirt and play at left-back when he made his international debut in front of 160,000 people in Brazil. Jimmy, I'm sure, would put any smattering of self-interest to one side and do the same here as the natural captain of this team. I first met him on Friday October 18th, 1963. It was the day before Blackpool's home game against Ipswich, and we were having a family half-term illuminations holiday on the Golden Mile. Being the precocious thirteen-year old that I was, I informed my folks that I was off to Bloomfield Road in the hope of seeing the players after training. One by one they came out and signed my book. Alan Ball, Ray Charnley, Tony Waiters, but still no sign of my main target and I wasn't going to leave until I had the autograph of the England captain. When Jim did eventually emerge in his car, I was standing at the wrong exit and had to do a personal best for the 100 metres sprinting in his direction. Jim saw me coming; he could hardly have missed me hurtling towards him and he waited understandingly for my breathless arrival. He opened his window, took my book and signed. When I told him this story twenty years later, he said that he had considered telling me to 'bugger off'. That would have been an impossibility. It was not part of his metabolism.

MARTIN O'NEILL

As you would have expected, many of the players who came under the influence of Brian Clough and Peter Taylor went on to make forays into management, and so far, Martin O'Neill has been the most convincing. I suspect that he subconsciously absorbed the positives and rejected the negatives of Clough's law-unto-himself eccentricity, and then, being his own man, added his own personal gloss. He regularly worked for us in those early days when he was building his foundations at Wycombe Wanderers in the way Clough did at Hartlepool. The embryonic talent was there for all to see as he learned quickly from experiences that would set him up nicely for a life in the fast lane. I remember him telling me once at a commentary match at Portsmouth how jaundiced he had been by what he perceived as a condescending attitude towards him by Newcastle when they signed his star player Steve Guppy for a knockdown price, then telling him, "Welcome to the Premier League." At Leicester City, O'Neill won two domestic trophies, which is two more than Newcastle have won in over sixty years. The greatest tribute I can think of to Martin as a person and a football manager is that Roy Keane, who is nobody's number two, was prepared to be his assistant. O'Neill's sacking by Nottingham Forest after only nineteen games in charge, said more about the power now being wielded by modern day players than it did about any perceived decline in his managerial ability.

JAN MOLBY

I don't know why I should have been, but on the few occasions that I heard Jan speak in his mother tongue of Danish when he met up with his fellow countrymen, I was always taken aback. I had completely forgotten that this 'native scouser' was from the kingdom of Hamlet and not Ken Dodd. As a player, he had always made the game look ridiculously easy as he caressed passes from midfield through to Dalglish and Rush. All that was missing was the cigar and slippers and he replicated this laidback style on radio. In what wasn't his first language, he was as naturally fluent as his football had always been. He only had one shortcoming; I would never have asked him to fill in a football pools coupon for me as he was a terrible tipster! This became a standing joke for us during the 2002 World Cup when we bumped into Jan while he was working for Danish TV and asked him for his prediction on the upcoming game. It was a bit like that scene in *Groundhog Day*, holding your breath and waiting for Punxsutawney Phil to confirm whether or not it would be an early spring. Jan's soothsaying at that tournament routinely backfired, and so when we arrived at the last sixteen game between England and Denmark, it was such a relief to hear him forecast with absolute certainty a Danish win. When we moved on to the quarter-final against Brazil, though, and were in need of some reassurance before kick-off, hearts were in our mouths when Jan was put on the spot and with unreserved confidence predicted, "I fancy England."

SIR TREVOR BROOKING

Trevor and Jimmy Armfield were peas from the same pod; one-club ambassadors who put so much back into the sport and the community. Archetypal English gentlemen who would have excelled as players in any era. As a supremely gifted footballer, when it came to striking up an understanding with colleagues, Trevor always seemed to be blessed with a built in sat nav system, and that was also a natural part of his armoury when he was analysing games for us on radio. I admired him greatly as a man of principle and resolve for shunning all temptation of alcohol; I'm only sorry that this sobriety didn't rub off on me. Like Jimmy, he set himself high standards of behaviour on the pitch. The only time that I ever saw him lose his rag was playing for the English press team in Georgia. One of the opposition brutalised him and drew blood. It was not a pretty sight, and the perpetrator of the assault then made a half-hearted attempt to show some remorse. Trevor looked up at him, and in declining his apology fixed him with a looks-could-kill glare, before mildly rebuking his assailant with a '*go away*'.

CHRIS WADDLE

As with Danny Mills, it was very easy to get the wrong first impression of Chris. As a wonderful player, he was renowned for having a style that appeared sometimes carefree and languid, but it would be wrong to jump to that conclusion about the man himself. Nobody held a more deep-rooted concern about how the game should be played and cared more about the development of the England team. He would still give anything to be a professional footballer, and that's why whenever he saw anybody abusing that privilege, he found it intolerable. Around the dinner table, sauce bottles and salt and pepper pots were made full use of whenever he was regaling us with stories about Jack Charlton or Bobby Robson and needed to illustrate a tactical point. At tournaments overseas, he would often wander off for a stroll in the hope of being able to join in with any old kickabout in a local park. In Japan, the youngsters who passed their ball to him probably had no idea of his background but were instantly made aware of a special presence in their midst when he treated them to tricks more associated with Hogwarts.

DENIS LAW

Denis was one of the greatest players the game has ever seen and in modern football would be priceless, yet never complained about missing out on the Monopoly money of today. He played iconically with his shirt cuffs rolled down, and his style as a summariser was very often off the cuff as well. I fondly remember doing a European game between Rangers and Dynamo Kyiv at Ibrox with him and Roddy Forsyth; a goal was scored just as he was trying to retrieve a cigarette that had dropped under his seat. He hadn't seen the incident or a replay, but with the strongest of conviction informed his audience, "Well, of course what happened there was that…" You believed him because he was Denis Law.

At the height of his fame, he told me that he had to give so many autographs to fans that he once sent a birthday card to his wife, Di, and signed it 'Best wishes, Denis Law'. Though he made it up to her and his young family by being available to spend Christmas at home with them miraculously often, after conveniently either picking up a booking that led to a one-game suspension or suddenly developing a niggly groin strain. I have checked the records from the early 1960s and am able to confirm this pattern of coincidence, but then, it's hard to be too critical because he was Denis Law.

STAN COLLYMORE

Not as many international caps as the others from a rollercoaster playing career that has been subsequently mirrored in his life as a broadcaster. When Stan joined us first time around as a summariser, his preparation and research was impressively thorough. He appeared to be very much at home, and it was a blow when Radio 5 Live dropped him after revelations about his private life. We had all really enjoyed working with Stan, believing that he enhanced our output and some of us lobbied strongly for him to make a return.

Stan was eventually re-employed and picked up from where he had left off. His status was restored to such an extent that he was selected for the 2008 Champions League final in Moscow between Chelsea and Manchester United and was also accredited for the European Championship in Austria and Switzerland but had to be precluded from attending that tournament for us after it was revealed that he was joining talkSPORT. We were in his company for two or three days in Russia and at no time did he feel obliged to tell any of us that he would be leaving, even though he knew that we had actively campaigned to get him back to the BBC. I remember one of his former Liverpool teammates once asking me how Stan was doing and when I enthused about the contribution he was making, he said pointedly, "He'll let you down, you know, he always does." In the end, I suppose he did, but he is still in my team ahead of many other outstanding candidates because of the time that he did spend with us, when he displayed all of those essential qualities that I listed to be a top summariser.

DAVID PLEAT

The Oracle. The definitive football man with an encyclopaedic knowledge of players and their potential. If you want to know about Ebbsfleet's third team keeper, contact David. If you need reassurance that a Solihull striker is worth a gamble, then call Mr Pleat. He is also a class act as a summariser and always reminded me of the actor Walter Matthau. If only we could have found a Jack Lemmon lookalike; we would have been able to put them together as The Odd Couple! David rang me at home during the 2018 World Cup, an illustration of what a considerate man he is. He knew that I would be suffering some withdrawal symptoms from no longer being involved and just wanted to let me know that he was thinking of me. It meant such a lot. Had Graham Taylor and Jimmy Armfield still been alive, they would have done the same.

GRAHAM TAYLOR

Graham loved being a valued member of the commentary team but sadly became disillusioned towards the end of his BBC Radio involvement. Some summarisers were becoming flavours of the month, and it became obvious to him that his work was becoming more irregular. All he ever wanted from BBC management was to be kept in the loop and to be told to his face if his services were no longer required. Instead, he became increasingly marginalised and remained in the dark. It is strange that a corporation supposedly in the communication business can be one of the worst communicators in the business when it comes to talking directly to valued employees. No better example of that than in early 2020 when the much respected Victoria Derbyshire had to discover that her daily television show was being cancelled by reading about it in the papers.

There was a flawed belief that some of the younger audience might not know anything about the background of some of the more veteran summarisers like Graham and Jimmy. This was a typically ageist attitude to take and also highly patronising to younger listeners.

When Graham Taylor so unexpectedly passed away, his funeral in the centre of Watford turned out to be a celebration of his life as a fine club manager, which was often overlooked and overshadowed by his traumatic England experience. The day was encapsulated for me by seeing the esteemed television commentator Martin Tyler standing with the fans in the rain. He hadn't asked for an entry ticket to the church but as a lover of the game, just wanted to be there to pay his final respects to a real football man. During the service, a common theme in all of the tributes to Graham was of kindness, dignity and respect. Sadly and depressingly, later that day we were brought shudderingly back to reality at Old Trafford after Manchester United's goalless draw against Hull. The then-United manager José Mourinho, attempting to camouflage the limitations of his team's performance, terminated his interview with the BBC by telling his inquisitor, "If you don't know football, you shouldn't be with a microphone in your hand." What a shame Pat Murphy hadn't been doing the interview, I could well have imagined him firing back with, "If you can't beat Hull at home, then you shouldn't be manager of Manchester United." Neither Graham Taylor nor Jimmy Armfield would have behaved so crassly as managers. To lose Jimmy so soon after Graham's death extinguished another light that had shone so brightly and touched so many.

IN MEMORY OF JIMMY

Every life is by definition unique, but in Jimmy Armfield's case, his truly was.

Member of the Armed Forces; a face on my bubble-gum cards in the 1950s; one-club man; captain of England; World Cup-winning squad member; European Cup final manager; journalist; organist;

radio broadcaster; PFA; pillar of community; FA kingmaker; awarded freedom of Blackpool; Sheriff of Lancashire; devoted family man; respected by the sporting world and, most important of all, a human being of the highest order.

If there is one picture that sums up the spirit of Jimmy Armfield, it is the one of him on the Wembley pitch as a squad member at the end of the 1966 World Cup final. There is not one ounce of visible disappointment at not being in the winning England team who are about to be presented with the trophy. There is only unbridled joy and pride to be part of something that may never ever be repeated, even though there would be no medal on that day to show for his involvement. The honour for the country overrode all other self-interest, and he was like that as a summariser. I probably worked with Jimmy more than any other summariser and never once did he make it about himself and say anything for effect. It was always only about the game and having been there himself as a distinguished player, he knew it was a tough profession and so was never over-critical, but everything he did say carried the weight of sage authority. I would look forward to a commentary even more than usual if I knew that Jimmy was going to be sitting alongside me.

This would be a typical Sunday afternoon match day with him in the North West. Jim would enter the press room about ninety minutes before kick-off after having chatted to supporters outside the ground. Off would come his flat cap, a quick comb through what remained of his hair, cheery greetings all round and then after firmly shaking my hand would say, "Well, son, if they play as well this afternoon as I did this morning, then we're in for a good game," a reference to his shift on the church organ at morning prayers. More often than not you would then be treated to a rendition of his latest joke, vintage end-of-the-pier stuff in the grand tradition of all those great Lancashire comedians. It was never blue and would nearly always start with 'this chap goes to the doctor'. After delivering the punchline, still chuckling, he would grab hold of you and insist, "It's a good 'un, that, did you like it?" Of course, you loved it because he did. In the commentary, he would have a few pet phrases and the one that I associate most of all with him was when he used to say, "He's what I call." Occasionally, like all of us attempting live radio, he might get his wires twisted and once observed about Aston Villa's Tony Morley: "He's what I call a down-and-out winger."

When we were together in Budapest for a European game between Honved and Manchester United, he was recognised in our hotel by a rather portly old boy who came over and gave him a bear hug. They had played against each other at Wembley in 1963 when Jimmy had captained England against the Rest of the World. It had turned out to be one of the greatest footballers of all time, and although Ferenc Puskás didn't speak English, the two men conversed in the language of football, ending with Jimmy playfully prodding the great Hungarian in the tummy. The so-called 'Galloping Major' had developed a galloping middle-aged spread. Whenever we were at Old Trafford in our position next to the directors' box, Jimmy would be on the lookout before kick-off for the arrival of any friends or former colleagues, and there would be many. He would suddenly jump to his feet and, like an excited schoolboy, call out '*Bally!*' on seeing Alan Ball or another favourite – '*Jack*' – when he spotted Lancashire cricket legend Jack Simmons. They would be just as thrilled to see him as well.

When he was commissioned by the FA to headhunt for two England managers, I naively assumed that as his friend, I would be given special favours and the odd steer about who was likely to be appointed. I called him many times, and we would chat at length. At the end of the call, I would look at my notepad and realise that nothing had been written down. This man of integrity had demonstrated why the FA had put their trust in him. When it was his seventieth birthday in 2005, I was invited by the Blackpool Supporters' Club to make a speech at a special dinner in his honour at Bloomfield Road. Sir Tom Finney was also there, as were Jim's England teammates from Blackburn, Ronnie Clayton and Bryan Douglas. Everyone there that night got a stick of tangerine Blackpool Rock with Jimmy's name on it to commemorate the occasion. That was Jimmy Armfield, the

Blackpool Rock. He would no doubt have been asked to approve the menu that night and insist that there should be no sauces or fancy stuff to spoil the taste. "Don't put anything on it," he would tell a puzzled *maître d'* at France '98. Jimmy belonged to the John Wayne School of fine dining when ordering his steak: "Just wipe its bottom and put it on the plate."

When still a teenager, Jimmy attended the Matthews Cup final in 1953 between Blackpool and Bolton. Nearly sixty years later, he was guest of honour at the FA Cup final between Chelsea and Liverpool, handing over the trophy to Frank Lampard and John Terry. I am able to say with great pride that when I did my final broadcast for the BBC in the summer of 2016, half a century on from the boys of '66, I was able to work for one last time with Jimmy Armfield.

Jimmy was awarded a CBE in 2010; it could easily stand for:

CAPTAIN
BLACKPOOL
ENGLAND

Talk, the divine amalgam that holds civilisation together. The lovely whitewash of words poured out over the asperities of life to make them more bearable.

Trust to Talk, Wynford Vaughan-Thomas, 1980

Who The F*** Are You?

IN THE EARLY HOURS OF THE MORNING IN THE LAND OF THE rising sun, a live feed of BBC television was made available in the Westin Hotel on Awaji Island, home to the 2002 England World Cup squad. It was of no interest to the players themselves, who were deep in sleep recovering from their opening game with Sweden and preparing for the next pivotal match against Argentina. However, thanks to self-induced insomnia that night, these pictures linked me to a musical event that I had been made to feel part of during months of its meticulous planning. On the lawn of Buckingham Palace in London, seven hours behind us in Japan, a Rock 'n' Roll Party was staged in honour of Her Majesty the Queen's Golden Jubilee and was produced for BBC Television by my wife, Lorna Dickinson.

All of the Royal Family were in attendance to watch among others: Ozzy Osbourne, Brian Wilson and Eric Clapton. Compared to some of Lorna's other productions, this one had been relatively straightforward in terms of booking artists, as most of those approached wanted to be involved, but that was counterbalanced by the colossal responsibility to make it all flow smoothly on the night. Lorna had decided to bring in the legendary American record producer Phil Ramone along with Sir George Martin to assist with artist liaison during two weeks of preparation at warehouse studios on the South Bank. There was a house band under the direction of

Phil Collins, who found himself drumming to music ranging from 'Paranoid' to 'Goldfinger'. Ozzy arrived for his run-through straight from Monsters of Rock at Donington, where he had kicked things off by yelling, "Let's go f***ing crazy." He conceded that for Her Majesty he would have to moderate it to, "Let's go incredibly very crazy," but he felt honoured to have been invited. An unforeseen spanner was thrown into the works during the final rehearsals at the palace when a fire alarm caused a forced evacuation of the site. There had been a leak in one of the royal toilets. Fan heaters used for drying had been left on for too long and began smoking. At the first sound of an alarm, the production team found themselves surrounded by security that suddenly appeared out of the undergrowth holding machine guns, ordering everyone to the back of the garden. At this point, all Lorna knew was that there was smoke coming out of the roof and as the BBC had assorted wires and technical equipment running through the building, she feared that she was about to become infamous as the producer who burnt down Buckingham Palace. All this drama was soon to be forgotten though when the concert started the next day.

I became very misty-eyed watching from afar, as so many of the ideas and musical collaborations nurtured by Lorna came together and reached glorious fruition. It was her suggestion, for example, to put Queen guitarist, Brian May, on top of the palace ramparts for his live rendition of the national anthem. Watching on, thousands of miles away, the most evocative moment of the show for me was to hear Joe Cocker once again redefine Sir Ringo Starr's 'With a Little Help from My Friends'. It takes something very special to put The Beatles in the shade, and his version always did. For Lorna, this was a climax to twenty years working in television and her reward from Her Majesty was to be made a Member of the Royal Victorian Order. However, when she had first been confirmed as the executive producer of this prestigious celebration, she had received a phone call from Harvey Goldsmith, the legendary promoter of so many major musical events, who had clearly been expecting to oversee this one as well. Goldsmith's abrupt, opening question to her was, "Who the f*** are you?" Allow me to answer that on her behalf...

Clearly, Lorna didn't do too bad a job, as she was invited back four years later to create the Children's Party at the Palace, to celebrate Her Majesty's eightieth birthday. Yet again it clashed with another World Cup, and this time I missed out on witnessing chimney sweeps dancing across the palace rooftops, Thomas the Tank Engine chuffing through the garden and the BFG whizz popping for real in front of the Queen. This was a live performance of a story written by David Wood using characters from children's books with help from Lord Julian Fellowes and J.K. Rowling. Rehearsals went smoothly this time, until the owl Hedwig set off alarms as she made a break for freedom to discover Hyde Park. The climax of the play was the appearance of the Queen herself, who was finally reunited with her missing handbag, and with perfect timing, Her Majesty delivered her line: "I do like a happy ending."

Lorna began her career at BBC Radio Nottingham, working with, among others, a young Simon Mayo. She was then taken on as a researcher by Richard Drewett in the light entertainment department at London Weekend Television. He had been Sir Michael Parkinson's producer during his golden era at the BBC. Her main duty was to meet up with a guest before an appearance on a chat show and do her own preparatory interview. This would enable her, then, to suggest questions for the presenter that might extract the most interesting stories. Unfortunately, at the time, some of the celebrities appeared to be confused about the role of a researcher, very often welcoming them into their hotel rooms in a state of partial undress. They appeared to assume that the girls, who became known as the Drewettes, were only there for their personal self-gratification. Lorna and her female colleagues would be routinely and pathetically propositioned and would need to have their wits about them at all times. However, it wasn't just the celebrities who were sex pests. In what was an all-male management in those days at LWT, one of Lorna's friends was assaulted in full view of others by a senior figure who, after forcing his tongue down her throat, declared, "Welcome to the wonderful world of AIDS," a virus that would later claim his life.

Fortunately for Lorna, the first chat show that she worked on was presented by Gloria Hunniford, who was seriously underappreciated as an interviewer. Gloria presided over a Sunday afternoon programme given the very original title of *Sunday Sunday*. Sadly it was unavailable to much of the country as it was only transmitted in a couple of regions, despite attracting notable guests like James Stewart, Bette Davis and Vincent Price. One of Lorna's early duties was to chaperone renowned Hollywood hellraiser Robert Mitchum. She was given the challenging responsibility of ensuring that he arrived at the studio sober. Perhaps it might have been better if he had been allowed a drop of the hard stuff to loosen him up, as he turned up grouchy and monosyllabic. Gloria needed all her skills to encourage him to speak rather than grunt. John Cleese tried to take advantage of Lorna as a researcher but only in the most professional way. He had been on the show to promote his film *Privates on Parade* and Lorna sent him a letter of thanks. When he replied, even this great comic performer appeared to be in need of some reassurance when confessing to a junior researcher just starting out in TV that he had been hoping to pick her brain:

> *Dear Lorna,*
>
> *I appreciate you writing very much. I did leave a message at one point, hoping to chat to you, because as it was the first of the batch of interviews I did for Privates, I was interested to get some feedback in case I could use any thoughts to improve the upcoming interviews. And I was slightly worried afterwards because everybody seemed a bit quiet and I wasn't sure whether I should have tried to be funnier?*

From the straightforward promotional interview style of *Sunday Sunday*, Lorna was then moved on to the rather more intellectual approach of *The Late Clive James* on Channel 4. As a viewer, I was often made to feel excluded from this entertainment, which at times felt like it was coming from a private club reserved for professional talking heads. Clive James, sadly no longer with us, was a considerable presence on television and Lorna was greatly stimulated by working with him. However, on this show, an over-embellished script was interwoven around ambiguous snapshots of contemporary figureheads like Yasser Arafat and Luciano Pavarotti, with the gags often being hit or miss. Where Clive came into his own away from the stilted autocue, though, was as a journalist with a razor-sharp instinct. This was never better demonstrated than when the unmissable opportunity came his way to meet one of the most notoriously private personalities in the movie business. Lorna spent a summer persuading a reluctant Katharine Hepburn to be interviewed by James at her Manhattan home. Hepburn wasn't plugging anything and had no reason for allowing her carefully guarded world to be invaded. James knew that during the cosy fireside chat, his audience would expect him to stick his chin out and breach territory that was usually off limits. A great deal of the pre-production that Lorna was involved in centred on how Clive might be able to make Hepburn feel relaxed enough to accept a question about her 'secret' love affair with actor Spencer Tracy. Lorna knew that the success or failure of the interview rested on his ability to extract even a morsel of comment. Clive did not plunge in head-first but sensitively built up to his moment of enquiry. Instinctively, Hepburn fired off an early warning signal – "I can tell you are going to tread too far" – but the drawbridge was never fully pulled in, and James skilfully took advantage of whatever limited opening came his way. The watery-eyed legendary actress wistfully recalled that Tracy 'found living difficult and found acting very easy, though [she thought] he thought it was a very silly profession'. Her bottom lip was quivering as she reflected on the fact that he didn't live to see her win the Oscar after they had appeared so memorably together in Guess Who's Coming to Dinner. Over the years Lorna would have the good fortune to work with some of the biggest entertainment stars, but none dazzled quite so radiantly and authentically as Katharine

Hepburn. Every time Lorna sees a red Amaryllis it reminds her of the beautiful gift she was sent after the interview; clearly, they didn't tread too far.

Clive James's interrogative instinct also came to the rescue of Michael Aspel. The Saturday night talk show *Aspel & Company* ran for nine years, and Lorna graduated from researcher to producer of a programme that spoon-fed its charming host with a conveyor belt of researched questions via autocue. There was the occasional breakdown of communication. Once when Aspel was prompted during the show to 'ask Cher about her tattoos', she was instead quizzed about her 'tomatoes'. The camera loved Michael Aspel, and he knew, with a twinkle in his eye, how to manipulate the lens. He was a safe pair of hands, the reliable go-to professional for any occasion, and Lorna enjoyed her working relationship with him. Michael never quite managed to cultivate chemistry between all of his guests in the way that Graham Norton now manages to achieve so naturally. He was, though, very much at home doing one-on-one interviews, especially in the company of glamorous and beguiling women like Dame Elizabeth Taylor and Barbra Streisand. No amount of research and careful planning, though, could have prepared the avuncular host for the anarchic arrival of a plastered Oliver Reed, complete with a jug of vodka and orange. Perhaps LWT had been lulled into a false sense of security. Lorna had once flown over to Spain to escort Reed away from all evil spirits and duty-free distraction, and as a result, he had been the personification of temperance. This time, though, it was a shambles and Aspel, confronted by total inebriation, was out of his depth but ploughed on regardless with his superfluous pre-arranged questions. Fortunately, Clive James was also on hand and intervened. When his patience ran out, he took it upon himself to ask the question all the audience had been waiting for and expected Reed to have to deal with: "Why do you drink?"

The show was renowned for putting together an unlikely combination of guests. Clint Eastwood is not someone who strikes you as being in need of a minder, but he was paired with Arthur

Daley's protector, Dennis Waterman. Lorna never forgot meeting the 'man with no name' for the first time in the hospitality area. "Hi, I'm Clint," he announced, shaking her hand firmly. Lorna was tempted to say, "Oh, that's who you are. I thought you reminded me of someone." George Harrison and Ringo Starr wanted to bring Eric Clapton with them, but instead, ITV preferred an actress from Coronation Street. When Sir David Jason was on the show, Lorna wanted his governor from *Open All Hours*, Ronnie Barker, to join him as well. Barker made a habit of declining these sorts of invitations but did so charmingly in this letter:

> *Please forgive me and tell Michael that had I been there, I would certainly have told you how pleased I am to see David [Jason] enjoying the success that a brilliant actor deserves. He is always, without exception, excellent in his characterisations and Granville in Open All Hours was one of the best – Nurse Gladys was two of the best!*
>
> *Kindest regards, Ronnie Barker.*

By a very long way, the most memorable of all of the shows was in February 1989. What was so wonderful about it was to see all the pomposity and pretension of the entertainment business and in particular, Hollywood, being systematically punctured. However, as with the Oliver Reed experience, Michael Aspel was helped by the intervention of a third party. The actor Richard Gere and his 'people' had made it known to Lorna in advance that the star of *American Gigolo* and *An Officer and a Gentleman* did not want any questions about being a sex symbol. Gere had wanted to focus primarily on talking about Tibet. This information was manna from heaven for another of the guests. Barry Humphries, aka Dame Edna Everage, was duly encouraged by Lorna beforehand to go for it. What was so fascinating was to monitor the reaction of the other guest Lauren Bacall, who was a little bemused at first but then, as Edna picks up the baton and charges with it, very quickly gets on the same page and finds it all hysterical. Aspel is effectively reduced to being a spectator as Edna informs Gere:

When I see you in some of those films, you're either wearing a military uniform or your little birthday suit aren't you. I see your little bits jigging around, your little front botty. You know when I see that, do you know what my fingers are doing, Miss Bacall? They are reaching for the talcum powder to give him a little dusting. I want to put a little nappy between those legs of yours because I am a very maternal person.

Gere does his best to feign amusement, but afterwards, this humanitarian activist and student of Zen Buddhism angrily confronted Lorna and her team. His management immediately demanded cuts; none were made. Gere believed that he was stitched up; he was, and it was compulsive viewing. Lorna adored working with Barry Humphries. One night when I was in their company, and he was dressed in full Edna regalia, Lorna would only ever address him as Edna. Let's just say, Edna and Barry have never been in the same room together. He is a genius.

As the countdown began to a new century, Lorna wanted to take advantage of what was a unique moment in history and make a television documentary in which people who had helped to shape the twentieth century offered their vision of the twenty-first. The programme would invite influential figures who had altered the course of history to not only reflect on the last hundred years but also, more importantly, express their hopes and fears for the next. A typical response from many of the networks that she approached was that they were already doing this, but none of them ever did. Her experience taught her just how tough it was to get any idea, no matter how brilliant, commissioned. Perhaps if she had facetiously proposed at the many meetings she had on both sides of the Atlantic that there would be zombies in the film, then it might have been made. For a period, she developed the idea with Quincy Jones, whom she had met on Aspel's show and had started up his own television production business. Quincy retained his enthusiasm throughout but there was never any momentum behind the project as there was such a fast turnover of executives in his company and as a result, never any continuity.

Undaunted, Lorna still wanted to do something creative to mark the turn of the century and became involved with the 'Children's Promise'. This was a campaign to encourage people to donate the last hour of their salary in the century to improve children's lives in the new millennium. Lorna had been hugely impressed by *Perfect Day*, the corporate film made by the BBC with a very healthy budget simply to promote its diverse music coverage. Her idea was to make something on a shoestring budget in conjunction with the Children's Promise and as part of that promise, hire a young first-time director and feature children in the video. For her, the greatest musical and cultural phenomenon of the twentieth century had been rock and roll, and so she suggested getting as many notable artists as possible to contribute to a version of 'It's Only Rock 'n' Roll (But I Like It)'. Over the autumn of 1999, lines were recorded from the song and filmed guerrilla-style in hotel rooms, tour buses, backstage and studios by performers that included BB King, James Brown, Mary J Blige, Joe Cocker, Iggy Pop, Annie Lennox, Ozzy Osbourne, Lionel Richie and then, finally, the original composers, Sir Mick Jagger and Keith Richards. Even the late great comedian Robin Williams made a cameo appearance. It was all done on a wing and a prayer and with very little finance. The BBC made limited funds available for a documentary about the making of the record and managed to leave some priceless interview material with some of the stars on the cutting room floor. Linda Womack, for example, had talked emotionally about her childhood as the daughter of Sam Cooke. When the record itself was released and then first played by Radio 1, it was immediately trivialised by Zoe Ball, because the Spice Girls had introduced themselves before singing their chorus. Compared to the rather plodding Stones original, this version produced by

Arthur Baker had more energy and vitality but above all was fun. It is something that Lorna can look back on with justifiable pride and should have been given much more support.

The new century began for Lorna with that question from Harvey Goldsmith: "Who the f*** are you?" He wouldn't have to wait much longer to find out; their paths were destined to cross, and it would be a painful experience. Twenty years on from Live Aid in July 2005, U2's Bono and Richard Curtis had joined forces to persuade Sir Bob Geldof to lead the global Live 8 movement and Goldsmith returned to stage London's contribution to the concerts, which were all taking place on the same day around the world. Unlike Live Aid, which was all about raising funds, Live 8 was more about raising awareness. It was timed to coincide with the meeting of the G8 superpowers in Scotland, calling upon them to sanction more debt relief and 'make poverty history'. Bob Geldof acknowledged that the role of live television on the day would be vital to spread the word around the globe. Lorna was appointed as the producer of the BBC's coverage and was set on a collision course with the Hyde Park event organiser, Harvey Goldsmith. He was only concerned about his stage and ensuring that it all ran to time and finished on schedule. Lorna had a bigger picture in mind. For her, one of the defining moments of the broadcast was going to be at 5pm UK time, when the Americans joined the coverage. The plan was for London to cue to Will Smith in Philadelphia, who would initiate a finger click every three seconds to represent the fact that somewhere in Africa a child died every three seconds. This would then be replicated live in Paris, Rome, Berlin and London. Just before handing over to Smith, there was a technical hitch, and Lorna had to send a text to the Americans saying, "Are you there?" Goldsmith's patience snapped, and he wanted Travis to get on stage instead. Lorna, wearing her TV hat, stuck to her guns and received a torrent of abuse from Goldsmith, who was sitting alongside her. At one stage, he even told her that she was fired. In the nick of time, America joined the party, and Will Smith was allowed to choreograph a visually stunning moment that only television could make happen. It was magical, but evidently lost on Goldsmith who showed his appreciation to Lorna by telling her, "Do that again, and you're out of here."

On the eve of the show, I jumped into a taxi with Lorna and headed off to a small studio near Millwall Football Ground, where the opening number to Live 8 was being rehearsed by U2 and Sir Paul McCartney. If only the locals had known what was on their doorstep. McCartney had never performed a live version of the opening to 'Sgt. Pepper's Lonely Hearts Club Band' before and this was going to begin proceedings in Hyde Park. U2's phenomenal guitarist, The Edge, was listening relentlessly to the original recording and trying to get to grips with what is quite a complex riff. What I recall most of all about this surreal experience, though, was that when it was time to take a break for fish and chips delivered in newspapers, Lorna had to step forward and address them all on behalf of the BBC. The biggest band in the world and the most famous individual musician on the planet being briefed by my wife. I would have freaked out, but she was completely unphased which is why she was so good at her job. Lorna was never star-struck, something she might have inherited from her dad. After he had retired as an engineer and came to live with us for a short time, Lorna discovered that 'extras' were required for a film being made in London and suggested to him that it might be an interesting way to spend a day. Michael ended up being quite prominent in his cameo, waving his walking stick at Brad Pitt, as the fighters made their way into the ring for the scene that climaxes Guy Ritchie's movie *Snatch*. When he returned home, we were anxious to grill him about his experience. "Very interesting," he said. "That woman was there." We wondered who? "Oh, you know, that singer, blonde girl, always on the telly." He was talking about Madonna.

Two months after Live 8, Lorna returned to her spiritual home at ITV's south bank after being invited to work on what would turn out to be the most frustrating and deceptive production of her career. To celebrate fifty years of ITV's London Studios on the South Bank, it was decided to construct a Hollywood Boulevard-style Avenue of Stars as a tribute to some of the biggest names associated over the years with

Independent Television. A live show was built around the awarding of these stars, and on the night, the executive in charge, Michael Hurll, assembled probably the greatest gathering of British show business celebrities under one roof. All of the recipients of this coveted award would have their star cemented into a special walkway in the grounds of St Paul's in Covent Garden, known as the actor's church. The stars were duly laid for this occasion and the sacred hall of fame was officially opened by Sir Michael Caine. In essence, it was all rather trite, but that is not the point here. Many of those being honoured were sadly deceased and were represented at the ceremony by family members who in effect had been lured there under false pretences. From the Ustinovs to the Thaws, they all proudly assembled, including my former BBC colleague Graham Jenkins, who was there on behalf of his brother Richard Burton. Les Dawson's daughter observed that, "In years to come, people who didn't know Dad will hopefully walk past and want to know more about him." Several artists were there that night receiving their stars who have sadly, subsequently passed away, including three knights of the realm: Richard Attenborough, David Frost and Bruce Forsyth. When the late Eric Sykes was honoured, he said that, "When they told me about this, I thought it was a joke." I am afraid it was. I challenge you to find this Avenue now. The stars were in place for less than a year before being removed from the flagstones and haven't been relocated. Nothing sums up the here today, gone tomorrow, sugar cane superficiality of television more than this charade. The most amazing thing of all is that nobody seems to have batted an eyelid over it. Hardly any attention has been given to what was, quite frankly, a scandal that exploited people's emotions.

Lorna was unwittingly part of a production that ITV, under new management, decided was no longer a priority and declined to fund. The handmade stars were packed up and are still in storage, waiting for that moment when they may be deemed worthy of another celebration. However, it is not only the Avenue of Stars that no longer exists, the South Bank studios themselves, the heartbeat of ITV in London for half a century, rather than becoming a listed building has ceased operation. Lorna feels the same way about this closure as I did vacating the old Broadcasting House. The end of this era was confirmed by Adam Crozier, once the FA's 'Golden Generation' man, now in his new role of chief executive at ITV. He explained that to continue with what was the hub of programme-making for his company 'would not be core to the strategic priorities of the ITV studio business'. Some might argue that surely the business of ITV was to make studio programmes. Within three months of making that announcement, Crozier had moved on again.

The London studios were the home of many happy memories for Lorna, particularly the *An Audience With...* shows. This involved many weeks working closely with artists such as Mel Brooks, Billy Connolly and the most satisfying of all, Ken Dodd. What made it even more fulfilling was to know that Dodd himself regarded this as his finest moment on television. He was a master in the theatre and the last major link to the old music hall days. In order for him to be able to deliver what turned out to be his definitive performance for the cameras, though, he needed to be gently steered in the right direction. Lorna spent hours watching Dodd's marathon stage shows and knew that editorially, the act would need a bit of fine tuning for the studio. It wasn't always plain-sailing; Dodd was fiercely protective and proud of all of his material. Together through mutual respect, they devised a formula and shape that would enable him to deliver a masterclass for any aspiring young comedian. When he was appearing in Torquay in September 2017, now as Sir Ken Dodd, Lorna wanted to go and see him, sensing that realistically it might be her last chance, as indeed it was. He went through his usual routine of gags like, "I'm not a chauvinist, I lift up my legs when she's hoovering," but then for the last half an hour of the show, he put his tickling stick away and talked more intimately to the audience about his unique life. He knew that Lorna was there and publicly thanked her again for her help. It reminded me a little of the night in Vienna sitting next to Graham Taylor, when Elton John paid tribute to him. We went backstage afterwards to meet Doddy with our son George. He knew that my background was in football and told me stories about what an inspiration Bill Shankly had been to him in Liverpool. It was after one o' clock in the morning when we finally emerged into the autumn night, and there were at least fifty fans still waiting patiently for him, hoping for one final chuckle.

Producers don't tend to be regarded as stars. I'm not sure that they are even designated as 'talent' these days by the BBC, but very few of the performing stars could have shone so brightly without their support. Lorna added something to every show that she worked on, and I was privileged by association to not only get an insight but also made to feel part of the preparation, as so many ideas were bounced around our kitchen table. Equally, I could not have been a football correspondent without her understanding on all of those occasions when I couldn't be at home. It helps so much to have a partner also in the media industry who can relate to what you are doing. One thing I am certain of is that after his disrespectful question to her, Harvey Goldsmith was able to discover the answer for himself.

Kernow

I must go down to the sea again,
For the call of the running tide
Is a wild call and a clear call
That may not be denied;
And all I ask is a windy day
With the white clouds flying
And the flung spray and the blown spume,
And the seagulls crying.

'Sea Fever', John Masefield, 1902

MY DAD USED TO TELL ME THAT IF YOU PUT A SEASHELL NEXT to your ear, that you could hear waves from the ocean, even in Derbyshire. When I retired, Lorna and I wanted to hear that sound again for real without having to rely on Otis Redding 'Sitting on the Dock of the Bay'. So where does a former football correspondent relocate to? Well, obviously over the Tamar Bridge to one of the few English counties devoid of any mainstream action in my sport, Cornwall. We moved to the authentic part that hasn't morphed into Hampstead-by-the-Sea and become an enclave for owners of multiple homes. The fishing port of Looe in the South East is the 'proper job'. It is a working town, affluent in spirit if not monetary wealth. An independently minded community where time-keeping is not a priority, which was exactly what I needed after so many years dictated by the stopwatch.

Time is what I have had in abundance to watch, listen, read and reflect on the two professions that have dominated my life, broadcasting and football, industries that have become unrecognisable from my fledgling years, for better and for worse. There are common denominators behind many of these monumental changes which I would like to now finally explore starting with broadcasting without, I hope, biting too many hands that used to feed me.

Time Is On My Side

IN MY RETIREMENT, I WAS ASSURED BY THE BBC THAT THEY didn't want me to disappear completely off the face of the earth and I was given a generous two-year contract to introduce 'special programmes' on Radio 5 Live. It was their initiative and not mine. I was keen to revisit my broadcasting roots as a presenter, as well as welcoming the opportunity to be able to continue exercising the grey matter. It didn't work out, and I have no idea why. Perhaps the writing was on the wall from the moment that I received a phone call offering me my first project about the footballers of the First World War with the ominous caveat that if I didn't do this, it might be a struggle to fit me into the rest of the schedules. It was an early indication that not everybody was apparently buying into the idea of me still being around.

For the money that I was being paid, the BBC had a right to expect my involvement in at least a dozen programmes over the twenty-four months. I came up with numerous ideas but was involved in only five. Without wishing to look a gift horse in the mouth, this was a colossal waste of licence payers' money and left me wondering how many other examples there might be of such profligacy. Graham Taylor, for example, was never asked to work the full quota of games that he was contracted and paid for, and this was a source of great frustration to him. It doesn't make any financial sense to axe football commentators for economic reasons and then fritter money away so needlessly like this.

As Director-General of the BBC, a quarter of a century earlier, John Birt initially had been quite correct in identifying a bloated organisation, hamstrung by bureaucracy. He set about ruthless reform and hundreds of jobs were culled. However, was it really necessary to be discussing the building of a new non-baronial BBC in management conferences at some of the most expensive hotels in the UK? What sort of a message was that sending out to the beleaguered troops, making decisions that would lead to redundancies and wreck family lives, while some of those in power continued to luxuriate in the manner to which they had become accustomed? Having gone through this pain barrier, rather than creating a more slimline and efficient programme-making machine, it seems to me that there have never been as many layers of middle management as exist today. Many of the posts you see advertised appear to have precious little to do with broadcasting. When I was eight, all I wanted to do was work for the BBC, but I don't recall ever fantasising about becoming an identity architect with this responsibility. "The role is empowered to identify the strategic direction required, define the delivery road map and drive projects to execute the vision for the identity service across the BBC." That's the one for me!

Lord Birt is proud of the fact that his regime was able to embrace the digital age. It's a shame, though, that in all of those extravagant 'away days', nobody appeared to have the strategy and vision to see the need for a TV sports channel instead of handing over all of the initiative to Sky. Children, Parliament and news would all be catered for with their own dedicated channels, but sport was not evidently viewed as such a priority. The great TV pioneers of yesteryear, like Peter Dimmock, would have seen this revolution coming. How horrified would he have been to see sport so completely disregarded in a special programme on BBC Two in July 2017 to mark sixty years of the best of British TV. This was a two-hour programme hosted by Lord Melvyn Bragg, and of the 7,200 seconds, only two were devoted to sport, a couple of subliminal flashed images of Bobby Moore and Andy Murray. Even though some of the largest audiences and some of the greatest technical advances had been generated by sports coverage, there was not one representative to talk about the subject.

I feel strongly about the need for football, the national game, to be shown more regularly live on network television. The trouble is you get so used to being spoiled by Sky and BT's coverage, which always leaves no stone unturned. After a match, you are treated to an in-depth discussion, hear from all of the central characters and all loose ends are tidied up. In my retirement as a viewer, I am afraid that on the fleeting occasions when a match is screened live by the BBC, I have often been left feeling short-changed. Sometimes, as soon as the action is over, after the briefest of summaries you are banished to the red button channel. The BBC will no doubt argue that this is still a *bona fide* service, but it is a subsidiary outlet and the message being conveyed is that the rest of this transmission is now not as important. For example, in June 2017, an England football team actually reached the final of a World Cup when the nation's Under-20s met Venezuela in South Korea. The BBC showed some enterprise by scheduling live afternoon coverage on BBC Two. Unfortunately, what was given with one hand was then taken away by the other. For the first time in over half a century, England emerged as World Champions, but in order to watch the presentation of the trophy, you had to press the red button so that BBC Two could focus on the UK leg of the World Triathlon. All very politically correct, but editorial nonsense. While all this was happening, BBC One was showing a repeat of *Homes Under the Hammer*.

Sadly, this was not to be a one-off aberration. Four months later, it was the turn of the Under-17s to reach a World Cup final, and their game against Spain in India was also shown live on BBC Two. England came back from two goals down to win the trophy, but to see it being handed over once again you had to press that red button so a repeat of *Gardeners' World* could take precedence. It's a bit like going to see a concert at Wembley Stadium and being told that if you want to watch the encore, then you have to move next door to the arena. To underline what a missed opportunity this had been to make the most of what might be a once in a lifetime experience, two years later in 2019, neither the England Under 17's nor the Under 20's even qualified for the two World Cups they should have been defending. Lessons though don't appear to have been learned. On December 21st 2019, the early Saturday evening schedule was cleared on BBC One to show Liverpool's Club World Cup final against South American champions Flamengo. This tournament has now been slimmed down and is more relevant than the one I attended in Brazil nearly twenty years ago. Liverpool won the trophy for the first time in their history and yet as soon as extra time had finished the audience was banished to the red button without any meaningful analysis and before the medal presentations. Why could this not have been screened on BBC Two which had only been showing a film and three repeated programmes? As my mum used to say to me, if a job is worth doing then do it properly or not at all.

Very few of the major sporting events that you always took for granted being shown on BBC TV remain and yet that has not prevented a grotesque amount of money being poured into the BBC Sports Personality of the Year show, which always used to be compulsive viewing. Once upon a time, this came live from TV Centre and was the definitive review of the year. Nothing demonstrates the changing face of broadcasting better than this modern version from an indoor arena that is more akin to the MTV video awards and succeeds only in drawing attention to what the BBC has lost, as many of the outstanding clips of the year credit other television companies. The award should now be renamed, 'Sports Personality of the Year as seen on the BBC'; how else to justify why both Anthony Joshua and Lewis Hamilton were passed over in 2017? To compound it all, the Manchester City footballer, Phil Foden, was named Young Sports Personality of that year as the star of the England Under-17's World Cup win. It was good to see him being presented with this because you wouldn't have seen him receive his World Cup medal on the BBC unless you had pressed the red button. The following year, at the end of 2018, the show was marginally improved. At least the winner was there in person this time to pick up the trophy. However, within seconds of cyclist Geraint Thomas being acclaimed as a deserved recipient, he had to take a back seat. The Tour de France champion was left to look on bemused and distinctly uncomfortable as his stage was handed over to George Ezra, wearing his best Gareth Southgate waistcoat, to perform a song entitled 'Paradise'. It was more a case of *Paradise Lost*. By December 2019, I had become almost immune to this extravagance with it's never ending capacity to shoot itself in the foot. On this occasion, the eventual winner, Ben Stokes, appeared to be inadvertently revealed even before voting had officially started. The great cricket all-rounder had been centre-stage in the most gripping sporting theatre of the year, yet all the dramatic tension surrounding this evening was not only tossed away but smashed for six through mid-wicket.

What Radio 5 Live would give for a fraction of the money spent on television's annual evening of back-slapping: money that could be more usefully invested in actually covering more sport. What is the point of staging such a lavish orgy of self-congratulation when the so-called home of live sport on BBC Radio can no longer afford to provide commentary on so many major events that used to be taken for granted? The BBC will no doubt argue that these are different budgets, as indeed they are, but that still doesn't make it right. It's a crying shame, because when BBC TV Sport does throw its weight behind an event, it is still in a class of its own, as was demonstrated by the unparalleled coverage of the 2019 Women's World Cup.

It is galling to see so much sport being lost when money still appears to be spent unnecessarily in other areas. As just one of many examples, Alan Yentob built up an empire overseeing arts documentaries at the BBC and over the years, many of his creations have been original and imaginative. However, more recently, there have also been a number that have been superbly crafted by independent companies, with only a token involvement from the BBC. Yentob, however, as presenter of the *Imagine* series, routinely feels the need gratuitously to project himself into the opening sequence, often on location, before introducing work that speaks for itself and does not need this unnecessary, time-wasting and expensive indulgence. A simple twenty seconds of text would suffice, as was the case when *Arena* presented a documentary about Bob Dylan that did require a brief explanation: that team certainly didn't feel the need to hire extra studio time or fly to America to film an introduction that would add nothing to the story. All this at a time when BBC Radio

Sport, for financial reasons, often finds itself having to rely on television material to sustain a documentary, rather than originating its own.

My final two programmes for the BBC about the 1966 World Cup and Euro '96 had no original radio interviews and were both illustrated only by television clips. Ironically for the Euro '96 show, permission was only granted for television to use the interview with Baddiel and Skinner about their 'Three Lions' anthem, even though radio play at the time of its release had been crucial to sales. Although there has never been as much airtime available to accommodate them, good, old-fashioned, crafted radio sport documentaries have mostly become obsolete. In their place, usually, are studio-based discussions, punctuated by the occasional pre-recorded insert. This is convenience broadcasting that doesn't require as much effort and can easily be halted in the event of a breaking news story. Many of the subjects tackled are thought-provoking and need to be dealt with in far greater depth. At least around the country, many BBC local radio stations are still upholding the traditional style of documentary making and, through skilful editing, ensure that every word counts. I feel very grateful to have experienced working in radio at a time when programme making was paramount. I do recognise, that as technology changes, other digital platforms emerge for listeners but this should never detract from radio's main objective. The broadcast and the podcast can happily coexist but there is no point making icing unless there is a cake.

Video may have done its best to 'kill the radio stars', but there has been no decline in broadcasting standards, especially in the art of reporting. Since I retired, there have been two occasions in particular that made me feel proud to have been part of the Radio Sport Academy. On the day of the Westminster Bridge terrorist attack in March 2017, I was watching live coverage on CNN. Renowned anchor, Wolf Blitzer, was in America and introduced an eyewitness on the phone from London. CNN didn't realise at that moment how fortunate they were to be joined by Alan Parry, a former radio colleague of mine and backbone of Sky's television football commentary team. Alan had been on his way to an appointment in the House of Lords when he was stopped in his tracks. Very often, eyewitnesses can be overcome with emotion and struggle to articulate what they have seen; not Alan. When it comes to simply describing what you can see, no one is more regularly tested than a sports reporter. Yet this skill is not always recognised within the BBC news hierarchy, to whom sport is always an 'and finally...'. All of Alan Parry's upbringing and instincts came to the fore as he painted measured word pictures of what he had seen on that appalling day. It was a model for any broadcaster and the result of years of experience in the field.

The same applies to the corporations man in the Midlands, Pat Murphy. On any media studies degree course, students should be shown Clive Anderson's excruciating exchanges with the Bee Gees as the definitive example of how not to conduct a TV chat show interview. Part of the syllabus should also involve listening to Pat Murphy standing up to the former Leicester City manager, Nigel Pearson, as an example of how to deal with any football personality whose tactics habitually extend to media intimidation. Murphy was just the man to do this shortly after Pearson had humiliated a local journalist, whom he referred to as 'son' and accused of being an ostrich with his head stuck in the sand. Pat was never going to tolerate this sort of pomposity on his patch and what I admired most of all about the way that he went in to bat against Pearson, was that he was taking up the cudgels on behalf of his profession. Far too many managers, protected by press officers, have been allowed to get away with victimising more junior local reporters, who rely on their co-operation and can never answer back; this was a red rag to a bull for Pat Murphy. Leicester's decision to make radio and television undertake a combined press conference backfired on that day, as Murphy's radio questions were filmed and reached an even wider audience than normal. The moment that made me cheer out loud was when he told Pearson: "Football gets a lot of money from the media, which should be treated with more respect." At the end, all that a chastened manager can muster as a last resort is a sarcastic, "Is the lecture over?"

A lecture that I did not approve of was delivered by another former BBC Radio colleague, Jeff Stelling. Jeff went on to become one of my favourite television hosts, after never really being given the chance to display his considerable talent at Broadcasting House. His Saturday afternoon show on Sky, which is essentially radio on TV, has become cult viewing, with Jeff, the indefatigable Hartlepool fan, as its irreplaceable ringmaster. Unfortunately, the cult of personality got the better of him on April 22nd, 2017. I thought that he overstepped the mark and abused his privileged position when he called for the sacking of Hartlepool manager, Dave Jones. While this might be fair game for one of his panel, this should never fall within the jurisdiction of the presenter. Even though he is also President of the club, I thought that he crossed a line when he said, "Dave Jones, for God's sake, for the good of the club, walk now, go now, this is not your level of football." Jones did leave twenty-four hours later, but this should all have been said in the privacy of a boardroom and not from a television studio.

Over the last quarter of century, Sky's coverage of sport has raised the crossbar and set new standards. My only issue is with their sports news channel, which seems to be influenced more by product placement than editorial judgment. One of the best examples of this occurred on Sunday June 2nd, 2019, the morning after two huge overnight stories. One had been featured live on Sky, the other hadn't and so boxer Anthony Joshua's first ever professional defeat by Andy Ruiz Jr in New York was prioritised ahead of Liverpool's victory over Spurs in an all-English Champions League final. Had that most important football match of the season been on Sky and the boxing on BT, I've no doubt the running order would have been reversed. In Sky's defence, the Joshua fight happened later in the night and might have been considered more of a breaking news story. However, what perplexed me was the extent of the imbalance of coverage given to the two events. It was nine minutes into the bulletin before Liverpool's victory was addressed. In my view, Sky should have started by reporting briefly on the bare bones of the fight, trailed more in-depth coverage and then comprehensively dealt with Liverpool's sixth European triumph.

Because of the regularity of live football on television, watching a game nowadays has become more commonplace and routine. Rather like buying a record, it's not the special event that it used to be. Punditry, though, has been taken to a new level, and the catalyst for that was Andy Gray, for whom there were never any shades of grey. More recently, another Scot, Graeme Souness, who as a player never shirked a challenge in his life, has for me become the outstanding football analyst on TV. Just as I want to know what a journalist like Martin Samuel is thinking about a particular issue when he appears on the unmissable *Sunday Supplement* programme, so in the afternoon I need to get Souness's insight whenever there is a big match taking place. Football's loss, in his case, has been television's gain, and it is a mystery to understand when you listen to him why he just fell short at the very top as a manager. Perhaps, like some other great players who ventured into management, he found it difficult to tolerate mediocrity and became disillusioned by the player power now being wielded by the stars of the modern game. Souness's experience shone through when he and Thierry Henry were analysing Arsenal's victory at Crystal Palace in December 2017. After scoring a goal in the game, Alexis Sanchez seemed to be surprised that the rest of his Arsenal colleagues hadn't run towards him to celebrate, probably because he had been making it transparently clear for some time that he wanted to leave the club. In the ensuing discussion, Henry still closely attached to his former club, sat on the fence. Souness listened with an exasperated expression and when it was his turn to pass comment, simply said that it had revealed to him a divided dressing room. He had never experienced it as a player at Anfield but had witnessed it as manager. He had hit the nail squarely on the head. This turned out to be the last game in which Sanchez would score for Arsenal, and a month later he had moved to Manchester United.

It has always surprised me why footballers have only ever gravitated towards becoming match summarisers or studio experts. Unlike other major sports, no former player has broken through as a commentator. There is no logical reason for this and it is something I would welcome. Articulate former players, like Danny Murphy, Jermaine Jenas and the emerging Alex Scott, with their inherent understanding of the sport, would be less inclined to feel the need to churn out endless facts and figures, and would only want to focus on the game in front of them. As a viewer, this obsession has become one of the banes of my life, and on occasions, I am forced to turn down the sound. 'Always be a good guest in somebody's living room' was the great Brian Moore's mantra as a television commentator and you were always pleased to have him as your guide operating on the principle that less is always best. When Barry Davies and John Motson both retired from the BBC, we were reminded of a remark by the former head of TV Sport Jonathan Martin when asked to compare and contrast their styles. "Barry commentates from the grandstand, John is talking from the terraces," was how he summed up the contrast. That might be so, but I have yet to watch a match from the terraces and be tapped on the shoulder and informed that this is going to be the fourth goalless draw between the clubs in their last nine meetings, so why would I want to hear this at home?

Whenever this retired potato leaves the couch, I rely in transit on radio for my football fix. The legacy of Peter Jones and Bryon Butler is in very safe hands with today's generation of commentators on 5 Live, who generally don't fall into the television trap of overdoing the homework, probably because they have less spare time to burn the midnight oil. Much to my chagrin though, for the latest news and sport, I will invariably desert the BBC for talkSPORT, not because they do it any better, but because they appear to feel more of a sense of obligation to deliver it on schedule. It's all very well adopting a relaxed and inclusive style, but bulletins need to be on time and rarely are on 5 Live. I find this *laissez-faire* attitude undisciplined and contrary to everything that I was brought up on; another reason, perhaps, for my eventual incompatibility with the network.

I will always hold the view that dispensing with a second commentator for some of the biggest games, a feature that had made, the BBC Radio output distinctive, was a retrograde step. It was a decision taken by management no longer involved in the day-to-day running of the department and devalued a sport once looked upon as the lifeblood of 5 Live; a cosmetic change designed not to sustain quality, but to justify redundancy. It's a bit like installing self-checkouts at supermarkets. They don't improve the service, just ensure less employment. An even better recent example of change for change's sake and unnecessary tinkering, was the decision to pair two of radio's finest broadcasters, Simon Mayo and Jo Whiley. They were both hugely popular and had a dedicated following for their own individual shows. Why did they need to be compromised in this way? Radio audiences, rather like some at the Football Association, are traditionally reticent about embracing change.

I feel blessed to have had my job. Anyone lucky enough to earn a living from what is essentially a hobby should go down on bended knee every day and give thanks. Your salary is, after all, being paid by many folks who have to do far more significant work for less financial return, like nurses and teachers.

Since I retired, the subject of BBC pay has been a hot topic. My view remains that you are indeed fortunate to be a BBC employee, and exorbitant salaries, if they have to be paid, should only be necessary to retain someone who is utterly irreplaceable. In my experience, I can think of only a select few that fall into this category. *5 Live Breakfast,* for example, is never the same radio programme if Nicky Campbell is not there. Television coverage of Wimbledon would be destitute without John McEnroe and on both platforms the ubiquitous political editor Laura Kuenssberg has such authority and clarity of perspective; but they are rare exceptions to the norm. I remember Des Lynam, who *was* indispensable and one of the few presenters to totally master TV and radio, once joking with colleagues on a flight to cover an Olympic Games that if the plane came down, it would 'put broadcasting back five minutes'. He was right. When I left, I was immediately and seamlessly replaced in both of my roles by the talented John Murray, and radio didn't miss a beat.

More of an issue than pay for me is the lack of value placed on experience. In the last year, five respected broadcasters with over one hundred and fifty years of service between them have been allowed to leave BBC Radio Sport. At the BBC, age concerns often surface when younger, more insecure members of management seem to perceive this as a potential threat to their authority. The BBC began to lose its way as soon as executives from the commercial sector were brought in and tried to operate it on the same lines, chasing ratings to support their own egos. A public service broadcaster should not be so preoccupied with this pursuit. There is now more of an obsession with quantity of audience than the quality of programme and one is not always compatible with the other. The uncannily accurate satire about the BBC, *W1A*, is not so much a comedy, more a reality show, though as Susan Sontag wrote, "Reality has come to seem more and more like what we are shown by the cameras." It is easy to identify many of the characters held up for ridicule in this spoof, especially the mate of the DG, who has managed to keep his nose clean, attended all of the right meetings and has never made a programme in his life, but looks good with a clipboard. New Broadcasting House in London prides itself on being at the hub of world broadcasting for virtually everyone, it seems, apart from sport, who are based in Salford. Before the 2014 World Cup, I had to attend a mandatory security briefing in that building, which warned us about all of the nasty insects and reptiles lying in wait for us in the Amazon rainforest. The seminar took place in one of the many open-plan seating areas with a constant distraction of passers-by touching base and slurping skinny lattes. *Bring on the insects and reptiles*, I thought. *It can't be worse than this.*

What can get lost amid all the corporate claptrap about strategy, branding and vision is that, ultimately, the job is about broadcasting. That is what the licence fee should be preserving and not propping up battalions of executives. Yet in January 2020 the BBC announced plans to terminate 450 newsroom jobs because "we are spending too much of our resources on traditional linear broadcasting." Pardon my ignorance but isn't that the main function of the organisation if it is not to be known in future as the British Bureaucratic Corporation?

How to get future generations to carry on listening is going to be the great challenge. On 5 Live there now appears to be an assumption that younger ears won't want to hear older voices, which is a highly patronising attitude. When I was a teenager, I was captivated by the avuncular, gravelly tones of World At One presenter William Hardcastle who oozed authority. His age was immaterial. At school most of my favourite teachers were veterans with years of experience. One of the reasons I was so stimulated by John Peel was that he didn't ever talk down to me or indulge in mindless banter and I thought it was profoundly symbolic that the last record he ever played on BBC Radio before his premature death was from an album entitled *No One's Listening Anymore*. My younger son George loves his football, but never listens to the radio in the way that I did. After I had taken him to see one of my closest colleagues, Garry Richardson, performing his very funny cabaret show, he said to me, "Dad, I know Garry is a comedian, but does he still report on sport?"

Radio is still going strong in the long-distance lorries, on Saturday afternoon market stalls and in student bed-sits, but will only survive if generations pass it on. For the sake of John Peel and John Arlott and all of the other pioneers who were the soundtrack to my life, I pray that it can, but I am not optimistic. We live in an age when people don't write letters to each other anymore, don't appear to have meal-table conversations and are too quick to dash out an insincere RIP on Twitter after someone they never knew passes away. I hope old habits will die hard and am so grateful while I am still here to have had this opportunity to look back over a life most treasured for family, friends and for allowing me to realise my dream as an eight-year-old, to work for what should still be regarded as the greatest broadcasting institution in the world. Radio may no longer be in the bloodstream of today's younger generation, and that is a source of great sadness because at its best, there is no better company.

I have never forgotten those two Preston fans standing next to me at the Cup final with one commentating for his blind friend, the very essence of what radio broadcasting means to me. When I retired, I received many kind, and generous messages and one that resonated deeply was this:

> *Mike, thank you for everything you've done over so many years.*
> *Enjoyed enormously your commentary, your wisdom and your professionalism.*
> *You will be sorely missed,*
> *Very best wishes, David.*

> Rt Hon David Blunkett MP, Member of Parliament for Sheffield Brightside
> and Hillsborough

Stop the Clock

IF BROADCASTING IS NO LONGER JUST ABOUT COMMUNICATION, then equally football no longer fits the description of being just 'the people's game'. Simplistically, I suppose you can put much of this down to the more commercially driven life of the twenty-first century. Whatever the reasons, one thing is for sure; the governance of both industries leaves a lot to be desired. Just as there are not enough actual broadcasters integrally involved in influencing the way ahead in that business, so there are not enough genuine football lovers helping to shape and protect the future of a great sport. Football is still one of our favourite universal pastimes, belonging to you, me and the folks next door, but as with the BBC, the sport's corridors of power can represent a gravy train for some. Broadcasting and football owe so much to many diehards at the coalface, who do sterling work, that are often taken for granted and sometimes even derided. At the sharp end of the operation, however, exist career opportunists who never stay in executive roles long enough to be found out but can do immeasurable damage in the short time that they are around.

I would need a second volume to address the charge sheet against FIFA and UEFA. Putting to one side politics and corruption and just dealing with football, they appear to be on a mission to exterminate the goose that lays their golden eggs by burning out their most precious assets. Without exceptional players to perform on their stages, FIFA and UEFA would become superfluous. It would be like watching *Swan Lake* without any dancers, yet they continue to ramp up the physical demands on these athletes with their ever-expanding tournaments. In a summer between a World Cup and a European Championship, what was to be gained by making England and Switzerland meet in a third-place play-off at the Nations League in Portugal when they should have all been on the beach? I also find it amusing that the world's governing body, FIFA, now has an Integrity and Compliance Unit for investigating alleged irregularities in the game. Whatever next? Metallica signing up to the Noise Abatement Society?

UEFA is like a modern-day King Canute attempting to hold back the tidal wave threat of a Super League breakaway. More and more it submits meekly to the so-called elite clubs in a bid to prevent something from happening that is surely as inevitable as a traffic light changing to red when you approach it. UEFA's largely unenforceable financial fair play rules (another misnomer) were effectively introduced to preserve the status quo and protect the established old guard from unwanted gate-crashers. The transfer window was born out of the same sort of thinking, and I am surprised that nobody has tested the validity of these restraint of trade regulations in a court of law. Whenever I hear the spine-chilling UEFA Champions League anthem, it is the closest I get to wishing I still had a microphone in my hand. For me, it is the ultimate hair-on-the-back-of-the-neck music in modern sport. However, it never ceases to amaze me that UEFA up until the quarter-final, manages to get away with its contrived Champions League draw. It is not so much a draw, more an arrangement of convenience for television and it does the credibility of the tournament a great disservice. It begs the question, why bother with this charade in the first place and not just announce it all on the website? However, that would be denying club and marketing officials an all-expenses-paid overseas trip to a ceremony as self-important as anything Hollywood has to offer. If only some of the money lavished on this absurdity could be invested back into more needy football causes.

As for the third member of the great administrative trio with whom I was involved, our Football Association, an ill-conceived proposal to sell off Wembley was apparently motivated by a desire to plough finance back into the foundations of the sport. In the end, it was so pleasantly ironic that the main dissenting voices against this sacrilege were the very people many of the corporate movers and shakers at the FA regard as being past their sell-by date. The so-called 'blazers' in the shires may be a legacy of Victorian times but are a representation that still cares deeply about the history of the sport. We were advised very publicly that the FA is in dire need of reform, and who said so? Why, only some of its most recent former policymakers. A collection of former chairmen and chief executives took the trouble of writing a letter to Parliament stating their case and expressing concern, a bit like Simon Cowell complaining about the quality of pop music in the charts.

One of the main issues that I have had with the FA over the years has been its ineffectiveness as a disciplinary body. There is no greater exercise in futility than when the FA charges someone with 'bringing the game into disrepute'. This never worked as a sanction forty years ago and is even less of a deterrent now when levied against multi-millionaires. Also, what caused you greater offence: watching José Mourinho allegedly mumble a Portuguese profanity at the end of a game for which he was put in the dock or hearing the then-FA chief executive Martin Glenn explain why it had been wrong for Pep Guardiola to wear a ribbon of support for imprisoned Spanish politicians? Glenn didn't think that political symbols should appear on football kits, and then went on to equate the Jewish Star of David with the Nazi swastika. This was the figurehead of an organisation overseeing a campaign to eradicate all racism from the sport.

Modernisation for Football Association administrators meant that when the new Wembley Stadium reopened, it was decided there should be a two-tiered system of admission. A Club Wembley with its VIP entrance might have boosted gate receipts but denied access to real fans and visually blemished nearly every showpiece occasion there. When Wembley re-opened, it was hard at times for us to focus on the game from our commentary box when so many people were still returning to their seats in front of us ten minutes into the second-half. Evidently, we were part of the Wembley junket experience in this exclusive enclosure, as phones would come out and we would have our photos taken as if we were some rare species in a zoo. Not too much 'strategy and vision' was employed when electing to accommodate the well-heeled selfie generation in their corporate zone on the halfway line, directly opposite the television cameras. For an example of why association football at the higher level is losing the plot and can no longer pride itself on being the 'people's game', look no further than the start of the second-half of any Wembley fixture. "Everyone here is utterly absorbed," excellent BBC TV commentator Steve Wilson informed us after the interval in the 2017 FA Cup semi-final, with Chelsea leading Tottenham 2-1. Not absorbed enough, evidently, to return from hospitality in time for the restart. Hundreds of seats were embarrassingly still unoccupied as Dele Alli equalised for Spurs. I have heard this justified on the basis that he who pays the piper calls the tune, but why bother going in the first place? It looked awful, and the same might well be said about the eventual Parliamentary discussion on the FA's continuing ability to govern the game.

This backbench debate took place in a glass house of stone throwing on Thursday February 9th, 2017. It was second only to Sam Fox and Mick Fleetwood's hosting of the Brits as the most shambolic television spectacle I have had the misfortune to witness. No more than five per cent of the entire house was in attendance as a motion was passed expressing no confidence in the FA. However, at the end of the session, it left me wondering which one of the two organisations had been more exposed as being unfit for purpose. Watching the factually flawed *The Damned United* film about Brian Clough had left me asking how many other such biopics might also be inaccurate. I had a similar emotion here, as I knew a little something about this subject as well and it made me question whether this superficiality had been typical of all Parliamentary debates. It was banal, vacuous and never got close to scratching the surface. Presentations were interrupted continuously by gratuitous offerings from the floor. One complained that a Huddersfield against Manchester City game hadn't been selected for live television and Leicester East MP Keith Vaz not once, but twice had to remind us that he was from the home of the reigning Premier League champions – and your point is?

So many trends seem to come from America, and if football at the top level is not careful, it will end up one day like the States, with authentic fans watching a game in a bar on TV, priced out of stadiums reserved for tunnel clubs and hospitality packages. Supporters who do attend games are given a raw deal, and scant respect is paid to them when football's paymasters schedule fixtures for television. One of the best examples of this was the Christmas programme in 2017. There were five Premier League clubs in the North West and five in London. Manchester City had to go to Crystal Palace, Liverpool to Arsenal, Chelsea to Everton and Tottenham to Burnley. Why not return to the old days of local Derby home and away doubleheaders to eliminate all unnecessary travelling? If Liverpool can play Manchester City twice in six days in the Champions League in April, why not over Christmas and New Year? Furthermore, if you are a supporter, working hard and earning around the national wage, you would need employment for 800 years to buy your club one average Premier League player and that doesn't even include the astronomical wages.

At least the 'people's game' is still alive and kicking out there in Frontierland. In retirement, I may not have been able to return in the way that I wanted to my broadcasting roots as a presenter but was able to do so watching football, going full circle and revisiting Home Park Plymouth. I wanted to enjoy a father-son experience going to a game like I had with my dad all those years ago and was never able to achieve with my eldest son, Marshall, because of my BBC commitments. My youngest son, George, and I were able to make the journey from our Cornish home to the ground in roughly the same amount of time it would have taken me to commentate on extra time and penalties. We became Plymouth Argyle season ticket holders and were able to savour one final season in the old Grandstand before it was demolished. It has been a welcome and refreshing culture shock. Plymouth is the largest city in the country to have never played in the top tier of league football. Attracting desirable players to venture to the South West has always been a handicap, and although their attendances for this level are substantial, investment in player recruitment has been inadequate. In the summer of 2018, having just flirted valiantly with a place in the play-offs, eleven additions were made to the squad, and though this provided extra depth, hardly any of the signings significantly improved the team. The ultimate, almost inevitable, relegation that followed was a heavy price to pay. The manager Derek Adams found himself on a slippery slope, from the moment he ill-advisedly made the decision not to talk to the local media apart from fulfilling his mandatory obligations. This is inexcusable. At a club that has a worldwide profile with a manager like Sir Alex Ferguson, you might be able to get away with the occasional banning orders, but a club like Argyle needs all the publicity it can get. Unless a Brian Clough, or indeed a Ferguson, materialises as their manager, I am afraid mediocrity will continue to prevail, which is sad for their remarkably loyal supporters. I used to think that my travelling was quite demanding, but it was a walk in the park compared to the distances covered to away games by Argyle's Green Army. Their vociferous contingent did make me laugh during one home game against Peterborough when they burst into a chorus of 'You dirty northern bastards'. When I got home, I did a quick Google search just to reconfirm that Peterborough was still only seventy-four miles north of London.

In my retirement, I have done my best to keep the local convenience store in business by hoovering up all of the daily newspapers, which I then devour and marvel over the standard of sports writing. Football has never truly acknowledged the debt it owes to journalism, often regarding it as an irritant, yet exploiting it when there might be something to be gained. I remember having a coffee with a well-known manager, who broke off to take a phone call. He told me that it had been from a reporter asking him if he would be interested in the Sunderland job. He had replied that he wasn't but was more than happy for the newspaper to link him with it, as it might improve his standing at his current club. Reading all of the papers and the views of so many writers whom I respect made me wonder what my opinion would have been on some of the issues, if I had still had a platform as correspondent. The sort of story that seemed to arouse me most was when I found myself saying, "Did he really say that?" Double standards are something else that broadcasting and football have in common.

I read with interest Martin Keown's newspaper column in January 2018 describing a spat between rival managers Antonio Conte and José Mourinho as 'an ugly row in public, a terrible advert for the game, showing such huge disrespect to one another'. In 2003, when Keown himself played for Arsenal at Old Trafford, on the final whistle, shortly after Manchester United's Ruud Van Nistelrooy had missed a penalty, Keown, for reasons best known to himself, snarled in his opponents face, jumped over a remarkably restrained player and brought his arms down hard on his back. Not the best of 'adverts' for a game being shown all around the world.

When he was the Chelsea manager, Antonio Conte had this to say about Manchester United: "I think this season it's very important to understand it's not always about who spends the most money. If they [Man Utd] think this is the right way to win the title, it's not always about who spends more money, who wins." Oh, really? Run that one past me again and remind me who was employing Conte. Roman Abramovich used his wealth to alter the financial terrain of English football overnight.

Among those to pass comment when Jamie Carragher was suspended by Sky after his regrettable spitting episode, was that model of etiquette and self-restraint, Joey Barton. On talkSPORT he said, "You just can't do that. I just don't get why he doesn't just, if he's that annoyed, keep his window up or wind it down and tell him to mind his own business." spot on Joey!

I also found it difficult to suppress mirth when Derby County, after dismissing Steve McClaren, said, "We need a manager who shares our values," and after removing Paul Clement from office claimed that 'he didn't do it the Derby way'. This from a club that has overseen fifteen managerial changes in the first nineteen years of this century.At what point does the penny drop and it occur to someone that those cherished "values" and the so called "Derby way"might need to be reassessed? The busiest person at Derby so far in the twenty-first century has been the poor soul who has had to sew the initials of the manager onto a tracksuit.

Incidentally on the subject of managerial appointments, I always find it amusing and a cliché, when a change is made, how the new man invariably abdicates responsibility when he attends the first game by distancing himself and letting it be known that he is not officially in charge yet. It's a no lose situation. If the team are beaten, well he's not taken over yet. However, if they rise to the occasion, well what a source of inspiration his presence has been!

Sometimes a lack of self-awareness in football can be quite staggering. Andy Carroll took it upon himself to berate West Ham fans who left with fourteen minutes to go when their team were losing 1-4 at home to Tottenham: "They really should be staying until the end, you never know what is going to happen, and they really should be helping us out a bit." The point might have carried a little more weight if it hadn't been made by a player who was a serial absentee from the West Ham team.

When he was at Liverpool, Carroll did play the full ninety minutes in a 1-3 defeat at Bolton. Three months before that game, the then-Liverpool managing director, Ian Ayre, had suggested that people didn't subscribe in Kuala Lumpur to watch Bolton on TV. He had effectively done Bolton manager Owen Coyle's team talk for him. Ayre was putting forward the case that the so-called bigger clubs in the Premier League should receive a greater share of the overseas television revenue. No other issue in recent times has raised my hackles more than this, as it goes right to the heart of so many of football's problems. It was a debate that just refused to go away. Liverpool's American owner, John W Henry, continued this campaign and voiced his disapproval of the egalitarian principle of sharing equally revenue raised from global exposure. "It's hard to imagine this continuing much longer," he said.

"Everyone in the league knows what the large clubs bring to the value of foreign rights." And so the case was made for the established elite to continue to prosper and prevail from a larger share of the pot. That was why Leicester City's upsetting of the applecart was the most joyful story of the modern era. Unfortunately, retiring Premier League chief executive Richard Scudamore appeared to blink first and instead of treating these selfish proposals with the contempt they deserved and kicking them into the long grass, the greedy demands were processed and a compromise was facilitated. Interestingly, though, when the idea was first mooted to reward Scudamore with a £5 million leaving present, there was never any talk of contributions being linked to league position, the initial plan was for equal shares all round.

When it comes to matters of high finance and politics, nobody has their finger more on the pulse than television presenter Robert Peston. However, he appeared to be less of an authority on football history. After there had been unpleasant scenes in London involving fans of the German club Cologne attending the Europa League game at Arsenal, he tweeted, "These Cologne fans are a disgrace, my European solidarity is being tested." It was a drop in the ocean compared to what mainland Europe, and especially Germany, had suffered from English marauders for over thirty years.

We now live in an age when football teams, after barely getting out of second gear for most of a game, will then expand more energy than seen before by chasing into the net to retrieve the ball and carrying it back to the halfway line after belatedly scoring a goal. This will then become the cue for the opposition to manage the rest of the game by deliberately taking as much time as they can to make a substitution. If a player who is being replaced cares so much about the fans he insincerely applauds in all corners of the stadium before he leaves, then stick around after the match and show them real appreciation. The problem for the spectator is that nobody has any real idea how many extra seconds are being added on for this gamesmanship and how much official time there is left to play. It all seems so arbitrary. I find it quite staggering that in such a billion-dollar industry where so many advances have been made and time equals money, that only a couple of people in a stadium actually know how much time there is left to be played. American sport may be littered with TV commercial breaks, but all venues are equipped with that old-fashioned mechanical device called a clock, visible to all and this stops whenever the action stops. All that is required in our league football is to have one official undistracted by having to keep the peace on the touchline, who is totally focused and able to stop the clock whenever the game is not in motion. Sir Alex Ferguson was right to be obsessed with how much time should be added on to a game; it always appears to be so random and never fully compensates for what has been so transparently wasted and lost. Goalkeepers, especially visiting ones, should not be given *carte blanche* to deliberately waste time for forty-five minutes before their nine lives finally run out in the second-half. Referees should have no jurisdiction to allow the taking of a corner or free kick to keep things neat and tidy before half-time or the final whistle. If the crowd and television audience could see for themselves on a big clock that time was up, then that discretion would be removed. Hasn't it ever struck you how strange it is that added time will always be a minimum of one, two, three, four – a nice rounded number of minutes – never one minute thirty-nine or two minutes sixteen. How can that be accurate? And remember, it only takes a second to score a goal. It might have become necessary for a referee to spray a white line before the taking of a free kick, and push the patience of mankind to the VAR limit by scrutinising whether an eyelash is off side but might it not also be a good idea to ensure that every game gets ninety minutes when the ball is actually in play? Does that sound like rocket science to you?

My time is almost up, and I must detain you no further. For all my petty neuroses about football, it is still and always will be the staff of life. There is nothing to beat hearing 40,000, or even 4,000, voices roaring a collective '*yes*' whenever there is a goal.

In my last conversation with my best friend Steve Cooper, three days before he succumbed to his terminal cancer, we talked football. We played together as kids, watched together as youths, and compared notes together as more cynical old-timers. He knew that I was writing this book and I told him that it would be dedicated to his memory. Steve had asked me to speak at his funeral and, in denial, clinging to the forlorn hope that he might defy medical science, I flippantly agreed, provided he spoke at mine. When it was time to perform that sad role, it was the most nervous and emotional that I have ever been. I wanted so much to find the right words to do justice to someone who had been such an integral part of my life. Rather like Brian Clough used to say about Peter Taylor: "He used to make me laugh." Steve would have seen the irony and funny side of me being made an Honorary Master of the University of Derby. All those years on from being denied a public presentation of my school cricket colours after shunning the 'short back and sides' barbers of Belper. Sporting those Hendrix curls, I remember in that landmark summer of 1967 being the furthest that I had ever been away from home in a fishing village in what was once Yugoslavia and now belongs to Slovenia. I went off in search of bread rolls and something edible as a filling. The proprietor of the local corner shop looked at me as if I was David Bowie in *The Man Who Fell to Earth* and enquired, "English?" When I confirmed the obvious, he boomed, "Bobby Charlton." And there you have it, not Shakespeare or even Her Majesty the Queen; he was focusing on a working-class boy from the coal mining community of Northumberland. That is the global pulling power of football for you.

When I was eight, I hadn't heard of any football administrators, club chairmen, agents or even referees, but I knew the names of all the teams, their star players and, of course, Charles Buchan. Strip away all of the extraneous and exploitative incidental trappings of the game and what you are left with in essence is those two young boys the morning after England's World Cup semi-final, having a kickabout in the yard. That is the fundamental ethos of the sport. All that is required on a beach, in a cobbled street, in a park or a school playground is something to replicate a ball. Without a ball, there is no game, and it is time for that ball to be returned to its rightful owners: you, me and the folks next door.

At the End of the Day

Towards the end of my commentating life, it was uncanny how many goals seemed to come off shins from a set piece, with anything up to eighteen players around the ball. Well, that's my excuse for sometimes finding instant identification with the naked eye increasingly more of a test. You could always rely on shirt numbers when it was 1 to 11; not so clear-cut when it's a 36 or 39. In my earlier years watching Liverpool, I sometimes confused Rush with Aldridge when they were both on the attack, and across Stanley Park, the follicly challenged Gravesen and Carsley were often a nightmare to tell apart in Everton's midfield, and as for the Berezutski twins in Russia's defence, don't get me started. Sometimes for preparation, I might play my own trivial pursuit game of dead ringers. I would try and think of a face, sometimes from the entertainment industry, resembling a football personality, then all I had to do in commentary was remind myself what that character looked like. It was quite a tortuous process, but good fun.

Some of my personal favourites, separated at birth include:

- Rafa Benítez – Paul Giamatti
- Zlatan Ibrahimović – Frank Zappa
- Gianluigi Buffon – Al Pacino

- Fabio Capello – Lou Reed
- Walter Mazzarri – Alec Baldwin
- Xherdan Shaqiri – Harry Enfield
- André Schürrle – Hugh Dennis
- Michael Ballack – Matt Damon
- Steve Bruce – Jay Leno
- Chris Kamara – Chris Kamara (there could only ever be one)

And so, while I am on the subject of lists and personal favourites, let me leave you with a few more. I must stress that this is highly subjective and there is no order of merit, often more an order of awareness. Number ten can mean just as much as number one. But first, an eleven.

THE BEST TEAM OF PLAYERS I WAS LUCKY ENOUGH TO COMMENTATE ON:

Buffon

Lahm Puyol Baresi Maldini

Gerrard Keane Xavi

Dalglish Messi Cristiano Ronaldo

Messi or Ronaldo as the greater is a fairly fatuous debate, rather like saying De Niro or Pacino? Does it really matter who is best when they are both from another planet? With my head on the block, I would just favour Messi because of his greater team ethic and less self-absorption. When the two met in the 2009 Champions League final in Rome, Ronaldo ran out like a show pony, with a team constructed around him, centre of attention, juggling a ball. Messi, by way of contrast, innocuously shuffled on, almost unnoticed and scored one of the two trophy-winning goals. When Real Madrid met Barcelona in the 2017 Spanish Super Cup, Ronaldo scored, whipped off his shirt almost as if to say 'look what I've been doing all summer', flashed his torso at the camera, invited a yellow card and promptly received one for this narcissism. Seconds later, he got a second yellow for diving and was sent off. He also manhandled the referee, and so his club had to do without him for five games. Away from the catwalk mentality though, he is a prodigious talent, and we are so lucky to have had them both around at the same time. Like many great players, Messi can also be a prima donna, but genuinely celebrates every goal for his side, no matter who has scored. One always plays for the team, the other sometimes only for himself; it can happen like that in broadcasting as well.

MOST DRAMATIC GOALS DESCRIBED

1. **1987** : Keith Houchen's diving header for Coventry City v Tottenham in the FA Cup final. The Cup may no longer be a priority for many clubs, but for all Coventry fans, this was their greatest day and is what they are most remembered for.
2. **1990:** David Platt's last-minute World Cup volley for England against Belgium in Bologna. Just as we were trying to work out who would be taking the penalties, Platt scored the goal that changed his life.
3. **1991:** Mark Hughes for Manchester United against Barcelona in the Cup Winners' Cup final in Rotterdam. Hughes scored from an almost impossible angle at the end of six years in the European wilderness for English clubs.
4. **1992:** Steve Watkin's winning goal for Fourth Division Wrexham at home to League champions Arsenal in the third round of the FA Cup. This is not only in my top ten but would also be included in the top ten of all-time shocks in the competition. If only another Welshman Peter Jones could have been there as well.

5. **1993:** Andy Linighan's extra-time winner for Arsenal against Sheffield Wednesday in the FA Cup final replay. Linighan's buzzer-beater header climaxed a typical comeback by George Graham's Arsenal, a season after that Wrexham humiliation.

6. **1996:** Paul Gascoigne for England against Scotland at the European Championship. Though his great days were starting to become numbered, this stunning individual goal was a moment that defined him as a very special player.

7. **1996:** Alan Shearer against the Netherlands at the European Championship. After Hurst's third goal against West Germany in '66, Shearer's second to put England 3-0 up at Wembley is my favourite England goal. Why couldn't it always be like this?

8. **2011:** Wayne Rooney for Manchester United against Manchester City. Rooney had been in dispute with the club after his lethargic World Cup in South Africa, but this breathtaking overhead kick propelled United to another League title and was the best goal he ever scored at Old Trafford.

9. **2012:** Sergio Agüero for Manchester City against QPR. The most dramatic goal in Premier League history to win Manchester City their first title in forty-four years. What is often overlooked is the crucial part played in the build-up to it by the much-maligned Mario Balotelli.

10. **2014:** Mario Götze for Germany against Argentina at the Maracanã Stadium in the World Cup final. This winning goal in extra time was the last that I ever described. It will live with me forever.

MOST EVOCATIVE COMMENTARY POSITIONS:

1. **Home Park, Plymouth:** Hard to imagine in 1958 that thirty years later I would find myself commentating on a couple of matches there from the directors' box with Peter Jones.

2. **Old Trafford, Manchester:** Going there as an eight-year-old made an everlasting impression, so there was nowhere more appropriate for me to do my first ever radio commentary.

3. **Moss Rose, Macclesfield:** An FA Cup tie there in 2002 against West Ham in the birthplace of my parents was the stuff of *Field of Dreams*.

4. **The Baseball Ground, Derby:** My spiritual home; nothing more to be said.

5. **The Old Wembley Stadium, London:** A quite stunning view, high in the sky from the stewards' box used for monitoring the greyhound racing. Trying to get to that position up in the rafters these days without a hard hat would never be approved by health and safety.

6. **Anfield, Liverpool:** The Centenary Stand gantry and the only access to it a ladder, which was removed as soon as the game started. Although we were effectively cut off from the outside world, we were granted a privileged vantage point in a unique theatre.

7. **Upton Park, West Ham:** Our old position in the front row of the press box, just a tape measure away from the pitch, immersed you in the action. This was a proper football atmosphere, especially under the lights.

8. **Celtic Park, Glasgow:** Roddy Forsyth told me in advance that I would never have experienced an

atmosphere like it overlooking the old jungle terrace and he was right. My only commentary position that vibrated and bounced.

9. **Stade de la Mosson, Montpellier:** Memorable for doing an England game there at the Tournoi against France in 1997 and discovering at the end of the match that all of the hospitality boxes with open windows behind our commentary seats had been vacated with several bottles of red wine left unattended. It would have been a shame to let it go to waste, a view that was endorsed by Terry Butcher.

10. **Millennium Stadium, Cardiff:** Although I missed the ritual of Cup final teams climbing those steps to the Royal Box, the Welsh capital did a wonderful job deputising for Wembley, and our commentary position was as near perfect as you could get.

MOST DIFFICULT VANTAGE POINTS FOR RADIO COMMENTARY:

1. **Camp Nou, Barcelona:** An awe-inspiring arena, heavenly football but always an outrageous commentary seat behind the corner flag.

2. **Goodison Park, Everton:** A classic, vintage stadium and a truly hospitable club, but a pillar allowed us only a partial view of the penalty area at the Gwladys Street End, and sod's law, of course, dictated that almost every goal I seemed to witness there was scored behind that obstruction.

3. **Atatürk Stadium, Izmir:** I went there three times with England in six years for games against Turkey and was a sitting duck for target practise in our unprotected commentary seats. Much of the game was spent dodging coins or phlegm spat in our direction.

4. **The Rose Bowl, Pasadena:** They don't need to build a roof over sporting venues in Southern California as it rarely rains. However in the height of summer, especially in the middle of the day, open to the elements, you might as well be sitting in the blast furnace of Death Valley. That was our experience at the 1994 World Cup final, trapped in a microwave oven for extra time and penalties.

5. **White Hart Lane, Tottenham:** The one thing you need at any commentary position is elevation to be able to get any sort of perspective. Once upon a time we had that in the main stand but were then moved to a box with a worm's eye view of the pitch, low down behind the press seats. Our hut was perfect for selling hot dogs but not for describing a football match. It was a pity, because I never felt that I was able to do justice to some really outstanding games there.

6. **The Olympic Stadium, Munich:** The complete polar opposite to Pasadena, but no protection here meant that on every visit hypothermia set in, even in early September. Thank goodness Bayern moved.

7. **The Workers' Stadium, Beijing:** I have no idea what our commentary position was like for England's friendly with China in 1996, as we were not allowed access to it unless we paid a king's ransom. The whole game was described on the phone.

8. **St James' Park, Newcastle:** Always one of my favourite venues, except during reconstruction and without a roof when the local derby with Sunderland was played in a monsoon. If I had jumped in the Tyne that night, I could not have been any wetter.

9. **Donbass Arena, Donetsk:** Two visits there during Euro 2012 meant coating myself beforehand with lashings of insect repellent, which might have persuaded other

humans to keep their distance but didn't prevent me from being bitten more times than I would have been in Dracula's castle.

10. **The New Wembley, London:** I get no pleasure from including the home of English football in this section, as before the stadium was rebuilt, it had provided so many cherished memories. After it reopened, broadcasting from an enclosed glass box behind the corporate enclosure gave me a feeling of complete disconnect and detachment. It was a bit like going to a rock concert and having to watch it all on a big screen.

COMMENTATORS WHO ENHANCED MY ENJOYMENT OF SPORT:

1. **John Arlott:** The sound of summer. My favourite example of the spontaneity of his work occurred when a streaker (or 'freaker', as John described him) invaded the 1975 Ashes Test at Lord's. The sense of disappointment in his voice was tangible when he sighed, "Not very shapely, and it's masculine."

2. **Richie Benaud:** Observed the golden rule on TV and allowed the pictures to tell the story. When he did interject, he always provided a unique insight, illuminated the action and made every word count. A sense of humour as dry as Luxor.

3. **David Coleman:** A voice that oozed authority. Masterful economy of words. He only had to say 'the final of the Olympic 100 metres' to make the hair rise on the back of your neck. Like all the great middle-distance runners, he always had an extra gear to climb into, never better demonstrated and synchronised than when he watched Ann Packer come with a late surge to win the 1964 Olympic 800 metres gold medal.

4. **Cliff Morgan:** Like Benaud, an outstanding former captain of his country. He was immortalised as a broadcaster when he came off the substitute's bench to describe the epic 1973 Barbarians v All Blacks match in Cardiff. Cliff had to deputise for Bill McLaren with only two hours' notice and found himself not only describing one of rugby's greatest tries but also delivering one of television's finest commentaries. I'm not a rugby man yet find it impossible to listen to Cliff's voice without having a tear in my eye. If you write the words that he used down as simple text, they hardly amount to purple prose, but they were conveyed with such raw emotion and relish for sport.

5. **Brian Moore:** Even on television with an audience of millions, always gave the impression that he was talking just to you. Treasured and cared about football and that bond with the game transparently shone through. Radiated warmth and was such a reassuring presence in any living room.

6. **Barry Davies:** Could have commentated on a fly climbing up a wall and had you transfixed. Never got bogged down with tedious statistics; he didn't need this crutch to fall back on. Barry allowed the action space to live and breathe as the great Francis Ford Coppola said "silence is a very powerful sound".

7. **Peter Jones:** Just simply the best all-around radio commentator there has ever been.

8. **Peter Bromley:** Along with John Arlott, probably the greatest radio commentator on one specialist sport. Razor-sharp accuracy and, aided by his racing specs, the eyesight of an eagle. Whatever the excitement, I don't ever remember his voice being out of control. Peter's perfect pitch and turn of phrase was never better demonstrated than when Shergar romped home in the 1981 Derby.

"There's only one horse in it," he declared. "You'll need a telescope to see the rest." An absolute thoroughbred.

9. **Alan Parry:** I can understand why he would want to progress into television but was a huge loss to the wireless. His passion for sport lit up the airwaves. Alan may not have waxed as lyrically as Peter Jones, but I regard him as technically the best radio commentator of my generation.

10. **Michael Holding:** Blessed with not only one of the finest bowling actions cricket has ever seen but also just about the most mellifluous commentary voice that I have ever heard. I am always disappointed when he is not at the broadcasting crease for Sky. Holding is a natural communicator, informs, educates and entertains and, along with John McEnroe and Graeme Souness, is now my favourite former player to pick up a microphone.

PRESENTERS AND ICONIC VOICES:

1. **Eamonn Andrews:** The voice of my childhood and the godfather of radio sport presentation.

2. **Alistair Cooke:** The master of radio script writing, talking his words on to the page and then making you feel that he had done that just for you. What would I give now to be able to hear just one *Letter from America* on President Trump?

3. **Brian Matthew:** The voice that cultivated my craving for popular music and transports me instantly back to the sixties.

4. **John Peel:** Picked up the baton from Brian Matthew and expanded my cultural education. If Peel liked a record, then that was usually good enough for me. His endorsement was the ultimate seal of approval. What made him so special to me was that like all the very best

presenters, he succeeded in maintaining the illusion of creating a one-on-one relationship with the listener. For a lonely student in bedsit land, this filled such a void.

5. **Desmond Lynam:** All that needs to be said is that he is in a class of his own and remains radio's greatest ever sports presenter.

6. **Bryon Butler:** Thank goodness the BBC's archives still make it possible for me to hear a voice that was such an influence on me and will forever generate a warm glow. A reminder that broadcasting, like football, at its best can be such a beautiful craft.

7. **Harriet Cass:** In the early hours of the morning, still a long way from home, accompanied by a convoy of truck drivers on a motorway reduced to one lane by essential roadworks, I would thank my lucky stars that at least I was still on dry land and listen for fifteen minutes to the comforting tones of Harriet Cass reading the shipping forecast on Radio 4.

8. **George Sephton:** Like that other famous George from Merseyside, this George also has a memorable voice. He is the PA announcer at Anfield, not a breed I normally take much notice of but George was the exception. It's hard to explain, but he's just got such a dulcet tone, that any child would adore listening to his bedtime stories. Not only that, but he played great music and was a top bloke.

9. **Howard Stern:** This is where I am in danger of being accused of losing my marbles. There have been many pale imitations but nobody else quite like this American radio host. I've heard him described as a 'shock jock', which frankly is an insult to a brilliantly imaginative and clever mind. A law unto himself, unafraid to venture where most others would fear to tread. I may find myself disagreeing with him on many

issues but am always stimulated and entertained, and there are not too many other shows that manage to achieve that.

10. **Nicky Campbell:** Inconceivable to imagine Radio 5 Live without him. Highly intelligent, quick-witted and the ultimate player of the devil's advocate card. I might have had my preconceived ideas about what I would like to say on the *Breakfast Show* the morning after a game, but Nicky skilfully always set the agenda, often leading me into potentially off-limits territory with a sniper lurking on every corner. He was always desperate to get me to say that England would win a World Cup or mention 1966, knowing that this is a red rag to a bull to all Scots. I like to think that there was a mutual respect; I do know that he is one of a rare breed of broadcasters who does merit being branded as a genuine member of BBC talent.

SPORTSWRITERS:

From 1989, the Sports Journalists' Association presented an annual Lifetime Achievement award and named the trophy after their former chairman and secretary Doug Gardner, who had been a member of the organisation for forty years. In 2015, it was given to me and was the most prestigious accolade of my lifetime. I was the first broadcaster to be honoured in this way and to be endorsed by my peers was what made it so extra special, especially as I had no formal journalistic upbringing myself. I was joined on stage for the presentation by four of the most respected sports writers in the industry, and this is quite possibly the last time they were ever photographed together.

These four gentlemen would all feature in my all-time top ten favourites, and for the record they were:

1. **Hugh McIlvanney:** He was a reference point for all sports journalists with a distinctive, poetic, unparalleled style. When I read his words, I hear his voice. Hugh's attention to detail was legendary, as rigorous as Dustin Hoffman preparing for any acting role. His BBC Arena film on *The Football Men* is my favourite documentary on the sport. If Bill Shankly, Matt Busby and Jock Stein were all defined by their Scottish roots, then so was Hugh.

2. **Jeff Powell:** I have been fortunate to interview Jeff a few times, and his natural fluency and communication skills always came to the fore in his writing, especially in his halcyon years covering football. Jeff's work in the aftermath of the Heysel Tragedy was a monumental blueprint.

3. **Patrick Collins:** No other columnist has been able to combine serious and sometimes grave subject matter with the more whimsical quite like Pat. What always set him apart from the rest on a Sunday was his pay-off line. Often it was deliberately understated and left dangling for the reader to contemplate but hit the bullseye every time.

4. **James Lawton:** There was so much thoughtful depth to his writing. At times I was profoundly moved by his words and even found myself becoming quite emotional. I certainly shed a tear when I heard of his sad passing. Jim never ever flaunted his status in the profession.

One of the great perks of doing my job was to travel with and be in the company of so many gifted sports journalists. I could quite easily list at least another twenty-six colleagues who meant so much to me, but have made a rod for my own back and can only nominate another six to be consistent with this final chapter:

5. **David Meek:** Hard to think of a more courteous and self-effacing journalist than David, who sadly died in 2018. He was a political specialist at the *Manchester Evening News* in 1958 and was asked as an emergency to switch from news to sport when the paper's Manchester United correspondent Tom Jackson was killed in the Munich air disaster. He went on to hold that position for thirty-seven years and was described by Sir Alex Ferguson as 'part of the fabric of the club'. If he wrote a story about United, then you know it had authenticity. David had no ego and was a gentleman of the highest order.

6. **David Lacey:** What I admired most of all about David, apart from the splendour of his writing, was that he was always independently minded and never ran with the pack. If we had both been at the same game, his report would be the first that I would seek out for reassurance that I had roughly been on the same wavelength as this astute observer. For some reason, whenever I see that gifted comedian Bill Bailey, he always reminds me of David.

7. **Paul Hayward:** In the same way that I always believed Barry Davies or Peter Jones could commentate on anything put in front of them, so Paul would be able to write about any subject under the sun with verve, elegance and style. Thankfully, he decided to give us the benefit of his talent in the sports pages. He sets such high standards and never ever fails to meet them.

8. **Henry Winter:** When I saw Martin Tyler standing in the rain with Watford fans outside the church at Graham Taylor's funeral, it reminded me of Henry. Both men share an undiminished boyhood love for football, and it shines through in their work. They are always still prepared to give the game, even in the most trying of circumstances, the benefit of the doubt. Henry, like Bryon Butler, will never take the easy way out and plump

for a lazy cliché. He can turn a phrase as adeptly as Derek Underwood could a cricket ball on a sticky wicket.

9. **Daniel Taylor:** The future of sports journalism is in safe hands as long as writers like Danny continue to emerge. He has carried on the great tradition of independent thinkers like David Lacey and Jim Lawton and added an extra, investigative ingredient. If only he, like another great writer, Richard Williams, wasn't a Forest fan!

10. **Martin Samuel:** I've saved Martin to the end, as one of the great pleasures in my career was to be able to see him, rather like a young apprentice at a football club, grow and mature into becoming one of the great players in the game. If I was only allowed to read one article every week, then it would be his. Apart from his perception and use of vocabulary, what sets him apart is his breadth of general knowledge and the amount of research undertaken before any word is committed to print. He must be an inspiration to the next generation of writers, and I hope that one day he will be able to find time to publish his own memoirs.

FILM AND TELEVISION

FIVE FILMS THAT MADE ME CRY EITHER TEARS OF EMOTION OR LAUGHTER:

1. 1931: *Monkey Business*, The Marx Brothers.
2. 1946: *It's a Wonderful Life*, James Stewart.
3. 1958: *The Inn of the Sixth Happiness*, Ingrid Bergman.
4. 1967: *Guess Who's Coming to Dinner*, Katharine Hepburn, Spencer Tracy, Sidney Poitier and Katharine Houghton.
5. 1972: *The Heartbreak Kid*, Charles Grodin, Cybill Shepherd and Eddie Albert.

FIVE TV SHOWS THAT I WILL NEVER TIRE OF WATCHING:

1. 1959: *The Untouchables,* narrated by Walter Winchell, greatest black-and-white TV of all time.
2. 1961: *The Avengers,* at its best from '65 with Diana Rigg. Time warp, classic opening Laurie Johnson theme.
3. 1967: *The High Chaparral,* an essential part of the sixth-form curriculum at school.
4. 1977: *Lou Grant,* probably too cheesy for real journalists but great admiration for Ed Asner.
5. 1979: *Minder,* genius.

MEMORABLE CONCERTS:

1. 1960: **Marty Wilde & the Wildcats,** Bournemouth Pavilion, confirmation that other music existed apart from the *Billy Cotton Band Show.*
2. 1966: **Gary Farr and the T-Bones,** Strutt Arms, Milford, Derbyshire. Tiny room, huge atmosphere. A group that like Geno Washington's Ram Jam Band had a cult following and was led by the son of legendary boxer Tommy Farr.
3. 1969: **Led Zeppelin,** Town Hall Birmingham. What I remember most of all was the encore, when they even managed to take Presley and Cochran classics to another level.
4. 1973: **David Bowie,** Town Hall Birmingham. It was a matinée and from another universe.
5. 1975: **Bob Marley and the Wailers,** Odeon New St Birmingham. The greatest party atmosphere I have experienced.
6. 1975: **Cat Stevens,** Bingley Hall Stafford. My first date with Lorna.

7. 1977: **Abba**, Royal Albert Hall. A guilty pleasure.
8. 1983: **The Everly Brothers**, Royal Albert Hall. The reunion after ten years. A spine-chilling experience. The brothers entered the stage from opposite directions and from the very first chord were in perfect harmony.
9. 1999: **Fun Lovin' Criminals**, The Viper Room, Los Angeles. How rock 'n' roll should be. Small room and in your face. Like turning the clock back thirty years.
10. 2016: **Alabama 3,** Looe Music Festival. On a beach, no backstage and an infectious rhythm; you would have to be inhuman not to want to dance to. Chatting afterwards to the band's co-founder Jake Black (Rev D Wayne Love) about his memories of Celtic's Lisbon Lions. Jake sadly passed away in May 2019 and is sorely missed.

DESERT ISLAND DISCS:

1. **'True Love'**, Bing Crosby – reminds me of Mum and Dad.
2. **'Funky Kingston'**, Toots and the Maytals – reminds me of Brian.
3. **'Be My Baby'**, The Ronettes – reminds me of Steve.
4. **'Green Onions'**, Booker T – reminds me of adolescence.
5. **'Lay It All At His Feet'**, Uncle Frank – reminds me of Lorna.
6. **'Blind Faith'**, Chase & Status – reminds me of Marshall.
7. **'Semper Fidelis'**, Royal Marines – reminds me of childhood and George.
8. **'The Champions League Anthem'** – reminds me of my career and especially my colleagues.

One luxury item:

- A shortwave radio.

One book:

- *The Football Man*, Arthur Hopcraft.

And these are the last words I have to say
That's why it took so long to write
There will be other words some other day
But that is the story of my life.

Bibliography And Sources

1. Armitage, Dave, *150 BC: Cloughie – The Inside Stories* Pub: Hot Air Publishing, 2009
2. Birt, John, *The Harder Path* Pub: Time Warner Books, 2002
3. Buchan, Charles, *Football Monthly*
4. Butler, Bryon, *Official Illustrated History of The FA Cup* Pub: Headline, 1996
5. Capote, Truman, *Portraits and Observations* Pub: Random House, 2007
6. Carragher, Jamie, *Carra: My Autobiography* Pub: Bantam Press, 2008
7. Cooper, Steve, *The Clown Joke*
8. *Daily Mail*
9. *Daily Mirror*
10. *Daily Telegraph*
11. *Derby Telegraph*
12. *Football Association Blueprint for the Future of Football*, 1991
13. *Football League Review*
14. Garner, Ken, *In Session Tonight: Complete Radio 1 Recordings* Pub: BBC, 1993
15. Greenwood, Ron, *Soccer Choice* Pub: Pelham Books, 1979

16. Hepworth, David, *1971 – Never a Dull Moment* Pub: Black Swan, 2017

17. Hornby, Nick, *Fever Pitch: The Screenplay* Pub: Indigo, 1997

18. *International Football Book for Boys* Pub: Souvenir Press, 1959

19. Johnston, Brian, *Chatterboxes* Pub: Methuen London, 1983

20. Keane, Roy, *Keane: The Autobiography* Pub: Penguin Michael Joseph, 2002

21. *Macclesfield Express*

22. Masefield, John, *The Collected Poems of John Masefield* Pub: William Heinemann Ltd, 1923

23. McMenemy, Lawrie, *A Lifetime's Obsession: My Autobiography* Pub: Sport Media, 2016

24. Millay, Edna St Vincent, *A Few Figs from Thistles* Pub: Harper & Brothers, NY & London, 1922

25. Milne, AA, *Winnie-the-Pooh* Pub: Methuen & Co London, 1926

26. Moberly, Sir Walter Hamilton, *The Crisis in the University*, Pub: London SCM press, 1949

27. *Private Eye*, Colemanballs

28. Simon, Neil, *The Heartbreak Kid* screenplay, 1972, based on *A Change of Plan* by Bruce Jay Friedman, Pub: Simon and Schuster, 1966

29. Sontag, Susan, *On Photography* Pub: Allen Lane Penguin books, 1978

30. *The Scroll* Herbert Strutt School, Belper

31. van Dyke, Henry, *Music and other Poems* Pub: Scribner's, NY, 1904

32. Vaughan-Thomas, Wynford, *Trust to Talk* Pub: Hutchinson and Co, 1980

33. *World Cup '66 England* Pub: Purnell, 1966

Acknowledgements

Mike would like to thank the following for making the publication of this book possible

Thom Axon – www.thomaxon.com
Mike Batt
Michael Bradley & The Undertones
Ian Darke
Andrew Dunkley
Andy Elliott – Sports Journalist Association
Richard Faulkner
Elaine Gallagher
Martin Heiron
George Ingham
Lorna Ingham
Marshall Ingham
Julia Lemagnen
Dean Moore Pipewell Studios – www.pipewellstudios.co.uk
Graham Nash – www.etsy.com/uk/shop/headfuzzbygrimboid
Charlotte Nicol
Nic Nicholas – www.indexers.org.uk/find-an-indexer/
    directory/nicolanicholas/
Garry Richardson

Janine Self – Sports Journalist Association
Bob Thomas Sports Photography
Daisy's Café Looe – for nourishment
Willington Hall Hotel, Cheshire
and from The Book Guild
Lauren Bailey. Philippa Iliffe, Megan Lockwood-Jones and
    Rosie Lowe

Index

Photographs are in *italics*. MI refers to Mike Ingham.

Owen, Michael 195, 223, 224
Oxford United F.C. 105

P

Pacino, Al 296
Packer, Ann 303
Paisley, Bob 220
Pallister, Gary 167
Parker, Scott 236
Parliament, FA and 223, 288–9
Parry, Alan *P1.5*, 277–8, 305
Parry, Rick 164
Party at the Palace (2002) 256–8
Peacock, Alan 25
Pearce, Stuart 184, 236
Pearson, Nigel 278
Peebles, Andy *P1.6*, 115, 136
Peel, John ix, *P2.8*, 64–5, 94, 283, 284,
    305–6
Pegg, David 31
Pelé 102, 171
Perry, Fred *P1.7*, 100
Perryman, Steve xiii
Peston, Robert 293
Peterborough United F.C. 290
Pickering, Ron 137
Pinter, Harold 66
Pitt, Brad 266
Plant, Robert 67
Platt, David 153–4, 298
Pleat, David 251
Plymouth Argyle F.C.
    Home Park 48–9, 300
    MI supports 15–16, 19–21, 22, 38,
    289–90
    players 20, 26, 27
Police, The 78
Portugal (football team) 216–17
Pougatch, Mark *P2.6*
Powell, Jeff *P1.8*, *P2.8*, 103, 308
Poxon, Kit 80
Premier League 130, 134, 156, 164, 289,
    292–3
Preston North End F.C. 52–4
Price, Vincent 259
Pulsford, Gill *P1.5*
Puskás, Ferenc 254

Q

Queens Park Rangers F.C. (QPR) 299

R

Radcliffe, Mark 155
Radio 4 (BBC) 111, 177
Radio 5 (BBC) 150, 155
Radio 5 Live (BBC)
    beginning of 169
    budget 276
    bulletins 172–3, 281
    commentators 237–8
    rebranding 177–80
    'special programmes' 272
Radio Derby (BBC) 73–7
Radio Sport (BBC) 53, 85–95, 189, 237,
    239
Radio Two (BBC) 205
Ramone, Phil 256
Ramsey, Aaron 239
Ramsey, Sir Alf *P1.3*, 231
Raphael, Adam 111
Raven, Mike 64
Rea, Chris 94–5
Reading F.C. 115
Redding, Otis 270
Redhead, Brian 93
Rednapp, Harry 153, 217
Reed, Lou 297
Reed, Oliver 261
referees 30, 166, 231, 294
Revie, Don 81
Richard, Sir Cliff 78–9
Richards, Keith 264
Richardson, Garry *P1.5*, *P2.6*, 107, 109, 148,
    185, 284
Richardson, John 197
Rimet, Jules 130
Robertson, Max *P1.7*, 94–5, 112
Robinson, Peter 124
Robson, Sir Bobby 114–15, 131, 139–40,
    146, 154, 232
Ronaldo, Cristiano 297–8
Rooney, Wayne 155–6, 218–19, 224–6, 231,
    234, 299
Roope, Graham 142
Rose Bowl, Pasadena 302
Rosenthal, Jim *P1.5*, 92, 95
Ross, Bill *P1.6*, 88, 105–7, 110
Rostron, Wilf 158
Rowley, Jack 16, 20
Rowley, Vi 16
Rowling, J.K. 258
Rudd, Alyson 229